FreeBSD Architecture Handbook

A catalogue record for this book is available from the Hong Kong Public Libraries.

Published in Hong Kong by Samurai Media Limited.

Email: info@samuraimedia.org

ISBN 978-988-8406-77-7

Table of Contents

List of Figures

List of Tables

List of Examples

Part I. Kernel

Table of Contents

Chapter 1. Bootstrapping and Kernel Initialization

Contributed by Sergey Lyubka.
Updated and enhanced by Sergio Andrés Gómez del Real.

1.1. Synopsis

This chapter is an overview of the boot and system initialization processes, starting from the BIOS (firmware) POST, to the first user process creation. Since the initial steps of system startup are very architecture dependent, the IA-32 architecture is used as an example.

The FreeBSD boot process can be surprisingly complex. After control is passed from the BIOS, a considerable amount of low-level configuration must be done before the kernel can be loaded and executed. This setup must be done in a simple and flexible manner, allowing the user a great deal of customization possibilities.

1.2. Overview

The boot process is an extremely machine-dependent activity. Not only must code be written for every computer architecture, but there may also be multiple types of booting on the same architecture. For example, a directory listing of /usr/src/sys/boot reveals a great amount of architecture-dependent code. There is a directory for each of the various supported architectures. In the x86-specific i386 directory, there are subdirectories for different boot standards like mbr (Master Boot Record), gpt (GUID Partition Table), and efi (Extensible Firmware Interface). Each boot standard has its own conventions and data structures. The example that follows shows booting an x86 computer from an MBR hard drive with the FreeBSD boot0 multi-boot loader stored in the very first sector. That boot code starts the FreeBSD three-stage boot process.

The key to understanding this process is that it is a series of stages of increasing complexity. These stages are boot1, boot2, and loader (see boot(8) for more detail). The boot system executes each stage in sequence. The last stage, loader, is responsible for loading the FreeBSD kernel. Each stage is examined in the following sections.

Here is an example of the output generated by the different boot stages. Actual output may differ from machine to machine:

FreeBSD Component	Output (may vary)
| boot0 | ```
F1    FreeBSD
F2    BSD
F5    Disk 2
``` |
| boot2 [a] | ```
>>FreeBSD/i386 BOOT
Default: 1:ad(1,a)/boot/loader
boot:
``` |
| loader | ```
BTX loader 1.00 BTX version is 1.02
Consoles: internal video/keyboard
BIOS drive C: is disk0
BIOS 639kB/2096064kB available memory

FreeBSD/x86 bootstrap loader, Revision 1.1
Console internal video/keyboard
(root@snap.freebsd.org, Thu Jan 16 ↵
22:18:05 UTC 2014)
Loading /boot/defaults/loader.conf
/boot/kernel/kernel text=0xed9008 ↵
data=0x117d28+0x176650 ↵
syms=[0x8+0x137988+0x8+0x1515f8]
``` |
```

kernel

```
Copyright (c) 1992-2013 The FreeBSD ↵
Project.
Copyright (c) 1979, 1980, 1983, 1986, ↵
1988, 1989, 1991, 1992, 1993, 1994
        The Regents of the University of ↵
California. All rights reserved.
FreeBSD is a registered trademark of The ↵
FreeBSD Foundation.
FreeBSD 10.0-RELEASE #0 r260789: Thu Jan ↵
16 22:34:59 UTC 2014
    root@snap.freebsd.org:/usr/obj/usr/src/
sys/GENERIC amd64
FreeBSD clang version 3.3 (tags/RELEASE_33/
final 183502) 20130610
```

[a]This prompt will appear if the user presses a key just after selecting an OS to boot at the boot0 stage.

1.3. The BIOS

When the computer powers on, the processor's registers are set to some predefined values. One of the registers is the *instruction pointer* register, and its value after a power on is well defined: it is a 32-bit value of 0xfffffff0 . The instruction pointer register (also known as the Program Counter) points to code to be executed by the processor. Another important register is the cr0 32-bit control register, and its value just after a reboot is 0. One of cr0's bits, the PE (Protection Enabled) bit, indicates whether the processor is running in 32-bit protected mode or 16-bit real mode. Since this bit is cleared at boot time, the processor boots in 16-bit real mode. Real mode means, among other things, that linear and physical addresses are identical. The reason for the processor not to start immediately in 32-bit protected mode is backwards compatibility. In particular, the boot process relies on the services provided by the BIOS, and the BIOS itself works in legacy, 16-bit code.

The value of 0xfffffff0 is slightly less than 4 GB, so unless the machine has 4 GB of physical memory, it cannot point to a valid memory address. The computer's hardware translates this address so that it points to a BIOS memory block.

The BIOS (Basic Input Output System) is a chip on the motherboard that has a relatively small amount of read-only memory (ROM). This memory contains various low-level routines that are specific to the hardware supplied with the motherboard. The processor will first jump to the address 0xfffffff0, which really resides in the BIOS's memory. Usually this address contains a jump instruction to the BIOS's POST routines.

The POST (Power On Self Test) is a set of routines including the memory check, system bus check, and other low-level initialization so the CPU can set up the computer properly. The important step of this stage is determining the boot device. Modern BIOS implementations permit the selection of a boot device, allowing booting from a floppy, CD-ROM, hard disk, or other devices.

The very last thing in the POST is the INT 0x19 instruction. The INT 0x19 handler reads 512 bytes from the first sector of boot device into the memory at address 0x7c00. The term *first sector* originates from hard drive architecture, where the magnetic plate is divided into a number of cylindrical tracks. Tracks are numbered, and every track is divided into a number (usually 64) of sectors. Track numbers start at 0, but sector numbers start from 1. Track 0 is the outermost on the magnetic plate, and sector 1, the first sector, has a special purpose. It is also called the MBR, or Master Boot Record. The remaining sectors on the first track are never used.

This sector is our boot-sequence starting point. As we will see, this sector contains a copy of our boot0 program. A jump is made by the BIOS to address 0x7c00 so it starts executing.

1.4. The Master Boot Record (boot0)

After control is received from the BIOS at memory address 0x7c00, boot0 starts executing. It is the first piece of code under FreeBSD control. The task of boot0 is quite simple: scan the partition table and let the user choose which partition to boot from. The Partition Table is a special, standard data structure embedded in the MBR (hence embedded in boot0) describing the four standard PC "partitions" [1]. boot0 resides in the filesystem as /boot/ boot0. It is a small 512-byte file, and it is exactly what FreeBSD's installation procedure wrote to the hard disk's MBR if you chose the "bootmanager" option at installation time. Indeed, boot0 *is* the MBR.

As mentioned previously, the INT 0x19 instruction causes the INT 0x19 handler to load an MBR (boot0) into memory at address 0x7c00. The source file for boot0 can be found in sys/boot/i386/boot0/boot0.S - which is an awesome piece of code written by Robert Nordier.

A special structure starting from offset 0x1be in the MBR is called the *partition table*. It has four records of 16 bytes each, called *partition records*, which represent how the hard disk is partitioned, or, in FreeBSD's terminology, sliced. One byte of those 16 says whether a partition (slice) is bootable or not. Exactly one record must have that flag set, otherwise boot0's code will refuse to proceed.

A partition record has the following fields:

- the 1-byte filesystem type

- the 1-byte bootable flag

- the 6 byte descriptor in CHS format

- the 8 byte descriptor in LBA format

A partition record descriptor contains information about where exactly the partition resides on the drive. Both descriptors, LBA and CHS, describe the same information, but in different ways: LBA (Logical Block Addressing) has the starting sector for the partition and the partition's length, while CHS (Cylinder Head Sector) has coordinates for the first and last sectors of the partition. The partition table ends with the special signature 0xaa55.

The MBR must fit into 512 bytes, a single disk sector. This program uses low-level "tricks" like taking advantage of the side effects of certain instructions and reusing register values from previous operations to make the most out of the fewest possible instructions. Care must also be taken when handling the partition table, which is embedded in the MBR itself. For these reasons, be very careful when modifying boot0.S.

Note that the boot0.S source file is assembled "as is": instructions are translated one by one to binary, with no additional information (no ELF file format, for example). This kind of low-level control is achieved at link time through special control flags passed to the linker. For example, the text section of the program is set to be located at address 0x600. In practice this means that boot0 must be loaded to memory address 0x600 in order to function properly.

It is worth looking at the Makefile for boot0 (sys/boot/i386/boot0/Makefile), as it defines some of the run-time behavior of boot0. For instance, if a terminal connected to the serial port (COM1) is used for I/O, the macro SIO must be defined (-DSIO). -DPXE enables boot through PXE by pressing F6. Additionally, the program defines a set of *flags* that allow further modification of its behavior. All of this is illustrated in the Makefile. For example, look at the linker directives which command the linker to start the text section at address 0x600, and to build the output file "as is" (strip out any file formatting):

```
BOOT_BOOT0_ORG?=0x600
LDFLAGS=-e start -Ttext ${BOOT_BOOT0_ORG} \
-Wl,-N,-S,--oformat,binary
```

Figure 1.1. sys/boot/i386/boot0/Makefile

Let us now start our study of the MBR, or boot0, starting where execution begins.

---

[1] http://en.wikipedia.org/wiki/Master_boot_record

Note

Some modifications have been made to some instructions in favor of better exposition. For example, some macros are expanded, and some macro tests are omitted when the result of the test is known. This applies to all of the code examples shown.

```
start:
    cld   # String ops inc
    xorw %ax,%ax # Zero
    movw %ax,%es # Address
    movw %ax,%ds #  data
    movw %ax,%ss # Set up
    movw 0x7c00,%sp #  stack
```

Figure 1.2. `sys/boot/i386/boot0/boot0.S`

This first block of code is the entry point of the program. It is where the BIOS transfers control. First, it makes sure that the string operations autoincrement its pointer operands (the `cld` instruction) [2]. Then, as it makes no assumption about the state of the segment registers, it initializes them. Finally, it sets the stack pointer register (`%sp`) to address `0x7c00`, so we have a working stack.

The next block is responsible for the relocation and subsequent jump to the relocated code.

```
    movw $0x7c00,%si # Source
    movw $0x600,%di  # Destination
    movw $512,%cx  # Word count
    rep   # Relocate
    movsb  #  code
    movw %di,%bp  # Address variables
    movb $16,%cl  # Words to clear
    rep   # Zero
    stosb  # them
    incb -0xe(%di)  # Set the S field to 1
    jmp main-0x7c00+0x600 # Jump to relocated code
```

Figure 1.3. `sys/boot/i386/boot0/boot0.S`

Because `boot0` is loaded by the BIOS to address `0x7C00`, it copies itself to address `0x600` and then transfers control there (recall that it was linked to execute at address `0x600`). The source address, `0x7c00`, is copied to register `%si`. The destination address, `0x600`, to register `%di`. The number of bytes to copy, 512 (the program's size), is copied to register `%cx`. Next, the `rep` instruction repeats the instruction that follows, that is, `movsb`, the number of times dictated by the `%cx` register. The `movsb` instruction copies the byte pointed to by `%si` to the address pointed to by `%di`. This is repeated another 511 times. On each repetition, both the source and destination registers, `%si` and `%di`, are incremented by one. Thus, upon completion of the 512-byte copy, `%di` has the value `0x600`+512= `0x800`, and `%si` has the value `0x7c00`+512= `0x7e00`; we have thus completed the code *relocation*.

Next, the destination register `%di` is copied to `%bp`. `%bp` gets the value `0x800`. The value 16 is copied to `%cl` in preparation for a new string operation (like our previous `movsb`). Now, `stosb` is executed 16 times. This instruction copies a 0 value to the address pointed to by the destination register (`%di`, which is `0x800`), and increments it. This is repeated another 15 times, so `%di` ends up with value `0x810`. Effectively, this clears the address range `0x800`-`0x80f`. This range is used as a (fake) partition table for writing the MBR back to disk. Finally, the sector field for the CHS addressing of this fake partition is given the value 1 and a jump is made to the main function from the relocated code. Note that until this jump to the relocated code, any reference to an absolute address was avoided.

---

[2]When in doubt, we refer the reader to the official Intel manuals, which describe the exact semantics for each instruction: http://www.intel.com/content/www/us/en/processors/architectures-software-developer-manuals.html.

The following code block tests whether the drive number provided by the BIOS should be used, or the one stored in boot0.

```
main:
      testb $SETDRV,-69(%bp) # Set drive number?
      jnz disable_update # Yes
      testb %dl,%dl  # Drive number valid?
      js save_curdrive  # Possibly (0x80 set)
```

Figure 1.4. `sys/boot/i386/boot0/boot0.S`

This code tests the SETDRV bit (0x20) in the *flags* variable. Recall that register %bp points to address location 0x800, so the test is done to the *flags* variable at address 0x800-69= 0x7bb. This is an example of the type of modifications that can be done to boot0. The SETDRV flag is not set by default, but it can be set in the Makefile. When set, the drive number stored in the MBR is used instead of the one provided by the BIOS. We assume the defaults, and that the BIOS provided a valid drive number, so we jump to save_curdrive.

The next block saves the drive number provided by the BIOS, and calls putn to print a new line on the screen.

```
save_curdrive:
      movb %dl, (%bp)  # Save drive number
      pushw %dx   # Also in the stack
#ifdef TEST /* test code, print internal bios drive */
      rolb $1, %dl
      movw $drive, %si
      call putkey
#endif
      callw putn  # Print a newline
```

Figure 1.5. `sys/boot/i386/boot0/boot0.S`

Note that we assume TEST is not defined, so the conditional code in it is not assembled and will not appear in our executable boot0.

Our next block implements the actual scanning of the partition table. It prints to the screen the partition type for each of the four entries in the partition table. It compares each type with a list of well-known operating system file systems. Examples of recognized partition types are NTFS (Windows®, ID 0x7), ext2fs (Linux®, ID 0x83), and, of course, ffs/ufs2 (FreeBSD, ID 0xa5). The implementation is fairly simple.

```
      movw $(partbl+0x4),%bx # Partition table (+4)
      xorw %dx,%dx   # Item number

read_entry:
      movb %ch,-0x4(%bx) # Zero active flag (ch == 0)
      btw %dx,_FLAGS(%bp) # Entry enabled?
      jnc next_entry  # No
      movb (%bx),%al  # Load type
      test %al, %al  # skip empty partition
      jz next_entry
      movw $bootable_ids,%di # Lookup tables
      movb $(TLEN+1),%cl # Number of entries
      repne   # Locate
      scasb   # type
      addw $(TLEN-1), %di # Adjust
      movb (%di),%cl  # Partition
      addw %cx,%di  # description
      callw putx  # Display it

next_entry:
      incw %dx   # Next item
      addb $0x10,%bl  # Next entry
      jnc read_entry  # Till done
```

Figure 1.6. `sys/boot/i386/boot0/boot0.S`

It is important to note that the active flag for each entry is cleared, so after the scanning, *no* partition entry is active in our memory copy of boot0. Later, the active flag will be set for the selected partition. This ensures that only one active partition exists if the user chooses to write the changes back to disk.

The next block tests for other drives. At startup, the BIOS writes the number of drives present in the computer to address 0x475. If there are any other drives present, boot0 prints the current drive to screen. The user may command boot0 to scan partitions on another drive later.

```
    popw %ax   # Drive number
    subb $0x79,%al  # Does next
    cmpb 0x475,%al  #  drive exist? (from BIOS?)
    jb print_drive  # Yes
    decw %ax   # Already drive 0?
    jz print_prompt  # Yes
```

Figure 1.7. sys/boot/i386/boot0/boot0.S

We make the assumption that a single drive is present, so the jump to print_drive is not performed. We also assume nothing strange happened, so we jump to print_prompt .

This next block just prints out a prompt followed by the default option:

```
print_prompt:
    movw $prompt,%si  # Display
    callw putstr  #  prompt
    movb _OPT(%bp),%dl # Display
    decw %si   #  default
    callw putkey  #  key
    jmp start_input  # Skip beep
```

Figure 1.8. sys/boot/i386/boot0/boot0.S

Finally, a jump is performed to start_input, where the BIOS services are used to start a timer and for reading user input from the keyboard; if the timer expires, the default option will be selected:

```
start_input:
    xorb %ah,%ah # BIOS: Get
    int $0x1a   #  system time
    movw %dx,%di  # Ticks when
    addw _TICKS(%bp),%di #  timeout
read_key:
    movb $0x1,%ah  # BIOS: Check
    int $0x16   #  for keypress
    jnz got_key  # Have input
    xorb %ah,%ah  # BIOS: int 0x1a, 00
    int $0x1a   #  get system time
    cmpw %di,%dx  # Timeout?
    jb read_key  # No
```

Figure 1.9. sys/boot/i386/boot0/boot0.S

An interrupt is requested with number 0x1a and argument 0 in register %ah. The BIOS has a predefined set of services, requested by applications as software-generated interrupts through the int instruction and receiving arguments in registers (in this case, %ah). Here, particularly, we are requesting the number of clock ticks since last midnight; this value is computed by the BIOS through the RTC (Real Time Clock). This clock can be programmed to work at frequencies ranging from 2 Hz to 8192 Hz. The BIOS sets it to 18.2 Hz at startup. When the request is satisfied, a 32-bit result is returned by the BIOS in registers %cx and %dx (lower bytes in %dx). This result (the %dx part) is copied to register %di, and the value of the TICKS variable is added to %di. This variable resides in boot0 at offset _TICKS (a negative value) from register %bp (which, recall, points to 0x800). The default value of this variable is 0xb6 (182 in decimal). Now, the idea is that boot0 constantly requests the time from the BIOS, and when the value returned in register %dx is greater than the value stored in %di, the time is up and the default selection will be made. Since the RTC ticks 18.2 times per second, this condition will be met after 10 seconds (this default behavior can be changed in the Makefile). Until this time has passed, boot0 continually asks the BIOS for any user input; this is done through int 0x16, argument 1 in %ah.

Whether a key was pressed or the time expired, subsequent code validates the selection. Based on the selection, the register %si is set to point to the appropriate partition entry in the partition table. This new selection overrides the previous default one. Indeed, it becomes the new default. Finally, the ACTIVE flag of the selected partition is set. If it was enabled at compile time, the in-memory version of boot0 with these modified values is written back to the MBR on disk. We leave the details of this implementation to the reader.

We now end our study with the last code block from the boot0 program:

```
movw $0x7c00,%bx  # Address for read
movb $0x2,%ah  # Read sector
callw intx13  #  from disk
jc beep  # If error
cmpw $0xaa55,0x1fe(%bx) # Bootable?
jne beep  # No
pushw %si  # Save ptr to selected part.
callw putn # Leave some space
popw %si  # Restore, next stage uses it
jmp *%bx  # Invoke bootstrap
```

Figure 1.10. sys/boot/i386/boot0/boot0.S

Recall that %si points to the selected partition entry. This entry tells us where the partition begins on disk. We assume, of course, that the partition selected is actually a FreeBSD slice.

Note

From now on, we will favor the use of the technically more accurate term "slice" rather than "partition".

The transfer buffer is set to 0x7c00 (register %bx), and a read for the first sector of the FreeBSD slice is requested by calling intx13. We assume that everything went okay, so a jump to beep is not performed. In particular, the new sector read must end with the magic sequence 0xaa55. Finally, the value at %si (the pointer to the selected partition table) is preserved for use by the next stage, and a jump is performed to address 0x7c00, where execution of our next stage (the just-read block) is started.

1.5. boot1 Stage

So far we have gone through the following sequence:

- The BIOS did some early hardware initialization, including the POST. The MBR (boot0) was loaded from absolute disk sector one to address 0x7c00. Execution control was passed to that location.

- boot0 relocated itself to the location it was linked to execute (0x600), followed by a jump to continue execution at the appropriate place. Finally, boot0 loaded the first disk sector from the FreeBSD slice to address 0x7c00. Execution control was passed to that location.

boot1 is the next step in the boot-loading sequence. It is the first of three boot stages. Note that we have been dealing exclusively with disk sectors. Indeed, the BIOS loads the absolute first sector, while boot0 loads the first sector of the FreeBSD slice. Both loads are to address 0x7c00. We can conceptually think of these disk sectors as containing the files boot0 and boot1, respectively, but in reality this is not entirely true for boot1. Strictly speaking, unlike boot0, boot1 is not part of the boot blocks [3]. Instead, a single, full-blown file, boot (/boot/boot), is what ultimately is written to disk. This file is a combination of boot1, boot2 and the Boot Extender (or BTX). This single file is greater in size than a single sector (greater than 512 bytes). Fortunately, boot1 occupies *exactly* the first 512 bytes of this single file, so when boot0 loads the first sector of the FreeBSD slice (512 bytes), it is actually loading boot1 and transferring control to it.

The main task of boot1 is to load the next boot stage. This next stage is somewhat more complex. It is composed of a server called the "Boot Extender", or BTX, and a client, called boot2. As we will see, the last boot stage, loader, is also a client of the BTX server.

Let us now look in detail at what exactly is done by boot1, starting like we did for boot0, at its entry point:

```
start:
 jmp main
```

Figure 1.11. sys/boot/i386/boot2/boot1.S

The entry point at start simply jumps past a special data area to the label main, which in turn looks like this:

```
main:
        cld   # String ops inc
        xor %cx,%cx  # Zero
        mov %cx,%es  # Address
        mov %cx,%ds  #  data
        mov %cx,%ss  # Set up
        mov $start,%sp  #  stack
        mov %sp,%si  # Source
        mov $0x700,%di  # Destination
        incb %ch   # Word count
        rep   # Copy
        movsw   #  code
```

Figure 1.12. sys/boot/i386/boot2/boot1.S

Just like boot0, this code relocates boot1, this time to memory address 0x700. However, unlike boot0, it does not jump there. boot1 is linked to execute at address 0x7c00, effectively where it was loaded in the first place. The reason for this relocation will be discussed shortly.

Next comes a loop that looks for the FreeBSD slice. Although boot0 loaded boot1 from the FreeBSD slice, no information was passed to it about this [4], so boot1 must rescan the partition table to find where the FreeBSD slice starts. Therefore it rereads the MBR:

```
        mov $part4,%si  # Partition
        cmpb $0x80,%dl  # Hard drive?
        jb main.4   # No
        movb $0x1,%dh  # Block count
        callw nread  # Read MBR
```

Figure 1.13. sys/boot/i386/boot2/boot1.S

In the code above, register %dl maintains information about the boot device. This is passed on by the BIOS and preserved by the MBR. Numbers 0x80 and greater tells us that we are dealing with a hard drive, so a call is made

---

[3]There is a file /boot/boot1 , but it is not the written to the beginning of the FreeBSD slice. Instead, it is concatenated with boot2 to form boot, which *is* written to the beginning of the FreeBSD slice and read at boot time.

[4]Actually we did pass a pointer to the slice entry in register %si. However, boot1 does not assume that it was loaded by boot0 (perhaps some other MBR loaded it, and did not pass this information), so it assumes nothing.

to nread, where the MBR is read. Arguments to nread are passed through %si and %dh. The memory address at label part4 is copied to %si. This memory address holds a "fake partition" to be used by nread. The following is the data in the fake partition:

```
    part4:
.byte 0x80, 0x00, 0x01, 0x00
.byte 0xa5, 0xfe, 0xff, 0xff
.byte 0x00, 0x00, 0x00, 0x00
.byte 0x50, 0xc3, 0x00, 0x00
```

Figure 1.14. sys/boot/i386/boot2/Makefile

In particular, the LBA for this fake partition is hardcoded to zero. This is used as an argument to the BIOS for reading absolute sector one from the hard drive. Alternatively, CHS addressing could be used. In this case, the fake partition holds cylinder 0, head 0 and sector 1, which is equivalent to absolute sector one.

Let us now proceed to take a look at nread:

```
nread:
      mov $0x8c00,%bx  # Transfer buffer
      mov 0x8(%si),%ax  # Get
      mov 0xa(%si),%cx  #  LBA
      push %cs  # Read from
      callw xread.1 #  disk
      jnc return  # If success, return
```

Figure 1.15. sys/boot/i386/boot2/boot1.S

Recall that %si points to the fake partition. The word [5] at offset 0x8 is copied to register %ax and word at offset 0xa to %cx. They are interpreted by the BIOS as the lower 4-byte value denoting the LBA to be read (the upper four bytes are assumed to be zero). Register %bx holds the memory address where the MBR will be loaded. The instruction pushing %cs onto the stack is very interesting. In this context, it accomplishes nothing. However, as we will see shortly, boot2, in conjunction with the BTX server, also uses xread.1. This mechanism will be discussed in the next section.

The code at xread.1 further calls the read function, which actually calls the BIOS asking for the disk sector:

```
xread.1:
  pushl $0x0  #  absolute
  push %cx  #  block
  push %ax  #  number
  push %es  # Address of
  push %bx  #  transfer buffer
  xor %ax,%ax  # Number of
  movb %dh,%al  #  blocks to
  push %ax  #  transfer
  push $0x10  # Size of packet
  mov %sp,%bp  # Packet pointer
  callw read  # Read from disk
  lea 0x10(%bp),%sp # Clear stack
  lret  # To far caller
```

Figure 1.16. sys/boot/i386/boot2/boot1.S

Note the long return instruction at the end of this block. This instruction pops out the %cs register pushed by nread, and returns. Finally, nread also returns.

With the MBR loaded to memory, the actual loop for searching the FreeBSD slice begins:

---

[5]In the context of 16-bit real mode, a word is 2 bytes.

```
 mov $0x1,%cx    # Two passes
main.1:
 mov $0x8dbe,%si # Partition table
 movb $0x1,%dh   # Partition
main.2:
 cmpb $0xa5,0x4(%si)  # Our partition type?
 jne main.3   # No
 jcxz main.5   # If second pass
 testb $0x80,(%si)  # Active?
 jnz main.5   # Yes
main.3:
 add $0x10,%si   # Next entry
 incb %dh   # Partition
 cmpb $0x5,%dh   # In table?
 jb main.2   # Yes
 dec %cx    # Do two
 jcxz main.1   #  passes
```

Figure 1.17. `sys/boot/i386/boot2/boot1.S`

If a FreeBSD slice is identified, execution continues at main.5. Note that when a FreeBSD slice is found %si points to the appropriate entry in the partition table, and %dh holds the partition number. We assume that a FreeBSD slice is found, so we continue execution at main.5:

```
main.5:
 mov %dx,0x900      # Save args
 movb $0x10,%dh      # Sector count
 callw nread      # Read disk
 mov $0x9000,%bx      # BTX
 mov 0xa(%bx),%si      # Get BTX length and set
 add %bx,%si      #  %si to start of boot2.bin
 mov $0xc000,%di      # Client page 2
 mov $0xa200,%cx      # Byte
 sub %si,%cx      #  count
 rep      # Relocate
 movsb      #  client
```

Figure 1.18. `sys/boot/i386/boot2/boot1.S`

Recall that at this point, register %si points to the FreeBSD slice entry in the MBR partition table, so a call to nread will effectively read sectors at the beginning of this partition. The argument passed on register %dh tells nread to read 16 disk sectors. Recall that the first 512 bytes, or the first sector of the FreeBSD slice, coincides with the boot1 program. Also recall that the file written to the beginning of the FreeBSD slice is not /boot/boot1 , but /boot/boot. Let us look at the size of these files in the filesystem:

```
-r--r--r--  1 root   wheel   512B Jan  8 00:15 /boot/boot0
-r--r--r--  1 root   wheel   512B Jan  8 00:15 /boot/boot1
-r--r--r--  1 root   wheel   7.5K Jan  8 00:15 /boot/boot2
-r--r--r--  1 root   wheel   8.0K Jan  8 00:15 /boot/boot
```

Both boot0 and boot1 are 512 bytes each, so they fit *exactly* in one disk sector. boot2 is much bigger, holding both the BTX server and the boot2 client. Finally, a file called simply boot is 512 bytes larger than boot2. This file is a concatenation of boot1 and boot2. As already noted, boot0 is the file written to the absolute first disk sector (the MBR), and boot is the file written to the first sector of the FreeBSD slice; boot1 and boot2 are *not* written to disk. The command used to concatenate boot1 and boot2 into a single boot is merely cat boot1 boot2 > boot .

So boot1 occupies exactly the first 512 bytes of boot and, because boot is written to the first sector of the FreeBSD slice, boot1 fits exactly in this first sector. Because nread reads the first 16 sectors of the FreeBSD slice, it effectively reads the entire boot file [6]. We will see more details about how boot is formed from boot1 and boot2 in the next section.

---

[6] 512*16=8192 bytes, exactly the size of boot

Recall that nread uses memory address 0x8c00 as the transfer buffer to hold the sectors read. This address is conveniently chosen. Indeed, because boot1 belongs to the first 512 bytes, it ends up in the address range 0x8c00-0x8dff. The 512 bytes that follows (range 0x8e00-0x8fff) is used to store the *bsdlabel* [7].

Starting at address 0x9000 is the beginning of the BTX server, and immediately following is the boot2 client. The BTX server acts as a kernel, and executes in protected mode in the most privileged level. In contrast, the BTX clients (boot2, for example), execute in user mode. We will see how this is accomplished in the next section. The code after the call to nread locates the beginning of boot2 in the memory buffer, and copies it to memory address 0xc000. This is because the BTX server arranges boot2 to execute in a segment starting at 0xa000. We explore this in detail in the following section.

The last code block of boot1 enables access to memory above 1MB [8] and concludes with a jump to the starting point of the BTX server:

```
seta20:
  cli   # Disable interrupts
seta20.1:
  dec %cx   # Timeout?
  jz seta20.3 # Yes

  inb $0x64,%al  # Get status
  testb $0x2,%al # Busy?
  jnz seta20.1 # Yes
  movb $0xd1,%al # Command: Write
  outb %al,$0x64 # output port
seta20.2:
  inb $0x64,%al  # Get status
  testb $0x2,%al # Busy?
  jnz seta20.2 # Yes
  movb $0xdf,%al # Enable
  outb %al,$0x60 # A20
seta20.3:
  sti   # Enable interrupts
  jmp 0x9010 # Start BTX
```

Figure 1.19. sys/boot/i386/boot2/boot1.S

Note that right before the jump, interrupts are enabled.

1.6. The BTX Server

Next in our boot sequence is the BTX Server. Let us quickly remember how we got here:

- The BIOS loads the absolute sector one (the MBR, or boot0), to address 0x7c00 and jumps there.

- boot0 relocates itself to 0x600, the address it was linked to execute, and jumps over there. It then reads the first sector of the FreeBSD slice (which consists of boot1) into address 0x7c00 and jumps over there.

- boot1 loads the first 16 sectors of the FreeBSD slice into address 0x8c00. This 16 sectors, or 8192 bytes, is the whole file boot. The file is a concatenation of boot1 and boot2. boot2, in turn, contains the BTX server and the boot2 client. Finally, a jump is made to address 0x9010, the entry point of the BTX server.

Before studying the BTX Server in detail, let us further review how the single, all-in-one boot file is created. The way boot is built is defined in its Makefile (/usr/src/sys/boot/i386/boot2/Makefile). Let us look at the rule that creates the boot file:

---

[7]Historically known as "disklabel". If you ever wondered where FreeBSD stored this information, it is in this region. See bsdlabel(8)

[8]This is necessary for legacy reasons. Interested readers should see http://en.wikipedia.org/wiki/A20_line.

```
      boot: boot1 boot2
cat boot1 boot2 > boot
```

Figure 1.20. `sys/boot/i386/boot2/Makefile`

This tells us that **boot1** and **boot2** are needed, and the rule simply concatenates them to produce a single file called **boot**. The rules for creating **boot1** are also quite simple:

```
      boot1: boot1.out
objcopy -S -O binary boot1.out boot1

      boot1.out: boot1.o
ld -e start -Ttext 0x7c00 -o boot1.out boot1.o
```

Figure 1.21. `sys/boot/i386/boot2/Makefile`

To apply the rule for creating **boot1**, **boot1.out** must be resolved. This, in turn, depends on the existence of **boot1.o**. This last file is simply the result of assembling our familiar **boot1.S**, without linking. Now, the rule for creating **boot1.out** is applied. This tells us that **boot1.o** should be linked with **start** as its entry point, and starting at address **0x7c00**. Finally, **boot1** is created from **boot1.out** applying the appropriate rule. This rule is the **objcopy** command applied to **boot1.out**. Note the flags passed to **objcopy**: -S tells it to strip all relocation and symbolic information; -O **binary** indicates the output format, that is, a simple, unformatted binary file.

Having **boot1**, let us take a look at how **boot2** is constructed:

```
      boot2: boot2.ld
@set -- `ls -l boot2.ld`; x=$$((7680-$$5)); \
    echo "$$x bytes available"; test $$x -ge 0
dd if=boot2.ld of=boot2 obs=7680 conv=osync

      boot2.ld: boot2.ldr boot2.bin ../btx/btx/btx
btxld -v -E 0x2000 -f bin -b ../btx/btx/btx -l boot2.ldr \
    -o boot2.ld -P 1 boot2.bin

      boot2.ldr:
dd if=/dev/zero of=boot2.ldr bs=512 count=1

      boot2.bin: boot2.out
objcopy -S -O binary boot2.out boot2.bin

      boot2.out: ../btx/lib/crt0.o boot2.o sio.o
ld -Ttext 0x2000 -o boot2.out

      boot2.o: boot2.s
${CC} ${ACFLAGS} -c boot2.s

      boot2.s: boot2.c boot2.h ${.CURDIR}/../../common/ufsread.c
${CC} ${CFLAGS} -S -o boot2.s.tmp ${.CURDIR}/boot2.c
sed -e '/align/d' -e '/nop/d' "MISSING" boot2.s.tmp > boot2.s
rm -f boot2.s.tmp

      boot2.h: boot1.out
${NM} -t d ${.ALLSRC} | awk '/([0-9])+ T xread/ \
    { x = $$1 - ORG1; \
    printf("#define XREADORG %#x\n", REL1 + x) }' \
    ORG1=`printf "%d" ${ORG1}` \
    REL1=`printf "%d" ${REL1}` > ${.TARGET}
```

Figure 1.22. `sys/boot/i386/boot2/Makefile`

The mechanism for building **boot2** is far more elaborate. Let us point out the most relevant facts. The dependency list is as follows:

```
boot2: boot2.ld
boot2.ld: boot2.ldr boot2.bin ${BTXDIR}/btx/btx
boot2.bin: boot2.out
boot2.out: ${BTXDIR}/lib/crt0.o boot2.o sio.o
boot2.o: boot2.s
boot2.s: boot2.c boot2.h ${.CURDIR}/../../common/ufsread.c
boot2.h: boot1.out
```

Figure 1.23. `sys/boot/i386/boot2/Makefile`

Note that initially there is no header file boot2.h, but its creation depends on boot1.out, which we already have. The rule for its creation is a bit terse, but the important thing is that the output, boot2.h, is something like this:

```
#define XREADORG 0x725
```

Figure 1.24. `sys/boot/i386/boot2/boot2.h`

Recall that boot1 was relocated (i.e., copied from 0x7c00 to 0x700). This relocation will now make sense, because as we will see, the BTX server reclaims some memory, including the space where boot1 was originally loaded. However, the BTX server needs access to boot1's xread function; this function, according to the output of boot2.h, is at location 0x725. Indeed, the BTX server uses the xread function from boot1's relocated code. This function is now accesible from within the boot2 client.

We next build boot2.s from files boot2.h, boot2.c and /usr/src/sys/boot/common/ufsread.c. The rule for this is to compile the code in boot2.c (which includes boot2.h and ufsread.c) into assembly code. Having boot2.s, the next rule assembles boot2.s, creating the object file boot2.o. The next rule directs the linker to link various files (crt0.o, boot2.o and sio.o). Note that the output file, boot2.out, is linked to execute at address 0x2000. Recall that boot2 will be executed in user mode, within a special user segment set up by the BTX server. This segment starts at 0xa000. Also, remember that the boot2 portion of boot was copied to address 0xc000, that is, offset 0x2000 from the start of the user segment, so boot2 will work properly when we transfer control to it. Next, boot2.bin is created from boot2.out by stripping its symbols and format information; boot2.bin is a *raw* binary. Now, note that a file boot2.ldr is created as a 512-byte file full of zeros. This space is reserved for the bsdlabel.

Now that we have files boot1, boot2.bin and boot2.ldr, only the BTX server is missing before creating the all-in-one boot file. The BTX server is located in /usr/src/sys/boot/i386/btx/btx; it has its own Makefile with its own set of rules for building. The important thing to notice is that it is also compiled as a *raw* binary, and that it is linked to execute at address 0x9000. The details can be found in /usr/src/sys/boot/i386/btx/btx/Makefile.

Having the files that comprise the boot program, the final step is to *merge* them. This is done by a special program called btxld (source located in /usr/src/usr.sbin/btxld). Some arguments to this program include the name of the output file (boot), its entry point (0x2000) and its file format (raw binary). The various files are finally merged by this utility into the file boot, which consists of boot1, boot2, the bsdlabel and the BTX server. This file, which takes exactly 16 sectors, or 8192 bytes, is what is actually written to the beginning of the FreeBSD slice during instalation. Let us now proceed to study the BTX server program.

The BTX server prepares a simple environment and switches from 16-bit real mode to 32-bit protected mode, right before passing control to the client. This includes initializing and updating the following data structures:

- Modifies the Interrupt Vector Table (IVT). The IVT provides exception and interrupt handlers for Real-Mode code.

- The Interrupt Descriptor Table (IDT) is created. Entries are provided for processor exceptions, hardware interrupts, two system calls and V86 interface. The IDT provides exception and interrupt handlers for Protected-Mode code.

- A Task-State Segment (TSS) is created. This is necessary because the processor works in the *least* privileged level when executing the client (boot2), but in the *most* privileged level when executing the BTX server.

- The GDT (Global Descriptor Table) is set up. Entries (descriptors) are provided for supervisor code and data, user code and data, and real-mode code and data. [9]

Let us now start studying the actual implementation. Recall that boot1 made a jump to address 0x9010, the BTX server's entry point. Before studying program execution there, note that the BTX server has a special header at address range 0x9000-0x900f, right before its entry point. This header is defined as follows:

```
start:         # Start of code
/*
 * BTX header.
 */
btx_hdr: .byte 0xeb   # Machine ID
  .byte 0xe   # Header size
  .ascii "BTX"   # Magic
  .byte 0x1   # Major version
  .byte 0x2   # Minor version
  .byte BTX_FLAGS   # Flags
  .word PAG_CNT-MEM_ORG>>0xc # Paging control
  .word break-start  # Text size
  .long 0x0   # Entry address
```

Figure 1.25. `sys/boot/i386/btx/btx/btx.S`

Note the first two bytes are 0xeb and 0xe. In the IA-32 architecture, these two bytes are interpreted as a relative jump past the header into the entry point, so in theory, boot1 could jump here (address 0x9000) instead of address 0x9010. Note that the last field in the BTX header is a pointer to the client's (boot2) entry point. This field is patched at link time.

Immediately following the header is the BTX server's entry point:

```
/*
 * Initialization routine.
 */
init:  cli     # Disable interrupts
  xor %ax,%ax   # Zero/segment
  mov %ax,%ss   # Set up
  mov $0x1800,%sp # stack
  mov %ax,%es   # Address
  mov %ax,%ds   # data
  pushl $0x2   # Clear
  popfl    # flags
```

Figure 1.26. `sys/boot/i386/btx/btx/btx.S`

This code disables interrupts, sets up a working stack (starting at address 0x1800) and clears the flags in the EFLAGS register. Note that the popfl instruction pops out a doubleword (4 bytes) from the stack and places it in the EFLAGS register. Because the value actually popped is 2, the EFLAGS register is effectively cleared (IA-32 requires that bit 2 of the EFLAGS register always be 1).

Our next code block clears (sets to 0) the memory range 0x5e00-0x8fff. This range is where the various data structures will be created:

```
/*
 * Initialize memory.
 */
  mov $0x5e00,%di  # Memory to initialize
  mov $(0x9000-0x5e00)/2,%cx # Words to zero
  rep    # Zero-fill
  stosw    # memory
```

Figure 1.27. `sys/boot/i386/btx/btx/btx.S`

---

[9]Real-mode code and data are necessary when switching back to real mode from protected mode, as suggested by the Intel manuals.

Recall that `boot1` was originally loaded to address `0x7c00`, so, with this memory initialization, that copy effectively dissapeared. However, also recall that `boot1` was relocated to `0x700`, so *that* copy is still in memory, and the BTX server will make use of it.

Next, the real-mode IVT (Interrupt Vector Table is updated. The IVT is an array of segment/offset pairs for exception and interrupt handlers. The BIOS normally maps hardware interrupts to interrupt vectors `0x8` to `0xf` and `0x70` to `0x77` but, as will be seen, the 8259A Programmable Interrupt Controller, the chip controlling the actual mapping of hardware interrupts to interrupt vectors, is programmed to remap these interrupt vectors from `0x8-0xf` to `0x20-0x27` and from `0x70-0x77` to `0x28-0x2f`. Thus, interrupt handlers are provided for interrupt vectors `0x20-0x2f`. The reason the BIOS-provided handlers are not used directly is because they work in 16-bit real mode, but not 32-bit protected mode. Processor mode will be switched to 32-bit protected mode shortly. However, the BTX server sets up a mechanism to effectively use the handlers provided by the BIOS:

```
/*
 * Update real mode IDT for reflecting hardware interrupts.
 */
  mov $intr20,%bx   # Address first handler
  mov $0x10,%cx   # Number of handlers
  mov $0x20*4,%di   # First real mode IDT entry
init.0:  mov %bx,(%di)   # Store IP
  inc %di   # Address next
  inc %di   #  entry
  stosw    # Store CS
  add $4,%bx   # Next handler
  loop init.0   # Next IRQ
```

Figure 1.28. `sys/boot/i386/btx/btx/btx.S`

The next block creates the IDT (Interrupt Descriptor Table). The IDT is analogous, in protected mode, to the IVT in real mode. That is, the IDT describes the various exception and interrupt handlers used when the processor is executing in protected mode. In essence, it also consists of an array of segment/offset pairs, although the structure is somewhat more complex, because segments in protected mode are different than in real mode, and various protection mechanisms apply:

```
/*
 * Create IDT.
 */
  mov $0x5e00,%di   # IDT's address
  mov $idtctl,%si   # Control string
init.1:  lodsb    # Get entry
  cbw   #  count
  xchg %ax,%cx   # as word
  jcxz init.4   # If done
  lodsb    # Get segment
  xchg %ax,%dx   # P:DPL:type
  lodsw    # Get control
  xchg %ax,%bx   #  set
  lodsw    # Get handler offset
  mov $SEL_SCODE,%dh # Segment selector
init.2:  shr %bx    # Handle this int?
  jnc init.3   # No
  mov %ax,(%di)   # Set handler offset
  mov %dh,0x2(%di)  #  and selector
  mov %dl,0x5(%di)  # Set P:DPL:type
  add $0x4,%ax   # Next handler
init.3:  lea 0x8(%di),%di # Next entry
  loop init.2   # Till set done
  jmp init.1   # Continue
```

Figure 1.29. `sys/boot/i386/btx/btx/btx.S`

Each entry in the IDT is 8 bytes long. Besides the segment/offset information, they also describe the segment type, privilege level, and whether the segment is present in memory or not. The construction is such that interrupt vectors from `0` to `0xf` (exceptions) are handled by function `intx00`; vector `0x10` (also an exception) is handled by `intx10`; hardware interrupts, which are later configured to start at interrupt vector `0x20` all the way to interrupt vector `0x2f`, are handled by function `intx20`. Lastly, interrupt vector `0x30`, which is used for system calls, is handled by `intx30`, and vectors `0x31` and `0x32` are handled by `intx31`. It must be noted that only descriptors for interrupt vectors `0x30`, `0x31` and `0x32` are given privilege level 3, the same privilege level as the `boot2` client, which means the client can execute a software-generated interrupt to this vectors through the `int` instruction without failing (this is the way `boot2` use the services provided by the BTX server). Also, note that *only* software-generated interrupts are protected from code executing in lesser privilege levels. Hardware-generated interrupts and processor-generated exceptions are *always* handled adequately, regardless of the actual privileges involved.

The next step is to initialize the TSS (Task-State Segment). The TSS is a hardware feature that helps the operating system or executive software implement multitasking functionality through process abstraction. The IA-32 architecture demands the creation and use of *at least* one TSS if multitasking facilities are used or different privilege levels are defined. Because the `boot2` client is executed in privilege level 3, but the BTX server does in privilege level 0, a TSS must be defined:

```
/*
 * Initialize TSS.
 */
init.4:  movb $_ESP0H,TSS_ESP0+1(%di) # Set ESP0
  movb $SEL_SDATA,TSS_SS0(%di) # Set SS0
  movb $_TSSIO,TSS_MAP(%di) # Set I/O bit map base
```

Figure 1.30. `sys/boot/i386/btx/btx/btx.S`

Note that a value is given for the Privilege Level 0 stack pointer and stack segment in the TSS. This is needed because, if an interrupt or exception is received while executing `boot2` in Privilege Level 3, a change to Privilege Level 0 is automatically performed by the processor, so a new working stack is needed. Finally, the I/O Map Base Address field of the TSS is given a value, which is a 16-bit offset from the beginning of the TSS to the I/O Permission Bitmap and the Interrupt Redirection Bitmap.

After the IDT and TSS are created, the processor is ready to switch to protected mode. This is done in the next block:

```
/*
 * Bring up the system.
 */
  mov $0x2820,%bx    # Set protected mode
  callw setpic   #  IRQ offsets
  lidt idtdesc   # Set IDT
  lgdt gdtdesc   # Set GDT
  mov %cr0,%eax   # Switch to protected
  inc %ax    #  mode
  mov %eax,%cr0   #
  ljmp $SEL_SCODE,$init.8 # To 32-bit code
  .code32
init.8:  xorl %ecx,%ecx   # Zero
  movb $SEL_SDATA,%cl  # To 32-bit
  movw %cx,%ss   # stack
```

Figure 1.31. `sys/boot/i386/btx/btx/btx.S`

First, a call is made to `setpic` to program the 8259A PIC (Programmable Interrupt Controller). This chip is connected to multiple hardware interrupt sources. Upon receiving an interrupt from a device, it signals the processor with the appropriate interrupt vector. This can be customized so that specific interrupts are associated with specific interrupt vectors, as explained before. Next, the IDTR (Interrupt Descriptor Table Register) and GDTR (Global Descriptor Table Register) are loaded with the instructions `lidt` and `lgdt`, respectively. These registers are loaded with the base address and limit address for the IDT and GDT. The following three instructions set the Protection Enable (PE) bit of the `%cr0` register. This effectively switches the processor to 32-bit protected mode. Next, a long jump is made to `init.8` using segment selector SEL_SCODE, which selects the Supervisor Code Segment. The processor is effectively executing in CPL 0, the most privileged level, after this jump. Finally, the Supervisor

Data Segment is selected for the stack by assigning the segment selector SEL_SDATA to the %ss register. This data segment also has a privilege level of 0.

Our last code block is responsible for loading the TR (Task Register) with the segment selector for the TSS we created earlier, and setting the User Mode environment before passing execution control to the **boot2** client.

```
/*
 * Launch user task.
 */
  movb $SEL_TSS,%cl  # Set task
  ltr %cx     #  register
  movl $0xa000,%edx  # User base address
  movzwl %ss:BDA_MEM,%eax  # Get free memory
  shll $0xa,%eax    # To bytes
  subl $ARGSPACE,%eax  # Less arg space
  subl %edx,%eax    # Less base
  movb $SEL_UDATA,%cl  # User data selector
  pushl %ecx     # Set SS
  pushl %eax     # Set ESP
  push $0x202    # Set flags (IF set)
  push $SEL_UCODE   # Set CS
  pushl btx_hdr+0xc  # Set EIP
  pushl %ecx     # Set GS
  pushl %ecx     # Set FS
  pushl %ecx     # Set DS
  pushl %ecx     # Set ES
  pushl %edx     # Set EAX
  movb $0x7,%cl    # Set remaining
init.9:  push $0x0   #  general
  loop init.9    #  registers
  popa     #  and initialize
  popl %es    # Initialize
  popl %ds    #  user
  popl %fs    #  segment
  popl %gs    #  registers
  iret     # To user mode
```

Figure 1.32. `sys/boot/i386/btx/btx/btx.S`

Note that the client's environment include a stack segment selector and stack pointer (registers %ss and %esp). Indeed, once the TR is loaded with the appropriate stack segment selector (instruction ltr), the stack pointer is calculated and pushed onto the stack along with the stack's segment selector. Next, the value 0x202 is pushed onto the stack; it is the value that the EFLAGS will get when control is passed to the client. Also, the User Mode code segment selector and the client's entry point are pushed. Recall that this entry point is patched in the BTX header at link time. Finally, segment selectors (stored in register %ecx) for the segment registers %gs, %fs, %ds and %es are pushed onto the stack, along with the value at %edx (0xa000). Keep in mind the various values that have been pushed onto the stack (they will be popped out shortly). Next, values for the remaining general purpose registers are also pushed onto the stack (note the loop that pushes the value 0 seven times). Now, values will be started to be popped out of the stack. First, the popa instruction pops out of the stack the latest seven values pushed. They are stored in the general purpose registers in order %edi, %esi, %ebp, %ebx, %edx, %ecx, %eax . Then, the various segment selectors pushed are popped into the various segment registers. Five values still remain on the stack. They are popped when the iret instruction is executed. This instruction first pops the value that was pushed from the BTX header. This value is a pointer to boot2's entry point. It is placed in the register %eip, the instruction pointer register. Next, the segment selector for the User Code Segment is popped and copied to register %cs. Remember that this segment's privilege level is 3, the least privileged level. This means that we must provide values for the stack of this privilege level. This is why the processor, besides further popping the value for the EFLAGS register, does two more pops out of the stack. These values go to the stack pointer (%esp) and the stack segment (%ss). Now, execution continues at boot0's entry point.

It is important to note how the User Code Segment is defined. This segment's *base address* is set to 0xa000. This means that code memory addresses are *relative* to address 0xa000; if code being executed is fetched from address 0x2000, the *actual* memory addressed is 0xa000+0x2000=0xc000.

1.7. boot2 Stage

boot2 defines an important structure, struct bootinfo. This structure is initialized by boot2 and passed to the loader, and then further to the kernel. Some nodes of this structures are set by boot2, the rest by the loader. This structure, among other information, contains the kernel filename, BIOS harddisk geometry, BIOS drive number for boot device, physical memory available, envp pointer etc. The definition for it is:

```
/usr/include/machine/bootinfo.h:
struct bootinfo {
 u_int32_t bi_version;
 u_int32_t bi_kernelname;  /* represents a char * */
 u_int32_t bi_nfs_diskless; /* struct nfs_diskless * */
    /* End of fields that are always present. */
#define bi_endcommon bi_n_bios_used
 u_int32_t bi_n_bios_used;
 u_int32_t bi_bios_geom[N_BIOS_GEOM];
 u_int32_t bi_size;
 u_int8_t bi_memsizes_valid;
 u_int8_t bi_bios_dev;  /* bootdev BIOS unit number */
 u_int8_t bi_pad[2];
 u_int32_t bi_basemem;
 u_int32_t bi_extmem;
 u_int32_t bi_symtab;  /* struct symtab * */
 u_int32_t bi_esymtab;  /* struct symtab * */
    /* Items below only from advanced bootloader */
 u_int32_t bi_kernend;  /* end of kernel space */
 u_int32_t bi_envp;  /* environment */
 u_int32_t bi_modulep;  /* preloaded modules */
};
```

boot2 enters into an infinite loop waiting for user input, then calls load(). If the user does not press anything, the loop breaks by a timeout, so load() will load the default file (/boot/loader). Functions ino_t lookup(char *filename) and int xfsread(ino_t inode, void *buf, size_t nbyte) are used to read the content of a file into memory. /boot/loader is an ELF binary, but where the ELF header is prepended with a.out's struct exec structure. load() scans the loader's ELF header, loading the content of /boot/loader into memory, and passing the execution to the loader's entry:

```
sys/boot/i386/boot2/boot2.c:
    __exec((caddr_t)addr, RB_BOOTINFO | (opts & RBX_MASK),
    MAKEBOOTDEV(dev_maj[dsk.type], 0, dsk.slice, dsk.unit, dsk.part),
    0, 0, 0, VTOP(&bootinfo));
```

1.8. loader Stage

loader is a BTX client as well. I will not describe it here in detail, there is a comprehensive manpage written by Mike Smith, loader(8). The underlying mechanisms and BTX were discussed above.

The main task for the loader is to boot the kernel. When the kernel is loaded into memory, it is being called by the loader:

```
sys/boot/common/boot.c:
    /* Call the exec handler from the loader matching the kernel */
    module_formats[km->m_loader]->l_exec(km);
```

1.9. Kernel Initialization

Let us take a look at the command that links the kernel. This will help identify the exact location where the loader passes execution to the kernel. This location is the kernel's actual entry point.

```
sys/conf/Makefile.i386:
```

```
ld -elf -Bdynamic -T /usr/src/sys/conf/ldscript.i386  -export-dynamic \
-dynamic-linker /red/herring -o kernel -X locore.o \
<lots of kernel .o files>
```

A few interesting things can be seen here. First, the kernel is an ELF dynamically linked binary, but the dynamic linker for kernel is /red/herring, which is definitely a bogus file. Second, taking a look at the file sys/conf/ldscript.i386 gives an idea about what ld options are used when compiling a kernel. Reading through the first few lines, the string

```
sys/conf/ldscript.i386:
ENTRY(btext)
```

says that a kernel's entry point is the symbol `btext'. This symbol is defined in locore.s:

```
sys/i386/i386/locore.s:
 .text
/*****************************************************************
 *
 * This is where the bootblocks start us, set the ball rolling...
 *
 */
NON_GPROF_ENTRY(btext)
```

First, the register EFLAGS is set to a predefined value of 0x00000002. Then all the segment registers are initialized:

```
sys/i386/i386/locore.s:
/* Don't trust what the BIOS gives for eflags. */
 pushl $PSL_KERNEL
 popfl

/*
 * Don't trust what the BIOS gives for %fs and %gs.  Trust the bootstrap
 * to set %cs, %ds, %es and %ss.
 */
 mov %ds, %ax
 mov %ax, %fs
 mov %ax, %gs
```

btext calls the routines recover_bootinfo(), identify_cpu(), create_pagetables(), which are also defined in locore.s. Here is a description of what they do:

recover_bootinfo	This routine parses the parameters to the kernel passed from the bootstrap. The kernel may have been booted in 3 ways: by the loader, described above, by the old disk boot blocks, or by the old diskless boot procedure. This function determines the booting method, and stores the struct bootinfo structure into the kernel memory.
identify_cpu	This functions tries to find out what CPU it is running on, storing the value found in a variable _cpu.
create_pagetables	This function allocates and fills out a Page Table Directory at the top of the kernel memory area.

The next steps are enabling VME, if the CPU supports it:

```
 testl $CPUID_VME, R(_cpu_feature)
 jz 1f
 movl %cr4, %eax
 orl $CR4_VME, %eax
 movl %eax, %cr4
```

Then, enabling paging:

```
/* Now enable paging */
 movl R(_IdlePTD), %eax
 movl %eax,%cr3    /* load ptd addr into mmu */
 movl %cr0,%eax    /* get control word */
 orl $CR0_PE|CR0_PG,%eax  /* enable paging */
 movl %eax,%cr0    /* and let's page NOW! */
```

The next three lines of code are because the paging was set, so the jump is needed to continue the execution in virtualized address space:

```
 pushl $begin      /* jump to high virtualized address */
 ret

/* now running relocated at KERNBASE where the system is linked to run */
begin:
```

The function init386() is called with a pointer to the first free physical page, after that mi_startup(). init386 is an architecture dependent initialization function, and mi_startup() is an architecture independent one (the 'mi_' prefix stands for Machine Independent). The kernel never returns from mi_startup(), and by calling it, the kernel finishes booting:

```
sys/i386/i386/locore.s:
 movl physfree, %esi
 pushl %esi    /* value of first for init386(first) */
 call _init386   /* wire 386 chip for unix operation */
 call _mi_startup  /* autoconfiguration, mountroot etc */
 hlt  /* never returns to here */
```

1.9.1. init386()

init386() is defined in sys/i386/i386/machdep.c and performs low-level initialization specific to the i386 chip. The switch to protected mode was performed by the loader. The loader has created the very first task, in which the kernel continues to operate. Before looking at the code, consider the tasks the processor must complete to initialize protected mode execution:

• Initialize the kernel tunable parameters, passed from the bootstrapping program.

• Prepare the GDT.

• Prepare the IDT.

• Initialize the system console.

• Initialize the DDB, if it is compiled into kernel.

• Initialize the TSS.

• Prepare the LDT.

• Set up proc0's pcb.

init386() initializes the tunable parameters passed from bootstrap by setting the environment pointer (envp) and calling init_param1() . The envp pointer has been passed from loader in the bootinfo structure:

```
sys/i386/i386/machdep.c:
 kern_envp = (caddr_t)bootinfo.bi_envp + KERNBASE;

 /* Init basic tunables, hz etc */
 init_param1();
```

init_param1() is defined in sys/kern/subr_param.c . That file has a number of sysctls, and two functions, init_param1() and init_param2() , that are called from init386() :

```
sys/kern/subr_param.c:
 hz = HZ;
 TUNABLE_INT_FETCH("kern.hz", &hz);
```

TUNABLE_<typename>_FETCH is used to fetch the value from the environment:

```
/usr/src/sys/sys/kernel.h:
#define TUNABLE_INT_FETCH(path, var) getenv_int((path), (var))
```

Sysctl kern.hz is the system clock tick. Additionally, these sysctls are set by init_param1() : kern.maxswzone, kern.maxbcache, kern.maxtsiz, kern.dfldsiz, kern.maxdsiz, kern.dflssiz, kern.maxssiz, kern.sgrowsiz.

Then init386() prepares the Global Descriptors Table (GDT). Every task on an x86 is running in its own virtual address space, and this space is addressed by a segment:offset pair. Say, for instance, the current instruction to be executed by the processor lies at CS:EIP, then the linear virtual address for that instruction would be "the virtual address of code segment CS" + EIP. For convenience, segments begin at virtual address 0 and end at a 4Gb boundary. Therefore, the instruction's linear virtual address for this example would just be the value of EIP. Segment registers such as CS, DS etc are the selectors, i.e., indexes, into GDT (to be more precise, an index is not a selector itself, but the INDEX field of a selector). FreeBSD's GDT holds descriptors for 15 selectors per CPU:

```
sys/i386/i386/machdep.c:
union descriptor gdt[NGDT * MAXCPU]; /* global descriptor table */

sys/i386/include/segments.h:
/*
 * Entries in the Global Descriptor Table (GDT)
 */
#define GNULL_SEL 0 /* Null Descriptor */
#define GCODE_SEL 1 /* Kernel Code Descriptor */
#define GDATA_SEL 2 /* Kernel Data Descriptor */
#define GPRIV_SEL 3 /* SMP Per-Processor Private Data */
#define GPROC0_SEL 4 /* Task state process slot zero and up */
#define GLDT_SEL 5 /* LDT - eventually one per process */
#define GUSERLDT_SEL 6 /* User LDT */
#define GTGATE_SEL 7 /* Process task switch gate */
#define GBIOSLOWMEM_SEL 8 /* BIOS low memory access (must be entry 8) */
#define GPANIC_SEL 9 /* Task state to consider panic from */
#define GBIOSCODE32_SEL 10 /* BIOS interface (32bit Code) */
#define GBIOSCODE16_SEL 11 /* BIOS interface (16bit Code) */
#define GBIOSDATA_SEL 12 /* BIOS interface (Data) */
#define GBIOSUTIL_SEL 13 /* BIOS interface (Utility) */
#define GBIOSARGS_SEL 14 /* BIOS interface (Arguments) */
```

Note that those #defines are not selectors themselves, but just a field INDEX of a selector, so they are exactly the indices of the GDT. for example, an actual selector for the kernel code (GCODE_SEL) has the value 0x08.

The next step is to initialize the Interrupt Descriptor Table (IDT). This table is referenced by the processor when a software or hardware interrupt occurs. For example, to make a system call, user application issues the INT 0x80 instruction. This is a software interrupt, so the processor's hardware looks up a record with index 0x80 in the IDT. This record points to the routine that handles this interrupt, in this particular case, this will be the kernel's syscall gate. The IDT may have a maximum of 256 (0x100) records. The kernel allocates NIDT records for the IDT, where NIDT is the maximum (256):

```
sys/i386/i386/machdep.c:
static struct gate_descriptor idt0[NIDT];
struct gate_descriptor *idt = &idt0[0]; /* interrupt descriptor table */
```

For each interrupt, an appropriate handler is set. The syscall gate for INT 0x80 is set as well:

```
sys/i386/i386/machdep.c:
 setidt(0x80, &IDTVEC(int0x80_syscall),
   SDT_SYS386TGT, SEL_UPL, GSEL(GCODE_SEL, SEL_KPL)));
```

So when a userland application issues the INT 0x80 instruction, control will transfer to the function _Xint0x80_syscall, which is in the kernel code segment and will be executed with supervisor privileges.

Console and DDB are then initialized:

```
sys/i386/i386/machdep.c:
 cninit();
/* skipped */
#ifdef DDB
 kdb_init();
 if (boothowto & RB_KDB)
  Debugger("Boot flags requested debugger");
#endif
```

The Task State Segment is another x86 protected mode structure, the TSS is used by the hardware to store task information when a task switch occurs.

The Local Descriptors Table is used to reference userland code and data. Several selectors are defined to point to the LDT, they are the system call gates and the user code and data selectors:

```
/usr/include/machine/segments.h:
#define LSYS5CALLS_SEL 0 /* forced by intel BCS */
#define LSYS5SIGR_SEL 1
#define L43BSDCALLS_SEL 2 /* notyet */
#define LUCODE_SEL 3
#define LSOL26CALLS_SEL 4 /* Solaris >= 2.6 system call gate */
#define LUDATA_SEL 5
/* separate stack, es,fs,gs sels ? */
/* #define LPOSIXCALLS_SEL 5*/ /* notyet */
#define LBSDICALLS_SEL 16 /* BSDI system call gate */
#define NLDT  (LBSDICALLS_SEL + 1)
```

Next, proc0's Process Control Block (struct pcb) structure is initialized. proc0 is a struct proc structure that describes a kernel process. It is always present while the kernel is running, therefore it is declared as global:

```
sys/kern/kern_init.c:
    struct proc proc0;
```

The structure struct pcb is a part of a proc structure. It is defined in /usr/include/machine/pcb.h and has a process's information specific to the i386 architecture, such as registers values.

1.9.2. mi_startup()

This function performs a bubble sort of all the system initialization objects and then calls the entry of each object one by one:

```
sys/kern/init_main.c:
 for (sipp = sysinit; *sipp; sipp++) {

  /* ... skipped ... */

  /* Call function */
  (*((*sipp)->func))((*sipp)->udata);
  /* ... skipped ... */
 }
```

Although the sysinit framework is described in the Developers' Handbook, I will discuss the internals of it.

Every system initialization object (sysinit object) is created by calling a SYSINIT() macro. Let us take as example an announce sysinit object. This object prints the copyright message:

```
sys/kern/init_main.c:
static void
print_caddr_t(void *data __unused)
{
 printf("%s", (char *)data);
}
SYSINIT(announce, SI_SUB_COPYRIGHT, SI_ORDER_FIRST, print_caddr_t, copyright)
```

The subsystem ID for this object is SI_SUB_COPYRIGHT (0x0800001), which comes right after the SI_SUB_CONSOLE (0x0800000). So, the copyright message will be printed out first, just after the console initialization.

Let us take a look at what exactly the macro SYSINIT() does. It expands to a C_SYSINIT() macro. The C_SYSINIT() macro then expands to a static struct sysinit structure declaration with another DATA_SET macro call:

```
/usr/include/sys/kernel.h:
      #define C_SYSINIT(uniquifier, subsystem, order, func, ident) \
      static struct sysinit uniquifier ## _sys_init = { \ subsystem, \
      order, \ func, \ ident \ }; \ DATA_SET(sysinit_set,uniquifier ##
      _sys_init);

#define SYSINIT(uniquifier, subsystem, order, func, ident) \
  C_SYSINIT(uniquifier, subsystem, order,   \
  (sysinit_cfunc_t)(sysinit_nfunc_t)func, (void *)ident)
```

The DATA_SET() macro expands to a MAKE_SET(), and that macro is the point where all the sysinit magic is hidden:

```
/usr/include/linker_set.h:
#define MAKE_SET(set, sym)         \
  static void const * const __set_##set##_sym_##sym = &sym; \
  __asm(".section .set." #set ",\"aw\"");      \
  __asm(".long " #sym);         \
  __asm(".previous")
#endif
#define TEXT_SET(set, sym) MAKE_SET(set, sym)
#define DATA_SET(set, sym) MAKE_SET(set, sym)
```

In our case, the following declaration will occur:

```
static struct sysinit announce_sys_init = {
 SI_SUB_COPYRIGHT,
 SI_ORDER_FIRST,
 (sysinit_cfunc_t)(sysinit_nfunc_t)  print_caddr_t,
 (void *) copyright
};

static void const *const __set_sysinit_set_sym_announce_sys_init =
    &announce_sys_init;
__asm(".section .set.sysinit_set" ",\"aw\"");
__asm(".long " "announce_sys_init");
__asm(".previous");
```

The first __asm instruction will create an ELF section within the kernel's executable. This will happen at kernel link time. The section will have the name .set.sysinit_set. The content of this section is one 32-bit value, the address of announce_sys_init structure, and that is what the second __asm is. The third __asm instruction marks the end of a section. If a directive with the same section name occurred before, the content, i.e., the 32-bit value, will be appended to the existing section, so forming an array of 32-bit pointers.

Running objdump on a kernel binary, you may notice the presence of such small sections:

```
% objdump -h /kernel
  7 .set.cons_set 00000014  c03164c0  c03164c0  002154c0  2**2
                  CONTENTS, ALLOC, LOAD, DATA
  8 .set.kbddriver_set 00000010  c03164d4  c03164d4  002154d4  2**2
                  CONTENTS, ALLOC, LOAD, DATA
  9 .set.scrndr_set 00000024  c03164e4  c03164e4  002154e4  2**2
```

```
                 CONTENTS, ALLOC, LOAD, DATA
10 .set.scterm_set 0000000c  c0316508  c0316508  00215508  2**2
                 CONTENTS, ALLOC, LOAD, DATA
11 .set.sysctl_set 0000097c  c0316514  c0316514  00215514  2**2
                 CONTENTS, ALLOC, LOAD, DATA
12 .set.sysinit_set 00000664  c0316e90  c0316e90  00215e90  2**2
                 CONTENTS, ALLOC, LOAD, DATA
```

This screen dump shows that the size of .set.sysinit_set section is 0x664 bytes, so 0x664/sizeof(void *) sysinit objects are compiled into the kernel. The other sections such as .set.sysctl_set represent other linker sets.

By defining a variable of type struct linker_set the content of .set.sysinit_set section will be "collected" into that variable:

```
sys/kern/init_main.c:
     extern struct linker_set sysinit_set; /* XXX */
```

The struct linker_set is defined as follows:

```
/usr/include/linker_set.h:
  struct linker_set {
  int ls_length;
  void *ls_items[1];  /* really ls_length of them, trailing NULL */
};
```

The first node will be equal to the number of a sysinit objects, and the second node will be a NULL-terminated array of pointers to them.

Returning to the mi_startup() discussion, it is must be clear now, how the sysinit objects are being organized. The mi_startup() function sorts them and calls each. The very last object is the system scheduler:

```
/usr/include/sys/kernel.h:
enum sysinit_sub_id {
  SI_SUB_DUMMY    = 0x0000000, /* not executed; for linker*/
  SI_SUB_DONE     = 0x0000001, /* processed*/
  SI_SUB_CONSOLE  = 0x0800000, /* console*/
  SI_SUB_COPYRIGHT = 0x0800001, /* first use of console*/
...
  SI_SUB_RUN_SCHEDULER = 0xfffffff /* scheduler: no return*/
};
```

The system scheduler sysinit object is defined in the file sys/vm/vm_glue.c , and the entry point for that object is scheduler(). That function is actually an infinite loop, and it represents a process with PID 0, the swapper process. The proc0 structure, mentioned before, is used to describe it.

The first user process, called *init*, is created by the sysinit object init:

```
sys/kern/init_main.c:
static void
create_init(const void *udata __unused)
{
  int error;
  int s;

  s = splhigh();
  error = fork1(&proc0, RFFDG | RFPROC, &initproc);
  if (error)
    panic("cannot fork init: %d\n", error);
  initproc->p_flag |= P_INMEM | P_SYSTEM;
  cpu_set_fork_handler(initproc, start_init, NULL);
  remrunqueue(initproc);
  splx(s);
}
SYSINIT(init,SI_SUB_CREATE_INIT, SI_ORDER_FIRST, create_init, NULL)
```

The create_init() allocates a new process by calling fork1(), but does not mark it runnable. When this new process is scheduled for execution by the scheduler, the start_init() will be called. That function is defined in init_main.c . It tries to load and exec the init binary, probing /sbin/init first, then /sbin/oinit , /sbin/init.bak , and finally /stand/sysinstall :

```
sys/kern/init_main.c:
static char init_path[MAXPATHLEN] =
#ifdef INIT_PATH
    __XSTRING(INIT_PATH);
#else
    "/sbin/init:/sbin/oinit:/sbin/init.bak:/stand/sysinstall";
#endif
```

Chapter 2. Locking Notes

This chapter is maintained by the FreeBSD SMP Next Generation Project.

This document outlines the locking used in the FreeBSD kernel to permit effective multi-processing within the kernel. Locking can be achieved via several means. Data structures can be protected by mutexes or lockmgr(9) locks. A few variables are protected simply by always using atomic operations to access them.

2.1. Mutexes

A mutex is simply a lock used to guarantee mutual exclusion. Specifically, a mutex may only be owned by one entity at a time. If another entity wishes to obtain a mutex that is already owned, it must wait until the mutex is released. In the FreeBSD kernel, mutexes are owned by processes.

Mutexes may be recursively acquired, but they are intended to be held for a short period of time. Specifically, one may not sleep while holding a mutex. If you need to hold a lock across a sleep, use a lockmgr(9) lock.

Each mutex has several properties of interest:

Variable Name
> The name of the struct mtx variable in the kernel source.

Logical Name
> The name of the mutex assigned to it by `mtx_init`. This name is displayed in KTR trace messages and witness errors and warnings and is used to distinguish mutexes in the witness code.

Type
> The type of the mutex in terms of the `MTX_*` flags. The meaning for each flag is related to its meaning as documented in mutex(9).

> `MTX_DEF`
>> A sleep mutex

> `MTX_SPIN`
>> A spin mutex

> `MTX_RECURSE`
>> This mutex is allowed to recurse.

Protectees
> A list of data structures or data structure members that this entry protects. For data structure members, the name will be in the form of `structure name.member name`.

Dependent Functions
> Functions that can only be called if this mutex is held.

Table 2.1. Mutex List

Variable Name	Logical Name	Type	Protectees	Dependent Functions
sched_lock	"sched lock"	MTX_SPIN | MTX_RE-CURSE	_gmonparam, cnt.v_swtch, cp_time, curpriority, mtx.mtx_blocked , mtx.mtx_contested, proc.p_procq, proc.p_slpq, proc.p_sflag, proc.p_stat,	setrunqueue, remrunqueue, mi_switch, chooseproc, schedclock, resetpriority, updatepri, maybe_resched , cpu_switch , cpu_throw ,

Variable Name	Logical Name	Type	Protectees	Dependent Functions
			`proc.p_estcpu`, `proc.p_cpticks` `proc.p_pctcpu`, `proc.p_wchan`, `proc.p_wmesg`, `proc.p_swtime`, `proc.p_slptime`, `proc.p_runtime`, `proc.p_uu`, `proc.p_su`, `proc.p_iu`, `proc.p_uticks`, `proc.p_sticks`, `proc.p_iticks`, `proc.p_oncpu`, `proc.p_lastcpu`, `proc.p_rqindex`, `proc.p_heldmtx`, `proc.p_blocked`, `proc.p_mtxname`, `proc.p_contested`, `proc.p_priority`, `proc.p_usrpri`, `proc.p_nativepri`, `proc.p_nice`, `proc.p_rtprio`, `pscnt`, `slpque`, `itqueuebits`, `itqueues`, `rtqueuebits`, `rtqueues`, `queuebits`, `queues`, `idqueuebits`, `idqueues`, `switchtime`, `switchticks`	`need_resched`, `resched_wanted`, `clear_resched`, `aston`, `astoff`, `astpending`, `calcru`, `proc_compare`
vm86pcb_lock	"vm86pcb lock"	MTX_DEF	vm86pcb	vm86_bioscall
Giant	"Giant"	MTX_DEF | MTX_RECURSE	nearly everything	lots
callout_lock	"callout lock"	MTX_SPIN | MTX_RECURSE	`callfree`, `callwheel`, `nextsoftcheck`, `proc.p_itcallout`, `proc.p_slpcallout`, `softticks`, `ticks`	

2.2. Shared Exclusive Locks

These locks provide basic reader-writer type functionality and may be held by a sleeping process. Currently they are backed by lockmgr(9).

Table 2.2. Shared Exclusive Lock List

Variable Name	Protectees
allproc_lock	allproc zombproc pidhashtbl proc.p_list proc.p_hash nextpid
proctree_lock	proc.p_children proc.p_sibling

2.3. Atomically Protected Variables

An atomically protected variable is a special variable that is not protected by an explicit lock. Instead, all data accesses to the variables use special atomic operations as described in atomic(9). Very few variables are treated this way, although other synchronization primitives such as mutexes are implemented with atomically protected variables.

• mtx.mtx_lock

Chapter 3. Kernel Objects

Kernel Objects, or *Kobj* provides an object-oriented C programming system for the kernel. As such the data being operated on carries the description of how to operate on it. This allows operations to be added and removed from an interface at run time and without breaking binary compatibility.

3.1. Terminology

Object
    A set of data - data structure - data allocation.

Method
    An operation - function.

Class
    One or more methods.

Interface
    A standard set of one or more methods.

3.2. Kobj Operation

Kobj works by generating descriptions of methods. Each description holds a unique id as well as a default function. The description's address is used to uniquely identify the method within a class' method table.

A class is built by creating a method table associating one or more functions with method descriptions. Before use the class is compiled. The compilation allocates a cache and associates it with the class. A unique id is assigned to each method description within the method table of the class if not already done so by another referencing class compilation. For every method to be used a function is generated by script to qualify arguments and automatically reference the method description for a lookup. The generated function looks up the method by using the unique id associated with the method description as a hash into the cache associated with the object's class. If the method is not cached the generated function proceeds to use the class' table to find the method. If the method is found then the associated function within the class is used; otherwise, the default function associated with the method description is used.

These indirections can be visualized as the following:

```
object->cache<->class
```

3.3. Using Kobj

3.3.1. Structures

```
struct kobj_method
```

3.3.2. Functions

```
void kobj_class_compile(kobj_class_t cls);
void kobj_class_compile_static(kobj_class_t cls, kobj_ops_t ops);
void kobj_class_free(kobj_class_t cls);
kobj_t kobj_create(kobj_class_t cls, struct malloc_type *mtype, int mflags);
void kobj_init(kobj_t obj, kobj_class_t cls);
void kobj_delete(kobj_t obj, struct malloc_type *mtype);
```

3.3.3. Macros

```
KOBJ_CLASS_FIELDS
KOBJ_FIELDS
DEFINE_CLASS(name, methods, size)
KOBJMETHOD(NAME, FUNC)
```

3.3.4. Headers

```
<sys/param.h>
<sys/kobj.h>
```

3.3.5. Creating an Interface Template

The first step in using Kobj is to create an Interface. Creating the interface involves creating a template that the script src/sys/kern/makeobjops.pl can use to generate the header and code for the method declarations and method lookup functions.

Within this template the following keywords are used: #include, INTERFACE, CODE, METHOD, STATICMETHOD , and DEFAULT.

The #include statement and what follows it is copied verbatim to the head of the generated code file.

For example:

```
#include <sys/foo.h>
```

The INTERFACE keyword is used to define the interface name. This name is concatenated with each method name as [interface name]_[method name]. Its syntax is INTERFACE [interface name];.

For example:

```
INTERFACE foo;
```

The CODE keyword copies its arguments verbatim into the code file. Its syntax is CODE { [whatever] };

For example:

```
CODE {
  struct foo * foo_alloc_null(struct bar *)
  {
    return NULL;
  }
};
```

The METHOD keyword describes a method. Its syntax is METHOD [return type] [method name] { [object [, arguments]] };

For example:

```
METHOD int bar {
  struct object *;
  struct foo *;
  struct bar;
};
```

The DEFAULT keyword may follow the METHOD keyword. It extends the METHOD key word to include the default function for method. The extended syntax is METHOD [return type] [method name] { [object; [other arguments]] }DEFAULT [default function];

For example:

```
METHOD int bar {
```

```
  struct object *;
  struct foo *;
  int bar;
} DEFAULT foo_hack;
```

The `STATICMETHOD` keyword is used like the `METHOD` keyword except the kobj data is not at the head of the object structure so casting to kobj_t would be incorrect. Instead `STATICMETHOD` relies on the Kobj data being referenced as 'ops'. This is also useful for calling methods directly out of a class's method table.

Other complete examples:

```
src/sys/kern/bus_if.m
src/sys/kern/device_if.m
```

3.3.6. Creating a Class

The second step in using Kobj is to create a class. A class consists of a name, a table of methods, and the size of objects if Kobj's object handling facilities are used. To create the class use the macro `DEFINE_CLASS()`. To create the method table create an array of kobj_method_t terminated by a NULL entry. Each non-NULL entry may be created using the macro `KOBJMETHOD()`.

For example:

```
DEFINE_CLASS(fooclass, foomethods, sizeof(struct foodata));

kobj_method_t foomethods[] = {
  KOBJMETHOD(bar_doo, foo_doo),
  KOBJMETHOD(bar_foo, foo_foo),
  { NULL, NULL}
};
```

The class must be "compiled". Depending on the state of the system at the time that the class is to be initialized a statically allocated cache, "ops table" have to be used. This can be accomplished by declaring a `struct kobj_ops` and using `kobj_class_compile_static()`; otherwise, `kobj_class_compile()` should be used.

3.3.7. Creating an Object

The third step in using Kobj involves how to define the object. Kobj object creation routines assume that Kobj data is at the head of an object. If this in not appropriate you will have to allocate the object yourself and then use `kobj_init()` on the Kobj portion of it; otherwise, you may use `kobj_create()` to allocate and initialize the Kobj portion of the object automatically. `kobj_init()` may also be used to change the class that an object uses.

To integrate Kobj into the object you should use the macro KOBJ_FIELDS.

For example

```
struct foo_data {
  KOBJ_FIELDS;
  foo_foo;
  foo_bar;
};
```

3.3.8. Calling Methods

The last step in using Kobj is to simply use the generated functions to use the desired method within the object's class. This is as simple as using the interface name and the method name with a few modifications. The interface name should be concatenated with the method name using a '_' between them, all in upper case.

For example, if the interface name was foo and the method was bar then the call would be:

```
[return value = -] FOO_BAR(object [, other parameters]);
```

3.3.9. Cleaning Up

When an object allocated through `kobj_create()` is no longer needed `kobj_delete()` may be called on it, and when a class is no longer being used `kobj_class_free()` may be called on it.

Chapter 4. The Jail Subsystem

Evan Sarmiento

<evms@cs.bu.edu >

On most UNIX® systems, root has omnipotent power. This promotes insecurity. If an attacker gained root on a system, he would have every function at his fingertips. In FreeBSD there are sysctls which dilute the power of root, in order to minimize the damage caused by an attacker. Specifically, one of these functions is called secure levels. Similarly, another function which is present from FreeBSD 4.0 and onward, is a utility called jail(8). Jail chroots an environment and sets certain restrictions on processes which are forked within the jail. For example, a jailed process cannot affect processes outside the jail, utilize certain system calls, or inflict any damage on the host environment.

Jail is becoming the new security model. People are running potentially vulnerable servers such as Apache, BIND, and sendmail within jails, so that if an attacker gains root within the jail, it is only an annoyance, and not a devastation. This article mainly focuses on the internals (source code) of jail. For information on how to set up a jail see the handbook entry on jails.

4.1. Architecture

Jail consists of two realms: the userland program, jail(8), and the code implemented within the kernel: the jail(2) system call and associated restrictions. I will be discussing the userland program and then how jail is implemented within the kernel.

4.1.1. Userland Code

The source for the userland jail is located in /usr/src/usr.sbin/jail , consisting of one file, jail.c. The program takes these arguments: the path of the jail, hostname, IP address, and the command to be executed.

4.1.1.1. Data Structures

In jail.c, the first thing I would note is the declaration of an important structure struct jail j; which was included from /usr/include/sys/jail.h .

The definition of the jail structure is:

```
/usr/include/sys/jail.h :

struct jail {
        u_int32_t       version;
        char            *path;
        char            *hostname;
        u_int32_t       ip_number;
};
```

As you can see, there is an entry for each of the arguments passed to the jail(8) program, and indeed, they are set during its execution.

```
/usr/src/usr.sbin/jail/jail.c
char path[PATH_MAX];
...
if (realpath(argv[0], path) == NULL)
    err(1, "realpath: %s", argv[0]);
if (chdir(path) != 0)
    err(1, "chdir: %s", path);
memset(&j, 0, sizeof(j));
j.version = 0;
```

```
j.path = path;
j.hostname = argv[1];
```

4.1.1.2. Networking

One of the arguments passed to the jail(8) program is an IP address with which the jail can be accessed over the network. jail(8) translates the IP address given into host byte order and then stores it in j (the jail structure).

```
/usr/src/usr.sbin/jail/jail.c :
struct in_addr in;
...
if (inet_aton(argv[2], &in) == 0)
    errx(1, "Could not make sense of ip-number: %s", argv[2]);
j.ip_number = ntohl(in.s_addr);
```

The inet_aton(3) function "interprets the specified character string as an Internet address, placing the address into the structure provided." The ip_number member in the jail structure is set only when the IP address placed onto the in structure by inet_aton(3) is translated into host byte order by ntohl(3).

4.1.1.3. Jailing the Process

Finally, the userland program jails the process. Jail now becomes an imprisoned process itself and then executes the command given using execv(3).

```
/usr/src/usr.sbin/jail/jail.c
i = jail(&j);
...
if (execv(argv[3], argv + 3) != 0)
    err(1, "execv: %s", argv[3]);
```

As you can see, the jail() function is called, and its argument is the jail structure which has been filled with the arguments given to the program. Finally, the program you specify is executed. I will now discuss how jail is implemented within the kernel.

4.1.2. Kernel Space

We will now be looking at the file /usr/src/sys/kern/kern_jail.c . This is the file where the jail(2) system call, appropriate sysctls, and networking functions are defined.

4.1.2.1. sysctls

In kern_jail.c , the following sysctls are defined:

```
/usr/src/sys/kern/kern_jail.c:

int     jail_set_hostname_allowed = 1;
SYSCTL_INT(_security_jail, OID_AUTO, set_hostname_allowed, CTLFLAG_RW,
    &jail_set_hostname_allowed, 0,
    "Processes in jail can set their hostnames");

int     jail_socket_unixiproute_only = 1;
SYSCTL_INT(_security_jail, OID_AUTO, socket_unixiproute_only, CTLFLAG_RW,
    &jail_socket_unixiproute_only, 0,
    "Processes in jail are limited to creating UNIX/IPv4/route sockets only");

int     jail_sysvipc_allowed = 0;
SYSCTL_INT(_security_jail, OID_AUTO, sysvipc_allowed, CTLFLAG_RW,
    &jail_sysvipc_allowed, 0,
    "Processes in jail can use System V IPC primitives");

static int jail_enforce_statfs = 2;
SYSCTL_INT(_security_jail, OID_AUTO, enforce_statfs, CTLFLAG_RW,
```

```
    &jail_enforce_statfs, 0,
    "Processes in jail cannot see all mounted file systems");

int    jail_allow_raw_sockets = 0;
SYSCTL_INT(_security_jail, OID_AUTO, allow_raw_sockets, CTLFLAG_RW,
    &jail_allow_raw_sockets, 0,
    "Prison root can create raw sockets");

int    jail_chflags_allowed = 0;
SYSCTL_INT(_security_jail, OID_AUTO, chflags_allowed, CTLFLAG_RW,
    &jail_chflags_allowed, 0,
    "Processes in jail can alter system file flags");

int    jail_mount_allowed = 0;
SYSCTL_INT(_security_jail, OID_AUTO, mount_allowed, CTLFLAG_RW,
    &jail_mount_allowed, 0,
    "Processes in jail can mount/unmount jail-friendly file systems");
```

Each of these sysctls can be accessed by the user through the sysctl(8) program. Throughout the kernel, these specific sysctls are recognized by their name. For example, the name of the first sysctl is `security.jail.set_hostname_allowed`.

4.1.2.2. jail(2) System Call

Like all system calls, the jail(2) system call takes two arguments, `struct thread *td` and `struct jail_args *uap` . td is a pointer to the `thread` structure which describes the calling thread. In this context, uap is a pointer to the structure in which a pointer to the `jail` structure passed by the userland `jail.c` is contained. When I described the userland program before, you saw that the jail(2) system call was given a `jail` structure as its own argument.

```
/usr/src/sys/kern/kern_jail.c:
/*
 * struct jail_args {
 *   struct jail *jail;
 * };
 */
int
jail(struct thread *td, struct jail_args *uap)
```

Therefore, `uap->jail` can be used to access the `jail` structure which was passed to the system call. Next, the system call copies the `jail` structure into kernel space using the copyin(9) function. copyin(9) takes three arguments: the address of the data which is to be copied into kernel space, `uap->jail` , where to store it, j and the size of the storage. The `jail` structure pointed by `uap->jail` is copied into kernel space and is stored in another `jail` structure, j.

```
/usr/src/sys/kern/kern_jail.c:
error = copyin(uap->jail, &j, sizeof(j));
```

There is another important structure defined in `jail.h`. It is the `prison` structure. The `prison` structure is used exclusively within kernel space. Here is the definition of the `prison` structure.

```
/usr/include/sys/jail.h :
struct prison {
      LIST_ENTRY(prison) pr_list;              /* (a) all prisons */
      int              pr_id;                  /* (c) prison id */
      int              pr_ref;                 /* (p) refcount */
      char             pr_path[MAXPATHLEN];    /* (c) chroot path */
      struct vnode     *pr_root;               /* (c) vnode to rdir */
      char             pr_host[MAXHOSTNAMELEN];/* (p) jail hostname */
      u_int32_t        pr_ip;                  /* (c) ip addr host */
      void             *pr_linux;              /* (p) linux abi */
      int              pr_securelevel;         /* (p) securelevel */
      struct task      pr_task;                /* (d) destroy task */
      struct mtx       pr_mtx;
    void             **pr_slots;               /* (p) additional data */
```

```
};
```

The jail(2) system call then allocates memory for a `prison` structure and copies data between the jail and `prison` structure.

```
/usr/src/sys/kern/kern_jail.c  :
MALLOC(pr, struct prison *, sizeof(*pr), M_PRISON, M_WAITOK | M_ZERO);
...
error = copyinstr(j.path, &pr->pr_path, sizeof(pr->pr_path), 0);
if (error)
    goto e_killmtx;
...
error = copyinstr(j.hostname, &pr->pr_host, sizeof(pr->pr_host), 0);
if (error)
     goto e_dropvnref;
pr->pr_ip = j.ip_number;
```

Next, we will discuss another important system call jail_attach(2), which implements the function to put a process into the jail.

```
/usr/src/sys/kern/kern_jail.c  :
/*
 * struct jail_attach_args {
 *       int jid;
 * };
 */
int
jail_attach(struct thread *td, struct jail_attach_args *uap)
```

This system call makes the changes that can distinguish a jailed process from those unjailed ones. To understand what jail_attach(2) does for us, certain background information is needed.

On FreeBSD, each kernel visible thread is identified by its `thread` structure, while the processes are described by their `proc` structures. You can find the definitions of the `thread` and `proc` structure in `/usr/include/sys/proc.h` . For example, the `td` argument in any system call is actually a pointer to the calling thread's `thread` structure, as stated before. The `td_proc` member in the `thread` structure pointed by `td` is a pointer to the `proc` structure which represents the process that contains the thread represented by `td`. The `proc` structure contains members which can describe the owner's identity(`p_ucred`), the process resource limits(`p_limit`), and so on. In the `ucred` structure pointed by `p_ucred` member in the `proc` structure, there is a pointer to the `prison` structure(`cr_prison`).

```
/usr/include/sys/proc.h:
struct thread {
    ...
    struct proc *td_proc;
    ...
};
struct proc {
    ...
    struct ucred *p_ucred;
    ...
};
/usr/include/sys/ucred.h
struct ucred {
    ...
    struct prison *cr_prison;
    ...
};
```

In `kern_jail.c` , the function `jail()` then calls function `jail_attach()` with a given `jid`. And `jail_attach()` calls function `change_root()` to change the root directory of the calling process. The `jail_attach()` then creates a new `ucred` structure, and attaches the newly created `ucred` structure to the calling process after it has successfully attached the `prison` structure to the `ucred` structure. From then on, the calling process is recognized as jailed. When the kernel routine `jailed()` is called in the kernel with the newly created `ucred` structure as its argument, it returns 1 to tell that the credential is connected with a jail. The public ancestor process of all the process forked within the jail, is the process which runs jail(8), as it calls the jail(2) system call. When a program is executed through execve(2), it inherits the jailed property of its parent's ucred structure, therefore it has a jailed ucred structure.

```
/usr/src/sys/kern/kern_jail.c
int
jail(struct thread *td, struct jail_args *uap)
{
...
    struct jail_attach_args jaa;
...
    error = jail_attach(td, &jaa);
    if (error)
        goto e_dropprref;
...
}

int
jail_attach(struct thread *td, struct jail_attach_args *uap)
{
    struct proc *p;
    struct ucred *newcred, *oldcred;
    struct prison *pr;
...
    p = td->td_proc;
...
    pr = prison_find(uap->jid);
...
    change_root(pr->pr_root, td);
...
    newcred->cr_prison = pr;
    p->p_ucred = newcred;
...
}
```

When a process is forked from its parent process, the fork(2) system call uses crhold() to maintain the credential for the newly forked process. It inherently keep the newly forked child's credential consistent with its parent, so the child process is also jailed.

```
/usr/src/sys/kern/kern_fork.c  :
p2->p_ucred = crhold(td->td_ucred);
...
td2->td_ucred = crhold(p2->p_ucred);
```

4.2. Restrictions

Throughout the kernel there are access restrictions relating to jailed processes. Usually, these restrictions only check whether the process is jailed, and if so, returns an error. For example:

```
if (jailed(td->td_ucred))
    return (EPERM);
```

4.2.1. SysV IPC

System V IPC is based on messages. Processes can send each other these messages which tell them how to act. The functions which deal with messages are: msgctl(3), msgget(3), msgsnd(3) and msgrcv(3). Earlier, I mentioned that there were certain sysctls you could turn on or off in order to affect the behavior of jail. One of these sysctls was security.jail.sysvipc_allowed. By default, this sysctl is set to 0. If it were set to 1, it would defeat the whole purpose of having a jail; privileged users from the jail would be able to affect processes outside the jailed environment. The difference between a message and a signal is that the message only consists of the signal number.

`/usr/src/sys/kern/sysv_msg.c` :

- `msgget(key, msgflg)` : `msgget` returns (and possibly creates) a message descriptor that designates a message queue for use in other functions.

- `msgctl(msgid, cmd, buf)` : Using this function, a process can query the status of a message descriptor.

- `msgsnd(msgid, msgp, msgsz, msgflg)`: `msgsnd` sends a message to a process.

- `msgrcv(msgid, msgp, msgsz, msgtyp, msgflg)`: a process receives messages using this function

In each of the system calls corresponding to these functions, there is this conditional:

```
/usr/src/sys/kern/sysv_msg.c :
if (!jail_sysvipc_allowed && jailed(td->td_ucred))
    return (ENOSYS);
```

Semaphore system calls allow processes to synchronize execution by doing a set of operations atomically on a set of semaphores. Basically semaphores provide another way for processes lock resources. However, process waiting on a semaphore, that is being used, will sleep until the resources are relinquished. The following semaphore system calls are blocked inside a jail: semget(2), semctl(2) and semop(2).

`/usr/src/sys/kern/sysv_sem.c` :

- `semctl(semid, semnum, cmd, ...)` : `semctl` does the specified `cmd` on the semaphore queue indicated by `semid`.

- `semget(key, nsems, flag)` : `semget` creates an array of semaphores, corresponding to `key`.

  `key and flag take on the same meaning as they do in msgget.`

- `semop(semid, array, nops)` : `semop` performs a group of operations indicated by `array`, to the set of semaphores identified by `semid`.

System V IPC allows for processes to share memory. Processes can communicate directly with each other by sharing parts of their virtual address space and then reading and writing data stored in the shared memory. These system calls are blocked within a jailed environment: shmdt(2), shmat(2), shmctl(2) and shmget(2).

`/usr/src/sys/kern/sysv_shm.c` :

- `shmctl(shmid, cmd, buf)` : `shmctl` does various control operations on the shared memory region identified by `shmid`.

- `shmget(key, size, flag)` : `shmget` accesses or creates a shared memory region of `size` bytes.

- `shmat(shmid, addr, flag)` : `shmat` attaches a shared memory region identified by `shmid` to the address space of a process.

- `shmdt(addr)`: `shmdt` detaches the shared memory region previously attached at `addr`.

4.2.2. Sockets

Jail treats the socket(2) system call and related lower-level socket functions in a special manner. In order to determine whether a certain socket is allowed to be created, it first checks to see if the sysctl `security.jail.socket_unixiproute_only` is set. If set, sockets are only allowed to be created if the family specified is either `PF_LOCAL`, `PF_INET` or `PF_ROUTE`. Otherwise, it returns an error.

```
/usr/src/sys/kern/uipc_socket.c :
int
```

```
socreate(int dom, struct socket **aso, int type, int proto,
    struct ucred *cred, struct thread *td)
{
    struct protosw *prp;
...
    if (jailed(cred) && jail_socket_unixiproute_only &&
        prp->pr_domain->dom_family != PF_LOCAL &&
        prp->pr_domain->dom_family != PF_INET &&
        prp->pr_domain->dom_family != PF_ROUTE) {
        return (EPROTONOSUPPORT);
    }
...
}
```

4.2.3. Berkeley Packet Filter

The Berkeley Packet Filter provides a raw interface to data link layers in a protocol independent fashion. BPF is now controlled by the devfs(8) whether it can be used in a jailed environment.

4.2.4. Protocols

There are certain protocols which are very common, such as TCP, UDP, IP and ICMP. IP and ICMP are on the same level: the network layer 2. There are certain precautions which are taken in order to prevent a jailed process from binding a protocol to a certain address only if the nam parameter is set. nam is a pointer to a sockaddr structure, which describes the address on which to bind the service. A more exact definition is that sockaddr "may be used as a template for referring to the identifying tag and length of each address". In the function in_pcbbind_setup(), sin is a pointer to a sockaddr_in structure, which contains the port, address, length and domain family of the socket which is to be bound. Basically, this disallows any processes from jail to be able to specify the address that does not belong to the jail in which the calling process exists.

```
/usr/src/sys/netinet/in_pcb.c  :
int
in_pcbbind_setup(struct inpcb *inp, struct sockaddr *nam, in_addr_t *laddrp,
    u_short *lportp, struct ucred *cred)
{
    ...
    struct sockaddr_in *sin;
    ...
    if (nam) {
        sin = (struct sockaddr_in *)nam;
        ...
        if (sin->sin_addr.s_addr != INADDR_ANY)
            if (prison_ip(cred, 0, &sin->sin_addr.s_addr))
                return(EINVAL);
        ...
        if (lport) {
            ...
            if (prison && prison_ip(cred, 0, &sin->sin_addr.s_addr))
                return (EADDRNOTAVAIL);
            ...
        }
    }
    if (lport == 0) {
        ...
        if (laddr.s_addr != INADDR_ANY)
            if (prison_ip(cred, 0, &laddr.s_addr))
                return (EINVAL);
        ...
    }
...
    if (prison_ip(cred, 0, &laddr.s_addr))
        return (EINVAL);
...
```

```
}
```

You might be wondering what function `prison_ip()` does. `prison_ip()` is given three arguments, a pointer to the credential(represented by `cred`), any flags, and an IP address. It returns 1 if the IP address does NOT belong to the jail or 0 otherwise. As you can see from the code, if it is indeed an IP address not belonging to the jail, the protocol is not allowed to bind to that address.

```
/usr/src/sys/kern/kern_jail.c:
int
prison_ip(struct ucred *cred, int flag, u_int32_t *ip)
{
    u_int32_t tmp;

    if (!jailed(cred))
        return (0);
    if (flag)
        tmp = *ip;
    else
        tmp = ntohl(*ip);
    if (tmp == INADDR_ANY) {
        if (flag)
            *ip = cred->cr_prison->pr_ip;
        else
            *ip = htonl(cred->cr_prison->pr_ip);
        return (0);
    }
    if (tmp == INADDR_LOOPBACK) {
        if (flag)
            *ip = cred->cr_prison->pr_ip;
        else
            *ip = htonl(cred->cr_prison->pr_ip);
        return (0);
    }
    if (cred->cr_prison->pr_ip != tmp)
        return (1);
    return (0);
}
```

4.2.5. Filesystem

Even root users within the jail are not allowed to unset or modify any file flags, such as immutable, append-only, and undeleteable flags, if the securelevel is greater than 0.

```
/usr/src/sys/ufs/ufs/ufs_vnops.c:
static int
ufs_setattr(ap)
    ...
{
    ...
        if (!priv_check_cred(cred, PRIV_VFS_SYSFLAGS, 0)) {
            if (ip->i_flags
                & (SF_NOUNLINK | SF_IMMUTABLE | SF_APPEND)) {
                    error = securelevel_gt(cred, 0);
                    if (error)
                        return (error);
            }
            ...
        }
}
/usr/src/sys/kern/kern_priv.c
int
priv_check_cred(struct ucred *cred, int priv, int flags)
{
    ...
    error = prison_priv_check(cred, priv);
```

```
    if (error)
        return (error);
    ...
}
/usr/src/sys/kern/kern_jail.c
int
prison_priv_check(struct ucred *cred, int priv)
{
    ...
    switch (priv) {
    ...
    case PRIV_VFS_SYSFLAGS:
        if (jail_chflags_allowed)
            return (0);
        else
            return (EPERM);
    ...
    }
    ...
}
```

Chapter 5. The SYSINIT Framework

SYSINIT is the framework for a generic call sort and dispatch mechanism. FreeBSD currently uses it for the dynamic initialization of the kernel. SYSINIT allows FreeBSD's kernel subsystems to be reordered, and added, removed, and replaced at kernel link time when the kernel or one of its modules is loaded without having to edit a statically ordered initialization routing and recompile the kernel. This system also allows kernel modules, currently called *KLD's*, to be separately compiled, linked, and initialized at boot time and loaded even later while the system is already running. This is accomplished using the "kernel linker" and "linker sets".

5.1. Terminology

Linker Set
    A linker technique in which the linker gathers statically declared data throughout a program's source files into a single contiguously addressable unit of data.

5.2. SYSINIT Operation

SYSINIT relies on the ability of the linker to take static data declared at multiple locations throughout a program's source and group it together as a single contiguous chunk of data. This linker technique is called a "linker set". SYSINIT uses two linker sets to maintain two data sets containing each consumer's call order, function, and a pointer to the data to pass to that function.

SYSINIT uses two priorities when ordering the functions for execution. The first priority is a subsystem ID giving an overall order for SYSINIT's dispatch of functions. Current predeclared ID's are in <sys/kernel.h> in the enum list sysinit_sub_id . The second priority used is an element order within the subsystem. Current predeclared subsystem element orders are in <sys/kernel.h> in the enum list sysinit_elem_order.

There are currently two uses for SYSINIT. Function dispatch at system startup and kernel module loads, and function dispatch at system shutdown and kernel module unload. Kernel subsystems often use system startup SYSINIT's to initialize data structures, for example the process scheduling subsystem uses a SYSINIT to initialize the run queue data structure. Device drivers should avoid using SYSINIT() directly. Instead drivers for real devices that are part of a bus structure should use DRIVER_MODULE() to provide a function that detects the device and, if it is present, initializes the device. It will do a few things specific to devices and then call SYSINIT() itself. For pseudo-devices, which are not part of a bus structure, use DEV_MODULE().

5.3. Using SYSINIT

5.3.1. Interface

5.3.1.1. Headers

```
<sys/kernel.h>
```

5.3.1.2. Macros

```
SYSINIT(uniquifier, subsystem, order, func, ident)
SYSUNINIT(uniquifier, subsystem, order, func, ident)
```

5.3.2. Startup

The SYSINIT() macro creates the necessary SYSINIT data in SYSINIT's startup data set for SYSINIT to sort and dispatch a function at system startup and module load. SYSINIT() takes a uniquifier that SYSINIT uses to identify the particular function dispatch data, the subsystem order, the subsystem element order, the function to call, and the data to pass the function. All functions must take a constant pointer argument.

Example 5.1. Example of a SYSINIT()

```
#include <sys/kernel.h>

void foo_null(void *unused)
{
        foo_doo();
}
SYSINIT(foo, SI_SUB_FOO, SI_ORDER_FOO, foo_null, NULL);

struct foo foo_voodoo = {
        FOO_VOODOO;
}

void foo_arg(void *vdata)
{
        struct foo *foo = (struct foo *)vdata;
        foo_data(foo);
}
SYSINIT(bar, SI_SUB_FOO, SI_ORDER_FOO, foo_arg, &foo_voodoo);
```

Note that SI_SUB_FOO and SI_ORDER_FOO need to be in the sysinit_sub_id and sysinit_elem_order enum's as mentioned above. Either use existing ones or add your own to the enum's. You can also use math for fine-tuning the order a SYSINIT will run in. This example shows a SYSINIT that needs to be run just barely before the SYSINIT's that handle tuning kernel parameters.

Example 5.2. Example of Adjusting SYSINIT() Order

```
static void
mptable_register(void *dummy __unused)
{

  apic_register_enumerator(&mptable_enumerator);
}

SYSINIT(mptable_register, SI_SUB_TUNABLES - 1, SI_ORDER_FIRST,
    mptable_register, NULL);
```

5.3.3. Shutdown

The SYSUNINIT() macro behaves similarly to the SYSINIT() macro except that it adds the SYSINIT data to SYSINIT's shutdown data set.

Example 5.3. Example of a SYSUNINIT()

```
#include <sys/kernel.h>
```

```
void foo_cleanup(void *unused)
{
        foo_kill();
}
SYSUNINIT(foobar, SI_SUB_FOO, SI_ORDER_FOO, foo_cleanup, NULL);

struct foo_stack foo_stack = {
        FOO_STACK_VOODOO;
}

void foo_flush(void *vdata)
{
}
SYSUNINIT(barfoo, SI_SUB_FOO, SI_ORDER_FOO, foo_flush, &foo_stack);
```

Chapter 6. The TrustedBSD MAC Framework

Chris Costello and Robert Watson.

6.1. MAC Documentation Copyright

This documentation was developed for the FreeBSD Project by Chris Costello at Safeport Network Services and Network Associates Laboratories, the Security Research Division of Network Associates, Inc. under DARPA/SPAWAR contract N66001-01-C-8035 ("CBOSS"), as part of the DARPA CHATS research program.

Redistribution and use in source (SGML DocBook) and 'compiled' forms (SGML, HTML, PDF, PostScript, RTF and so forth) with or without modification, are permitted provided that the following conditions are met:

1. Redistributions of source code (SGML DocBook) must retain the above copyright notice, this list of conditions and the following disclaimer as the first lines of this file unmodified.

2. Redistributions in compiled form (transformed to other DTDs, converted to PDF, PostScript, RTF and other formats) must reproduce the above copyright notice, this list of conditions and the following disclaimer in the documentation and/or other materials provided with the distribution.

6.2. Synopsis

FreeBSD includes experimental support for several mandatory access control policies, as well as a framework for kernel security extensibility, the TrustedBSD MAC Framework. The MAC Framework is a pluggable access control framework, permitting new security policies to be easily linked into the kernel, loaded at boot, or loaded dynamically at run-time. The framework provides a variety of features to make it easier to implement new security policies, including the ability to easily tag security labels (such as confidentiality information) onto system objects.

This chapter introduces the MAC policy framework and provides documentation for a sample MAC policy module.

6.3. Introduction

The TrustedBSD MAC framework provides a mechanism to allow the compile-time or run-time extension of the kernel access control model. New system policies may be implemented as kernel modules and linked to the kernel; if multiple policy modules are present, their results will be composed. The MAC Framework provides a variety of access control infrastructure services to assist policy writers, including support for transient and persistent policy-agnostic object security labels. This support is currently considered experimental.

This chapter provides information appropriate for developers of policy modules, as well as potential consumers of MAC-enabled environments, to learn about how the MAC Framework supports access control extension of the kernel.

6.4. Policy Background

Mandatory Access Control (MAC), refers to a set of access control policies that are mandatorily enforced on users by the operating system. MAC policies may be contrasted with Discretionary Access Control (DAC) protections, by which non-administrative users may (at their discretion) protect objects. In traditional UNIX systems, DAC protections include file permissions and access control lists; MAC protections include process controls preventing inter-user debugging and firewalls. A variety of MAC policies have been formulated by operating system designers and security researches, including the Multi-Level Security (MLS) confidentiality policy, the Biba integrity policy, Role-Based Access Control (RBAC), Domain and Type Enforcement (DTE), and Type Enforcement (TE). Each model bases decisions on a variety of factors, including user identity, role, and security clearance, as well as security labels on objects representing concepts such as data sensitivity and integrity.

The TrustedBSD MAC Framework is capable of supporting policy modules that implement all of these policies, as well as a broad class of system hardening policies, which may use existing security attributes, such as user and group IDs, as well as extended attributes on files, and other system properties. In addition, despite the name, the MAC Framework can also be used to implement purely discretionary policies, as policy modules are given substantial flexibility in how they authorize protections.

6.5. MAC Framework Kernel Architecture

The TrustedBSD MAC Framework permits kernel modules to extend the operating system security policy, as well as providing infrastructure functionality required by many access control modules. If multiple policies are simultaneously loaded, the MAC Framework will usefully (for some definition of useful) compose the results of the policies.

6.5.1. Kernel Elements

The MAC Framework contains a number of kernel elements:

- Framework management interfaces

- Concurrency and synchronization primitives.

- Policy registration

- Extensible security label for kernel objects

- Policy entry point composition operators

- Label management primitives

- Entry point API invoked by kernel services

- Entry point API to policy modules

- Entry points implementations (policy life cycle, object life cycle/label management, access control checks).

- Policy-agnostic label-management system calls

- `mac_syscall()` multiplex system call

- Various security policies implemented as MAC policy modules

6.5.2. Framework Management Interfaces

The TrustedBSD MAC Framework may be directly managed using sysctl's, loader tunables, and system calls.

In most cases, sysctl's and loader tunables of the same name modify the same parameters, and control behavior such as enforcement of protections relating to various kernel subsystems. In addition, if MAC debugging support is compiled into the kernel, several counters will be maintained tracking label allocation. It is generally advisable that per-subsystem enforcement controls not be used to control policy behavior in production environments, as they broadly impact the operation of all active policies. Instead, per-policy controls should be preferred, as they provide greater granularity and greater operational consistency for policy modules.

Loading and unloading of policy modules is performed using the system module management system calls and other system interfaces, including boot loader variables; policy modules will have the opportunity to influence load and unload events, including preventing undesired unloading of the policy.

6.5.3. Policy List Concurrency and Synchronization

As the set of active policies may change at run-time, and the invocation of entry points is non-atomic, synchronization is required to prevent loading or unloading of policies while an entry point invocation is in progress, freezing the set of active policies for the duration. This is accomplished by means of a framework busy count: whenever an entry point is entered, the busy count is incremented; whenever it is exited, the busy count is decremented. While the busy count is elevated, policy list changes are not permitted, and threads attempting to modify the policy list will sleep until the list is not busy. The busy count is protected by a mutex, and a condition variable is used to wake up sleepers waiting on policy list modifications. One side effect of this synchronization model is that recursion into the MAC Framework from within a policy module is permitted, although not generally used.

Various optimizations are used to reduce the overhead of the busy count, including avoiding the full cost of incrementing and decrementing if the list is empty or contains only static entries (policies that are loaded before the system starts, and cannot be unloaded). A compile-time option is also provided which prevents any change in the set of loaded policies at run-time, which eliminates the mutex locking costs associated with supporting dynamically loaded and unloaded policies as synchronization is no longer required.

As the MAC Framework is not permitted to block in some entry points, a normal sleep lock cannot be used; as a result, it is possible for the load or unload attempt to block for a substantial period of time waiting for the framework to become idle.

6.5.4. Label Synchronization

As kernel objects of interest may generally be accessed from more than one thread at a time, and simultaneous entry of more than one thread into the MAC Framework is permitted, security attribute storage maintained by the MAC Framework is carefully synchronized. In general, existing kernel synchronization on kernel object data is used to protect MAC Framework security labels on the object: for example, MAC labels on sockets are protected using the existing socket mutex. Likewise, semantics for concurrent access are generally identical to those of the container objects: for credentials, copy-on-write semantics are maintained for label contents as with the remainder of the credential structure. The MAC Framework asserts necessary locks on objects when invoked with an object reference. Policy authors must be aware of these synchronization semantics, as they will sometimes limit the types of accesses permitted on labels: for example, when a read-only reference to a credential is passed to a policy via an entry point, only read operations are permitted on the label state attached to the credential.

6.5.5. Policy Synchronization and Concurrency

Policy modules must be written to assume that many kernel threads may simultaneously enter one more policy entry points due to the parallel and preemptive nature of the FreeBSD kernel. If the policy module makes use of mutable state, this may require the use of synchronization primitives within the policy to prevent inconsistent views on that state resulting in incorrect operation of the policy. Policies will generally be able to make use of existing FreeBSD synchronization primitives for this purpose, including mutexes, sleep locks, condition variables, and counting semaphores. However, policies should be written to employ these primitives carefully, respecting existing kernel lock orders, and recognizing that some entry points are not permitted to sleep, limiting the use of primitives in those entry points to mutexes and wakeup operations.

When policy modules call out to other kernel subsystems, they will generally need to release any in-policy locks in order to avoid violating the kernel lock order or risking lock recursion. This will maintain policy locks as leaf locks in the global lock order, helping to avoid deadlock.

6.5.6. Policy Registration

The MAC Framework maintains two lists of active policies: a static list, and a dynamic list. The lists differ only with regards to their locking semantics: an elevated reference count is not required to make use of the static list. When kernel modules containing MAC Framework policies are loaded, the policy module will use SYSINIT to invoke a registration function; when a policy module is unloaded, SYSINIT will likewise invoke a de-registration function. Registration may fail if a policy module is loaded more than once, if insufficient resources are available for the registration (for example, the policy might require labeling and insufficient labeling state might be available), or other policy prerequisites might not be met (some policies may only be loaded prior to boot). Likewise, de-registration may fail if a policy is flagged as not unloadable.

6.5.7. Entry Points

Kernel services interact with the MAC Framework in two ways: they invoke a series of APIs to notify the framework of relevant events, and they provide a policy-agnostic label structure pointer in security-relevant objects. The label pointer is maintained by the MAC Framework via label management entry points, and permits the Framework to offer a labeling service to policy modules through relatively non-invasive changes to the kernel subsystem maintaining the object. For example, label pointers have been added to processes, process credentials, sockets, pipes, vnodes, Mbufs, network interfaces, IP reassembly queues, and a variety of other security-relevant structures. Kernel services also invoke the MAC Framework when they perform important security decisions, permitting policy modules to augment those decisions based on their own criteria (possibly including data stored in security labels). Most of these security critical decisions will be explicit access control checks; however, some affect more general decision functions such as packet matching for sockets and label transition at program execution.

6.5.8. Policy Composition

When more than one policy module is loaded into the kernel at a time, the results of the policy modules will be composed by the framework using a composition operator. This operator is currently hard-coded, and requires that all active policies must approve a request for it to return success. As policies may return a variety of error conditions (success, access denied, object does not exist, ...), a precedence operator selects the resulting error from the set of errors returned by policies. In general, errors indicating that an object does not exist will be preferred to errors indicating that access to an object is denied. While it is not guaranteed that the resulting composition will be useful or secure, we have found that it is for many useful selections of policies. For example, traditional trusted systems often ship with two or more policies using a similar composition.

6.5.9. Labeling Support

As many interesting access control extensions rely on security labels on objects, the MAC Framework provides a set of policy-agnostic label management system calls covering a variety of user-exposed objects. Common label types include partition identifiers, sensitivity labels, integrity labels, compartments, domains, roles, and types. By policy agnostic, we mean that policy modules are able to completely define the semantics of meta-data associated with an object. Policy modules participate in the internalization and externalization of string-based labels provides by user applications, and can expose multiple label elements to applications if desired.

In-memory labels are stored in slab-allocated `struct label`, which consists of a fixed-length array of unions, each holding a `void *` pointer and a `long`. Policies registering for label storage will be assigned a "slot" identifier, which may be used to dereference the label storage. The semantics of the storage are left entirely up to the policy module: modules are provided with a variety of entry points associated with the kernel object life cycle, including initialization, association/creation, and destruction. Using these interfaces, it is possible to implement reference counting and other storage models. Direct access to the object structure is generally not required by policy modules to retrieve a label, as the MAC Framework generally passes both a pointer to the object and a direct pointer to the object's label into entry points. The primary exception to this rule is the process credential, which must be manually dereferenced to access the credential label. This may change in future revisions of the MAC Framework.

Initialization entry points frequently include a sleeping disposition flag indicating whether or not an initialization is permitted to sleep; if sleeping is not permitted, a failure may be returned to cancel allocation of the label (and hence object). This may occur, for example, in the network stack during interrupt handling, where sleeping is not permitted, or while the caller holds a mutex. Due to the performance cost of maintaining labels on in-flight network packets (Mbufs), policies must specifically declare a requirement that Mbuf labels be allocated. Dynamically loaded policies making use of labels must be able to handle the case where their init function has not been called on an object, as objects may already exist when the policy is loaded. The MAC Framework guarantees that uninitialized label slots will hold a 0 or NULL value, which policies may use to detect uninitialized values. However, as allocation of Mbuf labels is conditional, policies must also be able to handle a NULL label pointer for Mbufs if they have been loaded dynamically.

In the case of file system labels, special support is provided for the persistent storage of security labels in extended attributes. Where available, extended attribute transactions are used to permit consistent compound updates of security labels on vnodes--currently this support is present only in the UFS2 file system. Policy authors may choose to implement multilabel file system object labels using one (or more) extended attributes. For efficiency reasons, the vnode label (v_label) is a cache of any on-disk label; policies are able to load values into the cache when the vnode is instantiated, and update the cache as needed. As a result, the extended attribute need not be directly accessed with every access control check.

Note

Currently, if a labeled policy permits dynamic unloading, its state slot cannot be reclaimed, which places a strict (and relatively low) bound on the number of unload-reload operations for labeled policies.

6.5.10. System Calls

The MAC Framework implements a number of system calls: most of these calls support the policy-agnostic label retrieval and manipulation APIs exposed to user applications.

The label management calls accept a label description structure, `struct mac`, which contains a series of MAC label elements. Each element contains a character string name, and character string value. Each policy will be given the chance to claim a particular element name, permitting policies to expose multiple independent elements if desired. Policy modules perform the internalization and externalization between kernel labels and user-provided labels via entry points, permitting a variety of semantics. Label management system calls are generally wrapped by user library functions to perform memory allocation and error handling, simplifying user applications that must manage labels.

The following MAC-related system calls are present in the FreeBSD kernel:

- `mac_get_proc()` may be used to retrieve the label of the current process.

- `mac_set_proc()` may be used to request a change in the label of the current process.

- `mac_get_fd()` may be used to retrieve the label of an object (file, socket, pipe, ...) referenced by a file descriptor.

- `mac_get_file()` may be used to retrieve the label of an object referenced by a file system path.

- `mac_set_fd()` may be used to request a change in the label of an object (file, socket, pipe, ...) referenced by a file descriptor.

- `mac_set_file()` may be used to request a change in the label of an object referenced by a file system path.

- `mac_syscall()` permits policy modules to create new system calls without modifying the system call table; it accepts a target policy name, operation number, and opaque argument for use by the policy.

- `mac_get_pid()` may be used to request the label of another process by process id.

- `mac_get_link()` is identical to `mac_get_file()`, only it will not follow a symbolic link if it is the final entry in the path, so may be used to retrieve the label on a symlink.

- `mac_set_link()` is identical to `mac_set_file()`, only it will not follow a symbolic link if it is the final entry in a path, so may be used to manipulate the label on a symlink.

- `mac_execve()` is identical to the `execve()` system call, only it also accepts a requested label to set the process label to when beginning execution of a new program. This change in label on execution is referred to as a "transition".

- `mac_get_peer()`, actually implemented via a socket option, retrieves the label of a remote peer on a socket, if available.

In addition to these system calls, the `SIOCSIGMAC` and `SIOCSIFMAC` network interface ioctls permit the labels on network interfaces to be retrieved and set.

6.6. MAC Policy Architecture

Security policies are either linked directly into the kernel, or compiled into loadable kernel modules that may be loaded at boot, or dynamically using the module loading system calls at runtime. Policy modules interact with the system through a set of declared entry points, providing access to a stream of system events and permitting the policy to influence access control decisions. Each policy contains a number of elements:

- Optional configuration parameters for policy.

- Centralized implementation of the policy logic and parameters.

- Optional implementation of policy life cycle events, such as initialization and destruction.

- Optional support for initializing, maintaining, and destroying labels on selected kernel objects.

- Optional support for user process inspection and modification of labels on selected objects.

- Implementation of selected access control entry points that are of interest to the policy.

- Declaration of policy identity, module entry points, and policy properties.

6.6.1. Policy Declaration

Modules may be declared using the `MAC_POLICY_SET()` macro, which names the policy, provides a reference to the MAC entry point vector, provides load-time flags determining how the policy framework should handle the policy, and optionally requests the allocation of label state by the framework.

```
static struct mac_policy_ops mac_policy_ops =
{
        .mpo_destroy = mac_policy_destroy,
        .mpo_init = mac_policy_init,
        .mpo_init_bpfdesc_label = mac_policy_init_bpfdesc_label,
        .mpo_init_cred_label = mac_policy_init_label,
/* ... */
        .mpo_check_vnode_setutimes = mac_policy_check_vnode_setutimes,
        .mpo_check_vnode_stat = mac_policy_check_vnode_stat,
        .mpo_check_vnode_write = mac_policy_check_vnode_write,
};
```

The MAC policy entry point vector, `mac_policy_ops` in this example, associates functions defined in the module with specific entry points. A complete listing of available entry points and their prototypes may be found in the MAC entry point reference section. Of specific interest during module registration are the .mpo_destroy and .mpo_init entry points. .mpo_init will be invoked once a policy is successfully registered with the module framework but prior to any other entry points becoming active. This permits the policy to perform any policy-specific allocation and initialization, such as initialization of any data or locks. .mpo_destroy will be invoked when a policy module is unloaded to permit releasing of any allocated memory and destruction of locks. Currently, these two entry points are invoked with the MAC policy list mutex held to prevent any other entry points from being invoked: this will be changed, but in the mean time, policies should be careful about what kernel primitives they invoke so as to avoid lock ordering or sleeping problems.

The policy declaration's module name field exists so that the module may be uniquely identified for the purposes of module dependencies. An appropriate string should be selected. The full string name of the policy is displayed to the user via the kernel log during load and unload events, and also exported when providing status information to userland processes.

6.6.2. Policy Flags

The policy declaration flags field permits the module to provide the framework with information about its capabilities at the time the module is loaded. Currently, three flags are defined:

MPC_LOADTIME_FLAG_UNLOADOK

> This flag indicates that the policy module may be unloaded. If this flag is not provided, then the policy framework will reject requests to unload the module. This flag might be used by modules that allocate label state and are unable to free that state at runtime.

MPC_LOADTIME_FLAG_NOTLATE

> This flag indicates that the policy module must be loaded and initialized early in the boot process. If the flag is specified, attempts to register the module following boot will be rejected. The flag may be used by policies that require pervasive labeling of all system objects, and cannot handle objects that have not been properly initialized by the policy.

MPC_LOADTIME_FLAG_LABELMBUFS

> This flag indicates that the policy module requires labeling of Mbufs, and that memory should always be allocated for the storage of Mbuf labels. By default, the MAC Framework will not allocate label storage for Mbufs unless at least one loaded policy has this flag set. This measurably improves network performance when policies do not require Mbuf labeling. A kernel option, MAC_ALWAYS_LABEL_MBUF, exists to force the MAC Framework to allocate Mbuf label storage regardless of the setting of this flag, and may be useful in some environments.

> ### Note
>
> Policies using the MPC_LOADTIME_FLAG_LABELMBUFS without the MPC_LOADTIME_FLAG_NOT-LATE flag set must be able to correctly handle NULL Mbuf label pointers passed into entry points. This is necessary as in-flight Mbufs without label storage may persist after a policy enabling Mbuf labeling has been loaded. If a policy is loaded before the network subsystem is active (i.e., the policy is not being loaded late), then all Mbufs are guaranteed to have label storage.

6.6.3. Policy Entry Points

Four classes of entry points are offered to policies registered with the framework: entry points associated with the registration and management of policies, entry points denoting initialization, creation, destruction, and other life cycle events for kernel objects, events associated with access control decisions that the policy module may influence, and calls associated with the management of labels on objects. In addition, a mac_syscall() entry point is provided so that policies may extend the kernel interface without registering new system calls.

Policy module writers should be aware of the kernel locking strategy, as well as what object locks are available during which entry points. Writers should attempt to avoid deadlock scenarios by avoiding grabbing non-leaf locks inside of entry points, and also follow the locking protocol for object access and modification. In particular, writers should be aware that while necessary locks to access objects and their labels are generally held, sufficient locks to modify an object or its label may not be present for all entry points. Locking information for arguments is documented in the MAC framework entry point document.

Policy entry points will pass a reference to the object label along with the object itself. This permits labeled policies to be unaware of the internals of the object yet still make decisions based on the label. The exception to this is the process credential, which is assumed to be understood by policies as a first class security object in the kernel.

6.7. MAC Policy Entry Point Reference

6.7.1. General-Purpose Module Entry Points

6.7.1.1. `mpo_init`

void **mpo_init**(*conf*);

struct mac_policy_conf **conf*;

Parameter	Description
conf	MAC policy definition

Policy load event. The policy list mutex is held, so sleep operations cannot be performed, and calls out to other kernel subsystems must be made with caution. If potentially sleeping memory allocations are required during policy initialization, they should be made using a separate module SYSINIT().

6.7.1.2. `mpo_destroy`

void **mpo_destroy**(*conf*);

struct mac_policy_conf **conf*;

Parameter	Description
conf	MAC policy defi-

Parameter	Description
...	...

Policy load event. The policy list mutex is held, so caution should be applied.

6.7.1.3. mpo_syscall

```
int mpo_syscall(td, call, arg);

struct thread *td;
int call;
void *arg;
```

Parameter	Description
td	Calling thread
call	Policy-specific syscall number
arg	Pointer to syscall arguments

This entry point provides a policy-multiplexed system call so that policies may provide additional services to user processes without registering specific system calls. The policy name provided during registration is used to demux calls from userland, and the arguments will be forwarded to this entry point. When implementing new services, security modules should be sure to invoke appropriate access control checks from the MAC framework as needed. For example, if a policy implements an augmented signal functionality, it should call the necessary signal access control checks to invoke the MAC framework and other registered policies.

Note

Modules must currently perform the copyin() of the syscall data on their own.

6.7.1.4. `mpo_thread_userret`

```
void mpo_thread_userret(td);
```

```
struct thread *td;
```

Parameter	Description
Pack- isagip- tiitea ter	Description
Rd- turn- ing thread	Returning thread

This entry point permits policy modules to perform MAC-related events when a thread returns to user space, via a system call return, trap return, or otherwise. This is required for policies that have floating process labels, as it is not always possible to acquire the process lock at arbitrary points in the stack during system call processing; process labels might represent traditional authentication data, process history information, or other data. To employ this mechanism, intended changes to the process credential label may be stored in the `p_label` protected by a per-policy spin lock, and then set the per-thread `TDF_ASTPENDING` flag and per-process `PS_MACPENDM` flag to schedule a call to the userret entry point. From this entry point, the policy may create a replacement credential with less concern about the locking context. Policy writers are cautioned that event ordering relating to scheduling an AST and the AST being performed may be complex and interlaced in multithreaded applications.

6.7.2. Label Operations

6.7.2.1. `mpo_init_bpfdesc_label`

```
void mpo_init_bpfdesc_label(label);
```

```
struct label *label;
```

Parameter	Description
Pack- isagip- tiitea ter	Description
New label bel to ap- ply	New label to apply

Initialize the label on a newly instantiated bpfdesc (BPF descriptor). Sleeping is permitted.

6.7.2.2. `mpo_init_cred_label`

```
void mpo_init_cred_label(label);
```

```
struct label *label;
```

Parameter	Description
Pack- isagip- tiitea ter	Description
New label	New label

Parameter	Description
label	Label to initialize

Initialize the label for a newly instantiated user credential. Sleeping is permitted.

6.7.2.3. `mpo_init_devfsdirent_label`

```
void mpo_init_devfsdirent_label(label);
```

```
struct label *label;
```

Parameter	Description
label	New label to apply

Initialize the label on a newly instantiated devfs entry. Sleeping is permitted.

6.7.2.4. `mpo_init_ifnet_label`

```
void mpo_init_ifnet_label(label);
```

```
struct label *label;
```

Parameter	Description
label	New label to apply

Initialize the label on a newly instantiated network interface. Sleeping is permitted.

6.7.2.5. `mpo_init_ipq_label`

```
void mpo_init_ipq_label(label, flag);
```

```
struct label *label;
```

```
int flag;
```

Parameter	Description
label	New label to apply
flag	Sleeping/non-sleeping malloc(9); see below

Initialize the label on a newly instantiated IP fragment reassembly queue. The *flag* field may be one of M_WAITOK and M_NOWAIT, and should be employed to avoid performing a sleeping malloc(9) during this initialization call. IP fragment reassembly queue allocation frequently occurs in performance sensitive environments, and the implementation should be careful to avoid sleeping or long-lived operations. This entry point is permitted to fail resulting in the failure to allocate the IP fragment reassembly queue.

6.7.2.6. `mpo_init_mbuf_label`

```
void mpo_init_mbuf_label(flag, label);

int flag;
struct label *label;
```

Parameter	Description
flag	Sleeping/non-sleeping malloc(9); see below
label	Policy label to

Parameter	Description
ter	
initialize	

Initialize the label on a newly instantiated mbuf packet header (*mbuf*). The *flag* field may be one of M_WAITOK and M_NOWAIT, and should be employed to avoid performing a sleeping malloc(9) during this initialization call. Mbuf allocation frequently occurs in performance sensitive environments, and the implementation should be careful to avoid sleeping or long-lived operations. This entry point is permitted to fail resulting in the failure to allocate the mbuf header.

6.7.2.7. `mpo_init_mount_label`

```
void mpo_init_mount_label(mntlabel, fslabel);

struct label *mntlabel;
struct label *fslabel;
```

Parameter	Description
ter	
mntlabel	label to be initialized for the mount itself
fslabel	label to be initialized for the file system

Initialize the labels on a newly instantiated mount point. Sleeping is permitted.

6.7.2.8. `mpo_init_mount_fs_label`

```
void mpo_init_mount_fs_label(label);

struct label *label;
```

Parameter	Description
label	Label to be initialized

Initialize the label on a newly mounted file system. Sleeping is permitted

6.7.2.9. `mpo_init_pipe_label`

```
void mpo_init_pipe_label(label);

struct label*label;
```

Parameter	Description
label	Label to be filled in

Initialize a label for a newly instantiated pipe. Sleeping is permitted.

6.7.2.10. `mpo_init_socket_label`

```
void mpo_init_socket_label(label, flag);

struct label *label;
int flag;
```

Parameter	Description
label	New label to ini-

Parameter	Description
label	New label to initialize
flag	malloc(9) flags

Initialize a label for a newly instantiated socket. The *flag* field may be one of M_WAITOK and M_NOWAIT, and should be employed to avoid performing a sleeping malloc(9) during this initialization call.

6.7.2.11. mpo_init_socket_peer_label

```
void mpo_init_socket_peer_label(label, flag);

struct label *label;
int flag;
```

Parameter	Description
label	New label to initialize
flag	malloc(9) flags

Initialize the peer label for a newly instantiated socket. The *flag* field may be one of M_WAITOK and M_NOWAIT, and should be employed to avoid performing a sleeping malloc(9) during this initialization call.

6.7.2.12. mpo_init_proc_label

```
void mpo_init_proc_label(label);

struct label *label;
```

Parameter	Description
label	New label to initialize

Initialize the label for a newly instantiated process. Sleeping is permitted.

6.7.2.13. mpo_init_vnode_label

```
void mpo_init_vnode_label(label);

struct label *label;
```

Parameter	Description
label	New label to initialize

Initialize the label on a newly instantiated vnode. Sleeping is permitted.

6.7.2.14. mpo_destroy_bpfdesc_label

```
void mpo_destroy_bpfdesc_label(label);

struct label *label;
```

Parameter	Description
label	bpfdesc label

Destroy the label on a BPF descriptor. In this entry point a policy should free any internal storage associated with *label* so that it may be destroyed.

6.7.2.15. mpo_destroy_cred_label

```
void mpo_destroy_cred_label(label);

struct label *label;
```

Parameter	Description
label	Label being destroyed

Destroy the label on a credential. In this entry point, a policy module should free any internal storage associated with *label* so that it may be destroyed.

6.7.2.16. mpo_destroy_devfsdirent_label

```
void mpo_destroy_devfsdirent_label(label);

struct label *label;
```

Parameter	Description
label	Label being destroyed

Destroy the label on a devfs entry. In this entry point, a policy module should free any internal storage associated with *label* so that it may be destroyed.

6.7.2.17. mpo_destroy_ifnet_label

```
void mpo_destroy_ifnet_label(label);

struct label *label;
```

Parameter	Description
label	Label being destroyed

Destroy the label on a removed interface. In this entry point, a policy module should free any internal storage associated with *label* so that it may be destroyed.

6.7.2.18. mpo_destroy_ipq_label

```
void mpo_destroy_ipq_label(label);

struct label *label;
```

Parameter	Description
label	Label be-

Parameter	Description
label	... being destroyed

Destroy the label on an IP fragment queue. In this entry point, a policy module should free any internal storage associated with *label* so that it may be destroyed.

6.7.2.19. mpo_destroy_mbuf_label

```
void mpo_destroy_mbuf_label(label);

struct label *label;
```

Parameter	Description
label	Label being destroyed

Destroy the label on an mbuf header. In this entry point, a policy module should free any internal storage associated with *label* so that it may be destroyed.

6.7.2.20. mpo_destroy_mount_label

```
void mpo_destroy_mount_label(label);

struct label *label;
```

Parameter	Description
label	Mount point label being destroyed

Destroy the labels on a mount point. In this entry point, a policy module should free the internal storage associated with *mntlabel* so that they may be destroyed.

6.7.2.21. mpo_destroy_mount_label

```
void mpo_destroy_mount_label(mntlabel, fslabel);
```

```
struct label *mntlabel;
struct label *fslabel;
```

Parameter	Description
mntlabel	Mount point label being destroyed
fslabel	File system label being destroyed>

Destroy the labels on a mount point. In this entry point, a policy module should free the internal storage associated with *mntlabel* and *fslabel* so that they may be destroyed.

6.7.2.22. mpo_destroy_socket_label

void **mpo_destroy_socket_label**(*label*);

```
struct label *label;
```

Parameter	Description
label	Socket label being destroyed

Destroy the label on a socket. In this entry point, a policy module should free any internal storage associated with *label* so that it may be destroyed.

6.7.2.23. mpo_destroy_socket_peer_label

void **mpo_destroy_socket_peer_label**(*peerlabel*);

```
struct label *peerlabel;
```

Parameter	Description
label	Socketpeer label being destroyed

Destroy the peer label on a socket. In this entry point, a policy module should free any internal storage associated with *label* so that it may be destroyed.

6.7.2.24. mpo_destroy_pipe_label

void **mpo_destroy_pipe_label**(*label*);

struct label **label*;

Parameter	Description
label	Pipe label

Destroy the label on a pipe. In this entry point, a policy module should free any internal storage associated with *label* so that it may be destroyed.

6.7.2.25. mpo_destroy_proc_label

void **mpo_destroy_proc_label**(*label*);

struct label **label*;

Parameter	Description
label	Process label

Destroy the label on a process. In this entry point, a policy module should free any internal storage associated with *label* so that it may be destroyed.

6.7.2.26. mpo_destroy_vnode_label

void **mpo_destroy_vnode_label**(*label*);

struct label **label*;

Parameter	Description
label	Policy label to be destroyed
plabel	Process label

Destroy the label on a vnode. In this entry point, a policy module should free any internal storage associated with *label* so that it may be destroyed.

6.7.2.27. mpo_copy_mbuf_label

```
void mpo_copy_mbuf_label(src, dest);

struct label *src;
struct label *dest;
```

Parameter	Description
src	Source label
dest	Destination label

Copy the label information in *src* into *dest*.

6.7.2.28. mpo_copy_pipe_label

```
void mpo_copy_pipe_label(src, dest);

struct label *src;
struct label *dest;
```

Parameter	Description
src	Source label
dest	Destination label

Copy the label information in *src* into *dest*.

6.7.2.29. `mpo_copy_vnode_label`

void **mpo_copy_vnode_label**(*src*, *dest*);

```
struct label *src;
struct label *dest;
```

Parameter	Description
src	Source label
dest	Destination label

Copy the label information in *src* into *dest*.

6.7.2.30. `mpo_externalize_cred_label`

int **mpo_externalize_cred_label**(*label*, *element_name*, *sb*, **claimed*);

```
struct label *label;
char *element_name;
struct sbuf *sb;
int *claimed;
```

Parameter	Description
label	Label to be externalized
element_name	Name of the policy whose

Description

Parameter

label
should
be
ex-
ter-
nal-
ized

String
buffer
to
be
filled
with
a
text
rep-
re-
sen-
ta-
tion
of
la-
bel

Claimed
be
in-
cre-
ment-
ed
when
*el-
e-
men-
t_da-
ta*
can
be
filled
in.

Produce an externalized label based on the label structure passed. An externalized label consists of a text representation of the label contents that can be used with userland applications and read by the user. Currently, all policies' externalize entry points will be called, so the implementation should check the contents of *element_name* before attempting to fill in *sb*. If *element_name* does not match the name of your policy, simply return 0. Only return nonzero if an error occurs while externalizing the label data. Once the policy fills in *element_data*, *claimed should be incremented.

6.7.2.31. mpo_externalize_ifnet_label

```
int mpo_externalize_ifnet_label(label, element_name, sb, *claimed);
```

```
struct label *label;
char *element_name;
struct sbuf *sb;
int *claimed;
```

Description

Parameter	Description
label	Label to be externalized
element_name	Name of the policy whose label should be externalized
sb	String buffer to be filled with a text representation of label
claimed	Should be incremented

Parameter	Description
	ter when *element_data* can be filled in.

Produce an externalized label based on the label structure passed. An externalized label consists of a text representation of the label contents that can be used with userland applications and read by the user. Currently, all policies' **externalize** entry points will be called, so the implementation should check the contents of *element_name* before attempting to fill in *sb*. If *element_name* does not match the name of your policy, simply return 0. Only return nonzero if an error occurs while externalizing the label data. Once the policy fills in *element_data*, *claimed* should be incremented.

6.7.2.32. mpo_externalize_pipe_label

```
int mpo_externalize_pipe_label(label, element_name, sb, *claimed);

struct label *label;
char *element_name;
struct sbuf *sb;
int *claimed;
```

Parameter	Description
	ter
	Label to be externalized
	Name of the policy whose label should be

Parameter	Description
	...ter externalized
sb	String buffer to be filled with a text representation of label
claimed	Should be incremented when element_data can be filled in.

Produce an externalized label based on the label structure passed. An externalized label consists of a text representation of the label contents that can be used with userland applications and read by the user. Currently, all policies' externalize entry points will be called, so the implementation should check the contents of element_name before attempting to fill in sb. If element_name does not match the name of your policy, simply return 0. Only return nonzero if an error occurs while externalizing the label data. Once the policy fills in element_data, *claimed should be incremented.

6.7.2.33. mpo_externalize_socket_label

```
int mpo_externalize_socket_label(label, element_name, sb, *claimed);

struct label *label;
char *element_name;
struct sbuf *sb;
```

```
int *claimed;
```

Parameter	Description
label	Label to be externalized
element_name	Name of the policy whose label should be externalized
sb	String buffer to be filled with a text representation of label
claimed	Should be incremented when ele-

Parameter	Description
ment_data	can be filled in.

Produce an externalized label based on the label structure passed. An externalized label consists of a text representation of the label contents that can be used with userland applications and read by the user. Currently, all policies' **externalize** entry points will be called, so the implementation should check the contents of *element_name* before attempting to fill in *sb*. If *element_name* does not match the name of your policy, simply return 0. Only return nonzero if an error occurs while externalizing the label data. Once the policy fills in *element_data*, *claimed* should be incremented.

6.7.2.34. mpo_externalize_socket_peer_label

```
int mpo_externalize_socket_peer_label(label, element_name, sb, *claimed);

struct label *label;
char *element_name;
struct sbuf *sb;
int *claimed;
```

Parameter	Description
label	Label to be externalized
element_name	Name of the policy whose label should be externalized

Parameter	Description
sb	String buffer to be filled with a text representation of label
claimed	Should be incremented when *element_data* can be filled in.

Produce an externalized label based on the label structure passed. An externalized label consists of a text representation of the label contents that can be used with userland applications and read by the user. Currently, all policies' externalize entry points will be called, so the implementation should check the contents of *element_name* before attempting to fill in *sb*. If *element_name* does not match the name of your policy, simply return 0. Only return nonzero if an error occurs while externalizing the label data. Once the policy fills in *element_data*, *claimed should be incremented.

6.7.2.35. mpo_externalize_vnode_label

```
int mpo_externalize_vnode_label(label, element_name, sb, *claimed);

struct label *label;
char *element_name;
struct sbuf *sb;
int *claimed;
```

parameter Description

Label to be externalized

Name of the policy whose label should be externalized

String buffer to be filled with a text representation of label

Chained be incremented when el-e-men-t_da-

Parameter	Description
ta	can be filled in.

Produce an externalized label based on the label structure passed. An externalized label consists of a text representation of the label contents that can be used with userland applications and read by the user. Currently, all policies' externalize entry points will be called, so the implementation should check the contents of *element_name* before attempting to fill in *sb*. If *element_name* does not match the name of your policy, simply return 0. Only return nonzero if an error occurs while externalizing the label data. Once the policy fills in *element_data*, *claimed* should be incremented.

6.7.2.36. mpo_internalize_cred_label

```
int mpo_internalize_cred_label(label, element_name, element_data, claimed);

struct label *label;
char *element_name;
char *element_data;
int *claimed;
```

Parameter	Description
label	Label to be filled in
element_name	Name of the policy whose label should be internalized
element_data	Text data...

Parameter	Description
to_data	Text to be internalized
claimed	Should be incremented when data can be successfully internalized.

Produce an internal label structure based on externalized label data in text format. Currently, all policies' `internalize` entry points are called when internalization is requested, so the implementation should compare the contents of *element_name* to its own name in order to be sure it should be internalizing the data in *element_data*. Just as in the `externalize` entry points, the entry point should return 0 if *element_name* does not match its own name, or when data can successfully be internalized, in which case *claimed should be incremented.

6.7.2.37. `mpo_internalize_ifnet_label`

```
int mpo_internalize_ifnet_label(label, element_name, element_data, claimed);

struct label *label;
char *element_name;
char *element_data;
int *claimed;
```

Parameter	Description
label	Label to be filled in

Parameter	Description
element_name	Name of the policy whose label should be internalized
element_data	Text data to be internalized
claimed	Should be incremented when data can be successfully internalized.

Produce an internal label structure based on externalized label data in text format. Currently, all policies' `internalize` entry points are called when internalization is requested, so the implementation should compare the contents of *element_name* to its own name in order to be sure it should be internalizing the data in *element_data*. Just as in the `externalize` entry points, the entry point should return 0 if *element_name* does not match its own name, or when data can successfully be internalized, in which case *claimed* should be incremented.

6.7.2.38. `mpo_internalize_pipe_label`

```
int mpo_internalize_pipe_label(label, element_name, element_data, claimed);

struct label *label;
char *element_name;
char *element_data;
int *claimed;
```

Parameter	Description
label	Label to be filled in
element_name	Name of the policy whose label should be internalized
element_data	Text data to be internalized
claimed	Should be incremented when data can be suc-

Parameter	Description
	ter cess- ful- ly in- ter- nal- ized.

Produce an internal label structure based on externalized label data in text format. Currently, all policies' **internalize** entry points are called when internalization is requested, so the implementation should compare the contents of *element_name* to its own name in order to be sure it should be internalizing the data in *element_data*. Just as in the **externalize** entry points, the entry point should return 0 if *element_name* does not match its own name, or when data can successfully be internalized, in which case *claimed should be incremented.

6.7.2.39. mpo_internalize_socket_label

int **mpo_internalize_socket_label**(*label, element_name, element_data, claimed*);

struct label *label;
char *element_name;
char *element_data;
int *claimed;

Parameter	Description
label	Label to be filled in
element_name	Name of the policy whose label should be internalized
element_data	Text data to in-

Parameter	Description
element_data	... to be internalized
claimed	Should be incremented when data can be successfully internalized.

Produce an internal label structure based on externalized label data in text format. Currently, all policies' `internalize` entry points are called when internalization is requested, so the implementation should compare the contents of *element_name* to its own name in order to be sure it should be internalizing the data in *element_data*. Just as in the `externalize` entry points, the entry point should return 0 if *element_name* does not match its own name, or when data can successfully be internalized, in which case *claimed* should be incremented.

6.7.2.40. `mpo_internalize_vnode_label`

```
int mpo_internalize_vnode_label(label, element_name, element_data, claimed);

struct label *label;
char *element_name;
char *element_data;
int *claimed;
```

Parameter	Description
label	Label to be filled in

Parameter	Description
element_name	Name of the policy whose label should be internalized
element_data	Text data to be internalized
claimed	Should be incremented when data can be successfully internalized.

Produce an internal label structure based on externalized label data in text format. Currently, all policies' `internalize` entry points are called when internalization is requested, so the implementation should compare the contents of *element_name* to its own name in order to be sure it should be internalizing the data in *element_data*. Just as in the `externalize` entry points, the entry point should return 0 if *element_name* does not match its own name, or when data can successfully be internalized, in which case *claimed* should be incremented.

6.7.3. Label Events

This class of entry points is used by the MAC framework to permit policies to maintain label information on kernel objects. For each labeled kernel object of interest to a MAC policy, entry points may be registered for relevant life cycle events. All objects implement initialization, creation, and destruction hooks. Some objects will also implement relabeling, allowing user processes to change the labels on objects. Some objects will also implement object-specific events, such as label events associated with IP reassembly. A typical labeled object will have the following life cycle of entry points:

```
Label initialization            o
(object-specific wait)           \
Label creation                   o
                                  \
Relabel events,                   o--<--.
Various object-specific,          |     |
Access control events             ~-->--o
                                         \
Label destruction                        o
```

Label initialization permits policies to allocate memory and set initial values for labels without context for the use of the object. The label slot allocated to a policy will be zeroed by default, so some policies may not need to perform initialization.

Label creation occurs when the kernel structure is associated with an actual kernel object. For example, Mbufs may be allocated and remain unused in a pool until they are required. mbuf allocation causes label initialization on the mbuf to take place, but mbuf creation occurs when the mbuf is associated with a datagram. Typically, context will be provided for a creation event, including the circumstances of the creation, and labels of other relevant objects in the creation process. For example, when an mbuf is created from a socket, the socket and its label will be presented to registered policies in addition to the new mbuf and its label. Memory allocation in creation events is discouraged, as it may occur in performance sensitive ports of the kernel; in addition, creation calls are not permitted to fail so a failure to allocate memory cannot be reported.

Object specific events do not generally fall into the other broad classes of label events, but will generally provide an opportunity to modify or update the label on an object based on additional context. For example, the label on an IP fragment reassembly queue may be updated during the MAC_UPDATE_IPQ entry point as a result of the acceptance of an additional mbuf to that queue.

Access control events are discussed in detail in the following section.

Label destruction permits policies to release storage or state associated with a label during its association with an object so that the kernel data structures supporting the object may be reused or released.

In addition to labels associated with specific kernel objects, an additional class of labels exists: temporary labels. These labels are used to store update information submitted by user processes. These labels are initialized and destroyed as with other label types, but the creation event is MAC_INTERNALIZE, which accepts a user label to be converted to an in-kernel representation.

6.7.3.1. File System Object Labeling Event Operations

6.7.3.1.1. mpo_associate_vnode_devfs

```
void mpo_associate_vnode_devfs(mp, fslabel, de, delabel, vp, vlabel);

struct mount *mp;
struct label *fslabel;
struct devfs_dirent *de;
struct label *delabel;
struct vnode *vp;
struct label *vlabel;
```

Pack-
isagip-
tiore
ter

Dp
vfs
mount
point

De-
vis
field
sys-
tem
la-
bel
(mp-
>mn-
t_f-
s-
la-
bel)

De-
vfs
di-
rec-
to-
ry
en-
try

Del
la-
bel
la-
bel
as-
so-
ci-
at-
ed
with
de

vp-
ode
as-
so-
ci-
at-
ed
with
de

Pol-
bel
cy

Parameter	Description
... ter	label associated with *vp*

Fill in the label (*vlabel*) for a newly created devfs vnode based on the devfs directory entry passed in *de* and its label.

6.7.3.1.2. mpo_associate_vnode_extattr

```
int mpo_associate_vnode_extattr(mp, fslabel, vp, vlabel);

struct mount *mp;
struct label *fslabel;
struct vnode *vp;
struct label *vlabel;
```

Parameter	Description
mp	File system mount point
fslabel	File system label
vp	Vnode to label
vlabel	Policy label associat-

Parameter	Description
	...tered with *vp*

Attempt to retrieve the label for *vp* from the file system extended attributes. Upon success, the value 0 is returned. Should extended attribute retrieval not be supported, an accepted fallback is to copy *fslabel* into *vlabel*. In the event of an error, an appropriate value for errno should be returned.

6.7.3.1.3. mpo_associate_vnode_singlelabel

void **mpo_associate_vnode_singlelabel**(*mp, fslabel, vp, vlabel*);

```
struct mount *mp;
struct label *fslabel;
struct vnode *vp;
struct label *vlabel;
```

Parameter	Description
mp	File system mount point
fslabel	File system label
vp	Vnode to label
vlabel	Policy label associated with *vp*

On non-multilabel file systems, this entry point is called to set the policy label for *vp* based on the file system label, *fslabel*.

6.7.3.1.4. `mpo_create_devfs_device`

```
void mpo_create_devfs_device(dev, devfs_dirent, label);

dev_t dev;
struct devfs_dirent *devfs_dirent;
struct label *label;
```

Parameter	Description
dev	Device corresponding with devfs_dirent
devfs_dirent	Devfs directory entry to be labeled.
label	Label for devfs_dirent to be filled in.

Fill out the label on a devfs_dirent being created for the passed device. This call will be made when the device file system is mounted, regenerated, or a new device is made available.

6.7.3.1.5. `mpo_create_devfs_directory`

```
void mpo_create_devfs_directory(dirname, dirnamelen, devfs_dirent, label);

char *dirname;
int dirnamelen;
```

```
struct devfs_dirent *devfs_dirent;
struct label *label;
```

Parameter	Description
dirname	Name of directory being created
namelen	Length of the string dirname
dd-dirent	Devfs directory entry for directory being created.

Fill out the label on a devfs_dirent being created for the passed directory. This call will be made when the device file system is mounted, regenerated, or a new device requiring a specific directory hierarchy is made available.

6.7.3.1.6. mpo_create_devfs_symlink

void **mpo_create_devfs_symlink**(*cred*, *mp*, *dd*, *ddlabel*, *de*, *delabel*);

```
struct ucred *cred;
struct mount *mp;
struct devfs_dirent *dd;
struct label *ddlabel;
struct devfs_dirent *de;
struct label *delabel;
```

Parameter	Description
cred	Subject credential
mp	Devfs mount point
link	Link destination
ddlabel	Label associated with dd
de	devfs symlink entry
delabel	Label associated with de

Fill in the label (*delabel*) for a newly created devfs(5) symbolic link entry.

6.7.3.1.7. mpo_create_vnode_extattr

```
int mpo_create_vnode_extattr(cred, mp, fslabel, dvp, dlabel, vp, vlabel, cnp);

struct ucred *cred;
struct mount *mp;
struct label *fslabel;
struct vnode *dvp;
struct label *dlabel;
struct vnode *vp;
struct label *vlabel;
```

```
struct componentname *cnp;
```

Parameter	Description
cred	Subject credential
mp	File system mount point
mntlabel	File system label
dvp	Parent directory vnode
dvlabel	Label associated with *dvp*
vp	Newly created vnode
vlabel	Policy label associ-

Parameter	Description
	...ter at-ed with *vp*
	Com-po-nent name for *vp*

Write out the label for *vp* to the appropriate extended attribute. If the write succeeds, fill in *vlabel* with the label, and return 0. Otherwise, return an appropriate error.

6.7.3.1.8. mpo_create_mount

```
void mpo_create_mount(cred, mp, mnt, fslabel);

struct ucred *cred;
struct mount *mp;
struct label *mnt;
struct label *fslabel;
```

Parameter	Description
	...ter
	Sub-ject cre-den-tial
	Ob-ject; file sys-tem be-ing mount-ed
	Pol-i-cy la-bel to be filled in

98

Parameter	Description
mp	Pointer for mp
fslabel	Policy label label for the file system mp mounts.

Fill out the labels on the mount point being created by the passed subject credential. This call will be made when a new file system is mounted.

6.7.3.1.9. mpo_create_root_mount

```
void mpo_create_root_mount(cred, mp, mntlabel, fslabel);

struct ucred *cred;
struct mount *mp;
struct label *mntlabel;
struct label *fslabel;
```

Parameter	Description
	See Section 6.7.3.1.8, "mpo_create_mount".

Fill out the labels on the mount point being created by the passed subject credential. This call will be made when the root file system is mounted, after mpo_create_mount;.

6.7.3.1.10. mpo_relabel_vnode

```
void mpo_relabel_vnode(cred, vp, vnodelabel, newlabel);

struct ucred *cred;
struct vnode *vp;
struct label *vnodelabel;
struct label *newlabel;
```

Parameter	Description
cred	Subject credential
vp	vnode to relabel
vlabel	Existing policy label for *vp*
intlabel	New, possibly partial label to replace vnode label

Update the label on the passed vnode given the passed update vnode label and the passed subject credential.

6.7.3.1.11. `mpo_setlabel_vnode_extattr`

```
int mpo_setlabel_vnode_extattr(cred, vp, vlabel, intlabel);

struct ucred *cred;
struct vnode *vp;
struct label *vlabel;
struct label *intlabel;
```

Parameter	Description
cred	Subject credential
vp	Vnode for which the label is being written
vlabel	Policy label associated with vp
intlabel	Label to label write out

Write out the policy from *intlabel* to an extended attribute. This is called from vop_stdcreatevnode_ea.

6.7.3.1.12. mpo_update_devfsdirent

```
void mpo_update_devfsdirent(devfs_dirent, direntlabel, vp, vnodelabel);

struct devfs_dirent *devfs_dirent;
struct label *direntlabel;
struct vnode *vp;
struct label *vnodelabel;
```

Parameter	Description
de_dirent	vfs directory entry object;
direntlabel	label for devfs_dirent to be updated.
vp	parent vnode
vnodelabel	label for vp

Update the *devfs_dirent* label from the passed devfs vnode label. This call will be made when a devfs vnode has been successfully relabeled to commit the label change such that it lasts even if the vnode is recycled. It will also be made when a symlink is created in devfs, following a call to mac_vnode_create_from_vnode to initialize the vnode label.

6.7.3.2. IPC Object Labeling Event Operations

6.7.3.2.1. mpo_create_mbuf_from_socket

```
void mpo_create_mbuf_from_socket(so, socketlabel, m, mbuflabel);

struct socket *so;
struct label *socketlabel;
struct mbuf *m;
struct label *mbuflabel;
```

Parameter	Description	Locking
socket	Socket	locking WIP
socketlabel	Socket label; label for socket object;	
mbuf	mbuf	
mbuflabel	mbuf label; label to fill in for m	

Set the label on a newly created mbuf header from the passed socket label. This call is made when a new datagram or message is generated by the socket and stored in the passed mbuf.

6.7.3.2.2. mpo_create_pipe

```
void mpo_create_pipe(cred, pipe, pipelabel);

struct ucred *cred;
struct pipe *pipe;
struct label *pipelabel;
```

Parameter	Description	Locking
cred	Subject credential	
pipe	Pipe	
pipelabel	Pipe label	

Parameter	Description
cred	Subject credential
pipelabel	Policy label associated with *pipe*

Set the label on a newly created pipe from the passed subject credential. This call is made when a new pipe is created.

6.7.3.2.3. mpo_create_socket

```
void mpo_create_socket(cred, so, socketlabel);

struct ucred *cred;
struct socket *so;
struct label *socketlabel;
```

Parameter	Description
cred	Subject credential
so	Object; socket to label
socketlabel	Label to fill in for *so*

Set the label on a newly created socket from the passed subject credential. This call is made when a socket is created.

6.7.3.2.4. mpo_create_socket_from_socket

```
void mpo_create_socket_from_socket(oldsocket, oldsocketlabel, newsocket, new-
socketlabel);
```

```
struct socket *oldsocket;
struct label *oldsocketlabel;
struct socket *newsocket;
struct label *newsocketlabel;
```

Parameter	Description
oldsocket	Existing socket
oldsocketlabel	Policy label associated with oldsocket
newsocket	New socket
newsocketlabel	Policy label associated with newsocketlabel

Label a socket, *newsocket*, newly accept(2)ed, based on the listen(2) socket, *oldsocket*.

6.7.3.2.5. mpo_relabel_pipe

void **mpo_relabel_pipe**(*cred, pipe, oldlabel, newlabel*);

```
struct ucred *cred;
```

```
struct pipe *pipe;
struct label *oldlabel;
struct label *newlabel;
```

Parameter	Description
cred	Subject credential
pipe	Existing policy label associated with pipe
newlabel	Policy label update to apply to pipe

Apply a new label, *newlabel*, to *pipe*.

6.7.3.2.6. mpo_relabel_socket

```
void mpo_relabel_socket(cred, so, oldlabel, newlabel);

struct ucred *cred;
struct socket *so;
struct label *oldlabel;
struct label *newlabel;
```

Parameter	Description
label	Embeddable injectable credential object; socket
socket	socket object
oldlabel	Old label for so
newlabel	New label update for so

Update the label on a socket from the passed socket label update.

6.7.3.2.7. mpo_set_socket_peer_from_mbuf

```
void mpo_set_socket_peer_from_mbuf(mbuf, mbuflabel, oldlabel, newlabel);

struct mbuf *mbuf;
struct label *mbuflabel;
struct label *oldlabel;
struct label *newlabel;
```

Parameter	Description
mbuf	mbuf datagram received over socket
mbuflabel	label of the mbuf

Parameter	Description
oldlabel	Existing label for the socket
newlabel	Policy label to be filled out for the socket

Set the peer label on a stream socket from the passed mbuf label. This call will be made when the first datagram is received by the stream socket, with the exception of Unix domain sockets.

6.7.3.2.8. mpo_set_socket_peer_from_socket

```
void mpo_set_socket_peer_from_socket(oldsocket, oldsocketlabel, newsocket,
newsocketpeerlabel);

struct socket *oldsocket;
struct label *oldsocketlabel;
struct socket *newsocket;
struct label *newsocketpeerlabel;
```

Parameter	Description
oldsocket	Old socket
oldsocketlabel	Policy label for old...

Parameter	Description	Locking
socket		
peer socket		
newsocketlabel	fill in for newsocket	
peerlabel		

Set the peer label on a stream UNIX domain socket from the passed remote socket endpoint. This call will be made when the socket pair is connected, and will be made for both endpoints.

6.7.3.3. Network Object Labeling Event Operations

6.7.3.3.1. mpo_create_bpfdesc

void **mpo_create_bpfdesc**(*cred*, *bpf_d*, *bpflabel*);

```
struct ucred *cred;
struct bpf_d *bpf_d;
struct label *bpflabel;
```

Parameter	Description	Locking
cred	Subject executable credential	
bpf_d	Object; bpf descriptor	
bpflabel	Policy label	

Parameter	Description
bpf_d	BPF descriptor label to be filled in for *bpf_d*

Set the label on a newly created BPF descriptor from the passed subject credential. This call will be made when a BPF device node is opened by a process with the passed subject credential.

6.7.3.3.2. `mpo_create_ifnet`

```
void mpo_create_ifnet(ifnet, ifnetlabel);

struct ifnet *ifnet;
struct label *ifnetlabel;
```

Parameter	Description
ifnet	Network interface
ifnetlabel	Policy label to fill in for *ifnet*

Set the label on a newly created interface. This call may be made when a new physical interface becomes available to the system, or when a pseudo-interface is instantiated during the boot or as a result of a user action.

6.7.3.3.3. `mpo_create_ipq`

```
void mpo_create_ipq(fragment, fragmentlabel, ipq, ipqlabel);

struct mbuf *fragment;
struct label *fragmentlabel;
struct ipq *ipq;
struct label *ipqlabel;
```

Parameter	Description
fragment	Received IP fragment
fragmentlabel	Policy label for *fragment*
ipq	Ipq reassembly queue to be labeled
ipqlabel	Policy label to be filled in for *ipq*

Set the label on a newly created IP fragment reassembly queue from the mbuf header of the first received fragment.

6.7.3.3.4. `mpo_create_datagram_from_ipq`

```
void mpo_create_create_datagram_from_ipq(ipq, ipqlabel, datagram, datagramla-
bel);

struct ipq *ipq;
struct label *ipqlabel;
struct mbuf *datagram;
struct label *datagramlabel;
```

Parameter	Description
ipq	IP reassembly queue
ipqlabel	Policy label for *ipq*
datagram	Datagram to be labeled
datagramlabel	Datagram label to be filled in for *datagramlabel*

Set the label on a newly reassembled IP datagram from the IP fragment reassembly queue from which it was generated.

6.7.3.3.5. `mpo_create_fragment`

```
void mpo_create_fragment(datagram, datagramlabel, fragment, fragmentlabel);

struct mbuf *datagram;
struct label *datagramlabel;
struct mbuf *fragment;
struct label *fragmentlabel;
```

Parameter	Description
datagram	Datagram

Parameter	Description
datagramlabel	Label for *datagram*
fragment	Fragment to be labeled
fraglabel	Fragment label to be filled in for *datagram*

Set the label on the mbuf header of a newly created IP fragment from the label on the mbuf header of the datagram it was generate from.

6.7.3.3.6. `mpo_create_mbuf_from_mbuf`

```
void mpo_create_mbuf_from_mbuf(oldmbuf, oldmbuflabel, newmbuf, newmbuflabel);

struct mbuf *oldmbuf;
struct label *oldmbuflabel;
struct mbuf *newmbuf;
struct label *newmbuflabel;
```

Parameter	Description
oldmbuf	Existing (source) mbuf
oldmbu-	Old mbu-

Parameter	Description
oldmbuflabel	Policy label for *oldmbuf*
newmbuf	New mbuf to be labeled
newmbuflabel	Policy label to be filled in for *newmbuf*

Set the label on the mbuf header of a newly created datagram from the mbuf header of an existing datagram. This call may be made in a number of situations, including when an mbuf is re-allocated for alignment purposes.

6.7.3.3.7. mpo_create_mbuf_linklayer

```
void mpo_create_mbuf_linklayer(ifnet, ifnetlabel, mbuf, mbuflabel);

struct ifnet *ifnet;
struct label *ifnetlabel;
struct mbuf *mbuf;
struct label *mbuflabel;
```

Parameter	Description
ifnet	Network interface
ifnetlabel	Policy label

114

Parameter	Description
ifnet	Interface pointer for *ifnet*
mbuf	mbuf header for new datagram
mbuflabel	Label to be filled in for mbuf

Set the label on the mbuf header of a newly created datagram generated for the purposes of a link layer response for the passed interface. This call may be made in a number of situations, including for ARP or ND6 responses in the IPv4 and IPv6 stacks.

6.7.3.3.8. `mpo_create_mbuf_from_bpfdesc`

void **mpo_create_mbuf_from_bpfdesc**(*bpf_d, bpflabel, mbuf, mbuflabel*);

```
struct bpf_d *bpf_d;
struct label *bpflabel;
struct mbuf *mbuf;
struct label *mbuflabel;
```

Parameter	Description
bpf_d	BPF descriptor
bpflabel	Policy label for *bpflabel*

Parameter	Description
mbuf	mbuf to be labeled
mbuflabel	label to fill in for mbuf

Set the label on the mbuf header of a newly created datagram generated using the passed BPF descriptor. This call is made when a write is performed to the BPF device associated with the passed BPF descriptor.

6.7.3.3.9. `mpo_create_mbuf_from_ifnet`

void **mpo_create_mbuf_from_ifnet**(*ifnet*, *ifnetlabel*, *mbuf*, *mbuflabel*);

```
struct ifnet *ifnet;
struct label *ifnetlabel;
struct mbuf *mbuf;
struct label *mbuflabel;
```

Parameter	Description
ifnet	Network interface
ifnetlabel	label for *ifnetlabel*
mbuf	mbuf head-

Parameter	Description
inter	er for new datagram
mbuflabel	flabel label to be filled in for mbuf

Set the label on the mbuf header of a newly created datagram generated from the passed network interface.

6.7.3.3.10. mpo_create_mbuf_multicast_encap

```
void mpo_create_mbuf_multicast_encap(oldmbuf, oldmbuflabel, ifnet, ifnetlabel,
newmbuf, newmbuflabel);

struct mbuf *oldmbuf;
struct label *oldmbuflabel;
struct ifnet *ifnet;
struct label *ifnetlabel;
struct mbuf *newmbuf;
struct label *newmbuflabel;
```

Parameter	Description
inter	ter
oldmbuf	header for existing datagram
oldmbuflabel	label for

Parameter	Description
oldmbuf	
ifnet	Network interface
ifnetlabel	Policy label for *ifnet*
newmbuf	Network buffer header to be labeled for new datagram
newmbuflabel	Policy label to be filled in for *newmbuf*

Set the label on the mbuf header of a newly created datagram generated from the existing passed datagram when it is processed by the passed multicast encapsulation interface. This call is made when an mbuf is to be delivered using the virtual interface.

6.7.3.3.11. mpo_create_mbuf_netlayer

void **mpo_create_mbuf_netlayer**(*oldmbuf, oldmbuflabel, newmbuf, newmbuflabel*);

```
struct mbuf *oldmbuf;
struct label *oldmbuflabel;
struct mbuf *newmbuf;
struct label *newmbuflabel;
```

Parameter	Description
oldmbuf	Received datagram
oldmbuflabel	Label for oldmbuf
newmbuf	Newly created datagram
newmbuflabel	Label for newmbuf

Set the label on the mbuf header of a newly created datagram generated by the IP stack in response to an existing received datagram (*oldmbuf*). This call may be made in a number of situations, including when responding to ICMP request datagrams.

6.7.3.3.12. mpo_fragment_match

```
int mpo_fragment_match(fragment, fragmentlabel, ipq, ipqlabel);

struct mbuf *fragment;
struct label *fragmentlabel;
struct ipq *ipq;
struct label *ipqlabel;
```

Parameter	Description
fragment	Datagram fragment

Parameter	Description
fragmentlabel	Policy label for *fragment*
ipq	IP fragment reassembly queue
ipqlabel	Policy label for *ipq*

Determine whether an mbuf header containing an IP datagram (*fragment*) fragment matches the label of the passed IP fragment reassembly queue (*ipq*). Return (1) for a successful match, or (0) for no match. This call is made when the IP stack attempts to find an existing fragment reassembly queue for a newly received fragment; if this fails, a new fragment reassembly queue may be instantiated for the fragment. Policies may use this entry point to prevent the reassembly of otherwise matching IP fragments if policy does not permit them to be reassembled based on the label or other information.

6.7.3.3.13. `mpo_relabel_ifnet`

void **mpo_relabel_ifnet**(*cred, ifnet, ifnetlabel, newlabel*);

```
struct ucred *cred;
struct ifnet *ifnet;
struct label *ifnetlabel;
struct label *newlabel;
```

Parameter	Description
cred	Subject credential
ifnet	Ifnet object;

Parameter	Description
ifnet	Network interface
ifnetlabel	Policy label for *ifnet*
newlabel	label update to apply to *ifnet*

Update the label of network interface, *ifnet*, based on the passed update label, *newlabel*, and the passed subject credential, *cred*.

6.7.3.3.14. `mpo_update_ipq`

void **mpo_update_ipq**(*fragment, fragmentlabel, ipq, ipqlabel*);

```
struct mbuf *fragment;
struct label *fragmentlabel;
struct ipq *ipq;
struct label *ipqlabel;
```

Parameter	Description
fragment	mbuf fragment
fragmentlabel	Policy label for *mbuf*
ipq	Ipq frag-

Parameter	Description
mbuf	Fragment reassembly queue
ipq	Policy label to be updated for ipq

Update the label on an IP fragment reassembly queue (*ipq*) based on the acceptance of the passed IP fragment mbuf header (*mbuf*).

6.7.3.4. Process Labeling Event Operations

6.7.3.4.1. mpo_create_cred

```
void mpo_create_cred(parent_cred, child_cred);

struct ucred *parent_cred;
struct ucred *child_cred;
```

Parameter	Description
parent_cred	Parent subject credential
child_cred	Child subject credential

Set the label of a newly created subject credential from the passed subject credential. This call will be made when crcopy(9) is invoked on a newly created struct ucred. This call should not be confused with a process forking or creation event.

6.7.3.4.2. mpo_execve_transition

```
void mpo_execve_transition(old, new, vp, vnodelabel);

struct ucred *old;
struct ucred *new;
struct vnode *vp;
struct label *vnodelabel;
```

Parameter	Description
old	Existing subject credential
new	New subject credential to be labeled
vp	File that was executed to execute
vnodelabel	Policy label to be updated / Policy label for vp

Update the label of a newly created subject credential (*new*) from the passed existing subject credential (*old*) based on a label transition caused by executing the passed vnode (*vp*). This call occurs when a process executes the passed vnode and one of the policies returns a success from the mpo_execve_will_transition entry point. Policies may choose to implement this call simply by invoking mpo_create_cred and passing the two subject credentials so as not to implement a transitioning event. Policies should not leave this entry point unimplemented if they implement mpo_create_cred, even if they do not implement mpo_execve_will_transition.

6.7.3.4.3. mpo_execve_will_transition

```
int mpo_execve_will_transition(old, vp, vnodelabel);

struct ucred *old;
```

```
struct vnode *vp;
struct label *vnodelabel;
```

Parameter	Description
subject	Subject executable credential prior to execve(2)
vp	File to execute
vnodelabel	Policy label for vp

Determine whether the policy will want to perform a transition event as a result of the execution of the passed vnode by the passed subject credential. Return 1 if a transition is required, 0 if not. Even if a policy returns 0, it should behave correctly in the presence of an unexpected invocation of mpo_execve_transition, as that call may happen as a result of another policy requesting a transition.

6.7.3.4.4. mpo_create_proc0

```
void mpo_create_proc0(cred);

struct ucred *cred;
```

Parameter	Description
cred	Subject credential to be filled in

Create the subject credential of process 0, the parent of all kernel processes.

6.7.3.4.5. `mpo_create_proc1`

void **mpo_create_proc1**(*cred*);

struct ucred *cred;

Parameter	Description	Locking
cred	Subject credential to be filled in	

Create the subject credential of process 1, the parent of all user processes.

6.7.3.4.6. `mpo_relabel_cred`

void **mpo_relabel_cred**(*cred*, *newlabel*);

struct ucred *cred;
struct label *newlabel;

Parameter	Description	Locking
cred	Subject credential	
newlabel	Label update to apply to cred	

Update the label on a subject credential from the passed update label.

6.7.4. Access Control Checks

Access control entry points permit policy modules to influence access control decisions made by the kernel. Generally, although not always, arguments to an access control entry point will include one or more authorizing credentials, information (possibly including a label) for any other objects involved in the operation. An access control entry point may return 0 to permit the operation, or an errno(2) error value. The results of invoking the entry point across various registered policy modules will be composed as follows: if all modules permit the operation to succeed, success will be returned. If one or modules returns a failure, a failure will be returned. If more than one module returns a failure, the errno value to return to the user will be selected using the following precedence, implemented by the error_select() function in kern_mac.c :

Most precedence	EDEADLK
	EINVAL
	ESRCH
	EACCES
Least precedence	EPERM

If none of the error values returned by all modules are listed in the precedence chart then an arbitrarily selected value from the set will be returned. In general, the rules provide precedence to errors in the following order: kernel failures, invalid arguments, object not present, access not permitted, other.

6.7.4.1. mpo_check_bpfdesc_receive

```
int mpo_check_bpfdesc_receive(bpf_d, bpflabel, ifnet, ifnetlabel);

struct bpf_d *bpf_d;
struct label *bpflabel;
struct ifnet *ifnet;
struct label *ifnetlabel;
```

Parameter	Description
bpf_d	Object; BPF descriptor
Bpflabel	Policy label for bpf_d
ifnet	Object; network interface
ifnetlabel	Policy label

Parameter	Description
bpf_d	Packet filter label for *ifnet*

Determine whether the MAC framework should permit datagrams from the passed interface to be delivered to the buffers of the passed BPF descriptor. Return (0) for success, or an `errno` value for failure Suggested failure: EACCES for label mismatches, EPERM for lack of privilege.

6.7.4.2. mpo_check_kenv_dump

```
int mpo_check_kenv_dump(cred);
```

```
struct ucred *cred;
```

Parameter	Description
cred	Subject credential

Determine whether the subject should be allowed to retrieve the kernel environment (see kenv(2)).

6.7.4.3. mpo_check_kenv_get

```
int mpo_check_kenv_get(cred, name);
```

```
struct ucred *cred;
char *name;
```

Parameter	Description
cred	Subject credential
name	Kernel environment variable name

Determine whether the subject should be allowed to retrieve the value of the specified kernel environment variable.

6.7.4.4. mpo_check_kenv_set

```
int mpo_check_kenv_set(cred, name);

struct ucred *cred;
char *name;
```

Parameter	Description
cred	Subject credential
name	Kernel environment variable name

Determine whether the subject should be allowed to set the specified kernel environment variable.

6.7.4.5. mpo_check_kenv_unset

```
int mpo_check_kenv_unset(cred, name);

struct ucred *cred;
char *name;
```

Parameter	Description
cred	Subject credential
name	Kernel environment vari-

128

Parameter	Description
	...ter able name

Determine whether the subject should be allowed to unset the specified kernel environment variable.

6.7.4.6. `mpo_check_kld_load`

```
int mpo_check_kld_load(cred, vp, vlabel);

struct ucred *cred;
struct vnode *vp;
struct label *vlabel;
```

Parameter	Description
cred	Subject credential
vp	Kernel module vnode
vlabel	Label associated with vp

Determine whether the subject should be allowed to load the specified module file.

6.7.4.7. `mpo_check_kld_stat`

```
int mpo_check_kld_stat(cred);

struct ucred *cred;
```

Parameter	Description
cred	Subject

Parameter	Description
cre-den-tial

Determine whether the subject should be allowed to retrieve a list of loaded kernel module files and associated statistics.

6.7.4.8. `mpo_check_kld_unload`

```
int mpo_check_kld_unload(cred);

struct ucred *cred;
```

Parameter	Description
cred	Sub-ject cre-den-tial

Determine whether the subject should be allowed to unload a kernel module.

6.7.4.9. `mpo_check_pipe_ioctl`

```
int mpo_check_pipe_ioctl(cred, pipe, pipelabel, cmd, data);

struct ucred *cred;
struct pipe *pipe;
struct label *pipelabel;
unsigned long cmd;
void *data;
```

Parameter	Description
cred	Sub-ject cre-den-tial
pipe
pipelabel	Pol-i-cy la-bel as-

Parameter	Description	Lock
	...ter sociated with *pipe*	
cmd	ioctl(2) command	
data	ioctl(2) data	

Determine whether the subject should be allowed to make the specified ioctl(2) call.

6.7.4.10. `mpo_check_pipe_poll`

```
int mpo_check_pipe_poll(cred, pipe, pipelabel);

struct ucred *cred;
struct pipe *pipe;
struct label *pipelabel;
```

Parameter	Description	Lock
cred	Subject credential	
pipe	Pipe	
pipelabel	Policy label associated with *pipe*	

Determine whether the subject should be allowed to poll *pipe*.

6.7.4.11. `mpo_check_pipe_read`

```
int mpo_check_pipe_read(cred, pipe, pipelabel);
```

```
struct ucred *cred;
struct pipe *pipe;
struct label *pipelabel;
```

Parameter	Description	Locking
cred	Subject credential	
pipe	Pipe	
pipelabel	Policy label associated with pipe	

Determine whether the subject should be allowed read access to *pipe*.

6.7.4.12. mpo_check_pipe_relabel

```
int mpo_check_pipe_relabel(cred, pipe, pipelabel, newlabel);

struct ucred *cred;
struct pipe *pipe;
struct label *pipelabel;
struct label *newlabel;
```

Parameter	Description	Locking
cred	Subject credential	
pipe	Pipe	
pipelabel	Current policy la- bel	

Parameter	Description
	...ter bel associated with pipe
newlabel	New label update to pipelabel

Determine whether the subject should be allowed to relabel *pipe*.

6.7.4.13. mpo_check_pipe_stat

```
int mpo_check_pipe_stat(cred, pipe, pipelabel);

struct ucred *cred;
struct pipe *pipe;
struct label *pipelabel;
```

Parameter	Description
cred	Subject credential
pipe	Pipe
pipelabel	Policy label associated with pipe

Determine whether the subject should be allowed to retrieve statistics related to *pipe*.

6.7.4.14. `mpo_check_pipe_write`

```
int mpo_check_pipe_write(cred, pipe, pipelabel);

struct ucred *cred;
struct pipe *pipe;
struct label *pipelabel;
```

Parameter	Description
cred	Subject credential
pipe	Pipe
pipelabel	Policy label associated with pipe

Determine whether the subject should be allowed to write to *pipe*.

6.7.4.15. `mpo_check_socket_bind`

```
int mpo_check_socket_bind(cred, socket, socketlabel, sockaddr);

struct ucred *cred;
struct socket *socket;
struct label *socketlabel;
struct sockaddr *sockaddr;
```

Parameter	Description
cred	Subject credential
socket	Socket to

Parameter	Description
	ter be bound
socketlabel	bel for socket
sockaddr	Address of socket

6.7.4.16. mpo_check_socket_connect

```
int mpo_check_socket_connect(cred, socket, socketlabel, sockaddr);

struct ucred *cred;
struct socket *socket;
struct label *socketlabel;
struct sockaddr *sockaddr;
```

Parameter	Description
cred	Subject credential
socket	Socket to be connected
socketlabel	bel for socket

Parameter	Description
sockaddr	Address of socket

Determine whether the subject credential (*cred*) can connect the passed socket (*socket*) to the passed socket address (*sockaddr*). Return 0 for success, or an errno value for failure. Suggested failure: EACCES for label mismatches, EPERM for lack of privilege.

6.7.4.17. mpo_check_socket_receive

```
int mpo_check_socket_receive(cred, so, socketlabel);

struct ucred *cred;
struct socket *so;
struct label *socketlabel;
```

Parameter	Description
cred	Subject credential
so	Socket
socketlabel	Socket label associated with so

Determine whether the subject should be allowed to receive information from the socket *so*.

6.7.4.18. mpo_check_socket_send

```
int mpo_check_socket_send(cred, so, socketlabel);

struct ucred *cred;
struct socket *so;
```

```
struct label *socketlabel;
```

Parameter	Description
cred	Subject credential
so	Socket
socketlabel	Policy label associated with so

Determine whether the subject should be allowed to send information across the socket *so*.

6.7.4.19. mpo_check_cred_visible

```
int mpo_check_cred_visible(u1, u2);

struct ucred *u1;
struct ucred *u2;
```

Parameter	Description
u1	Subject credential
u2	Object credential

Determine whether the subject credential *u1* can "see" other subjects with the passed subject credential *u2*. Return 0 for success, or an errno value for failure. Suggested failure: EACCES for label mismatches, EPERM for lack of privilege, or ESRCH to hide visibility. This call may be made in a number of situations, including inter-process status sysctl's used by ps, and in procfs lookups.

6.7.4.20. `mpo_check_socket_visible`

`int` **`mpo_check_socket_visible`**`(cred, socket, socketlabel);`

```
struct ucred *cred;
struct socket *socket;
struct label *socketlabel;
```

Parameter	Description
cred	Subject credential
socket	Object; socket
socketlabel	Socket label; label for socket

6.7.4.21. `mpo_check_ifnet_relabel`

`int` **`mpo_check_ifnet_relabel`**`(cred, ifnet, ifnetlabel, newlabel);`

```
struct ucred *cred;
struct ifnet *ifnet;
struct label *ifnetlabel;
struct label *newlabel;
```

Parameter	Description
cred	Subject credential
ifnet	Object; network interface

Parameter	Description
ifnetlabel	Policy label for *ifnet*
newlabel	Policy label update to later be applied to *ifnet*

Determine whether the subject credential can relabel the passed network interface to the passed label update.

6.7.4.22. mpo_check_socket_relabel

```
int mpo_check_socket_relabel(cred, socket, socketlabel, newlabel);

struct ucred *cred;
struct socket *socket;
struct label *socketlabel;
struct label *newlabel;
```

Parameter	Description
cred	Subject credential
socket	Socket

Parameter	Description
label	Existing policy label for *socket*
newlabel	Label update to later be applied to *socket-label*

Determine whether the subject credential can relabel the passed socket to the passed label update.

6.7.4.23. `mpo_check_cred_relabel`

```
int mpo_check_cred_relabel(cred, newlabel);

struct ucred *cred;
struct label *newlabel;
```

Parameter	Description
cred	Subject credential
newlabel	Label update to

140

Parameter	Description
cred	ter later be applied to cred

Determine whether the subject credential can relabel itself to the passed label update.

6.7.4.24. mpo_check_vnode_relabel

```
int mpo_check_vnode_relabel(cred, vp, vnodelabel, newlabel);

struct ucred *cred;
struct vnode *vp;
struct label *vnodelabel;
struct label *newlabel;
```

Parameter	Description
cred	Subject credential
vp	Object; vnode
vnodelabel	Existing policy label for vp
newlabel	Policy label update to

Parameter		Description
		ter later be applied to *vp*

Determine whether the subject credential can relabel the passed vnode to the passed label update.

6.7.4.25. mpo_check_mount_stat

```
int mpo_check_mount_stat(cred, mp, mountlabel);

struct ucred *cred;
struct mount *mp;
struct label *mountlabel;
```

Parameter		Description
cred	in	Subject credential
mp	in	Object; file system mount
mountlabel	in	Mount label; label for *mp*

Determine whether the subject credential can see the results of a statfs performed on the file system. Return 0 for success, or an errno value for failure. Suggested failure: EACCES for label mismatches or EPERM for lack of privilege. This call may be made in a number of situations, including during invocations of statfs(2) and related calls, as well as to determine what file systems to exclude from listings of file systems, such as when getfsstat(2) is invoked.

6.7.4.26. mpo_check_proc_debug

```
int mpo_check_proc_debug(cred, proc);

struct ucred *cred;
```

```
struct proc *proc;
```

Parameter *proc* Description process subject credential *proc* object; process

Determine whether the subject credential can debug the passed process. Return 0 for success, or an `errno` value for failure. Suggested failure: EACCES for label mismatch, EPERM for lack of privilege, or ESRCH to hide visibility of the target. This call may be made in a number of situations, including use of the ptrace(2) and ktrace(2) APIs, as well as for some types of procfs operations.

6.7.4.27. mpo_check_vnode_access

```
int mpo_check_vnode_access(cred, vp, label, flags);

struct ucred *cred;
struct vnode *vp;
struct label *label;
int flags;
```

Parameter *cred* Description subject credential *Object*; vnode *Label* cy label for *vp* *flags* cess(2) flags

Determine how invocations of access(2) and related calls by the subject credential should return when performed on the passed vnode using the passed access flags. This should generally be implemented using the same semantics used in mpo_check_vnode_open. Return 0 for success, or an errno value for failure. Suggested failure: EACCES for label mismatches or EPERM for lack of privilege.

6.7.4.28. mpo_check_vnode_chdir

```
int mpo_check_vnode_chdir(cred, dvp, dlabel);

struct ucred *cred;
struct vnode *dvp;
struct label *dlabel;
```

Parameter	Description	
cred	Subject credential	
dvp	Object; vnode to chdir(2) into	
dlabel	Policy label for dvp	

Determine whether the subject credential can change the process working directory to the passed vnode. Return 0 for success, or an errno value for failure. Suggested failure: EACCES for label mismatch, or EPERM for lack of privilege.

6.7.4.29. mpo_check_vnode_chroot

```
int mpo_check_vnode_chroot(cred, dvp, dlabel);

struct ucred *cred;
struct vnode *dvp;
struct label *dlabel;
```

Parameter	Description
cred	Subject cre-

Parameter	Description
cred	enter dential
dvp	Directory vnode
dlabel	Policy label associated with *dvp*

Determine whether the subject should be allowed to chroot(2) into the specified directory (*dvp*).

6.7.4.30. mpo_check_vnode_create

```
int mpo_check_vnode_create(cred, dvp, dlabel, cnp, vap);

struct ucred *cred;
struct vnode *dvp;
struct label *dlabel;
struct componentname *cnp;
struct vattr *vap;
```

Parameter	Description
cred	Subject credential
dvp	Object; vnode
dlabel	Policy la-

Parameter	Description
	...ter bel for dvp
	Component name for dvp
vap	Vnode attributes for vap

Determine whether the subject credential can create a vnode with the passed parent directory, passed name information, and passed attribute information. Return 0 for success, or an errno value for failure. Suggested failure: EACCES for label mismatch, or EPERM for lack of privilege. This call may be made in a number of situations, including as a result of calls to open(2) with O_CREAT, mkfifo(2), and others.

6.7.4.31. mpo_check_vnode_delete

```
int mpo_check_vnode_delete(cred, dvp, dlabel, vp, label, cnp);

struct ucred *cred;
struct vnode *dvp;
struct label *dlabel;
struct vnode *vp;
void *label;
struct componentname *cnp;
```

Parameter	Description
cred	Subject credential
dvp	Parent directory vnode

146

Parameter		Description
dlabel		Policy label for dvp
vp		Object; vnode to delete
label		Policy label for vp
cnp		Component name for vp

Determine whether the subject credential can delete a vnode from the passed parent directory and passed name information. Return 0 for success, or an errno value for failure. Suggested failure: EACCES for label mismatch, or EPERM for lack of privilege. This call may be made in a number of situations, including as a result of calls to unlink(2) and rmdir(2). Policies implementing this entry point should also implement mpo_check_rename_to to authorize deletion of objects as a result of being the target of a rename.

6.7.4.32. mpo_check_vnode_deleteacl

```
int mpo_check_vnode_deleteacl(cred, vp, label, type);

struct ucred *cred;
struct vnode *vp;
struct label *label;
acl_type_t type;
```

Parameter		Description
cred		Subject credential

Parameter	Description
vp	Object; vnode
label	Policy label for vp
type	ACL type

Determine whether the subject credential can delete the ACL of passed type from the passed vnode. Return 0 for success, or an errno value for failure. Suggested failure: EACCES for label mismatch, or EPERM for lack of privilege.

6.7.4.33. mpo_check_vnode_exec

```
int mpo_check_vnode_exec(cred, vp, label);

struct ucred *cred;
struct vnode *vp;
struct label *label;
```

Parameter	Description
cred	Subject credential
vp	Object; vnode to execute
label	Policy label for vp

Chapter 6. The TrustedBSD MAC Framework

Determine whether the subject credential can execute the passed vnode. Determination of execute privilege is made separately from decisions about any transitioning event. Return 0 for success, or an errno value for failure. Suggested failure: EACCES for label mismatch, or EPERM for lack of privilege.

6.7.4.34. mpo_check_vnode_getacl

```
int mpo_check_vnode_getacl(cred, vp, label, type);

struct ucred *cred;
struct vnode *vp;
struct label *label;
acl_type_t type;
```

Parameter	Description	Locking
cred	Subject credential	
vp	Object; vnode	
label	Policy label for vp	
type	Type	

Determine whether the subject credential can retrieve the ACL of passed type from the passed vnode. Return 0 for success, or an errno value for failure. Suggested failure: EACCES for label mismatch, or EPERM for lack of privilege.

6.7.4.35. mpo_check_vnode_getextattr

```
int mpo_check_vnode_getextattr(cred, vp, label, attrnamespace, name, uio);

struct ucred *cred;
struct vnode *vp;
struct label *label;
int attrnamespace;
const char *name;
struct uio *uio;
```

Parameter	Description	Locking
cred	Subject	

Parameter	Description
cred	Subject credential
vp	Object; vnode
label	Policy label for vp
namespace	Extended attribute namespace
name	Extended attribute name
uio	UIO structure pointer; see uio(9)

Determine whether the subject credential can retrieve the extended attribute with the passed namespace and name from the passed vnode. Policies implementing labeling using extended attributes may be interested in special handling of operations on those extended attributes. Return 0 for success, or an errno value for failure. Suggested failure: EACCES for label mismatch, or EPERM for lack of privilege.

6.7.4.36. mpo_check_vnode_link

```
int mpo_check_vnode_link(cred, dvp, dlabel, vp, label, cnp);

struct ucred *cred;
struct vnode *dvp;
struct label *dlabel;
struct vnode *vp;
struct label *label;
```

```
struct componentname *cnp;
```

Parameter	Description
cred	Subject credential
dvp	Directory vnode
dlabel	Policy label associated with dvp
vp	Link destination vnode
label	Policy label associated with vp
cnp	Component name for

Parameter	Description
	ter
	the link being created

Determine whether the subject should be allowed to create a link to the vnode *vp* with the name specified by *cnp*.

6.7.4.37. mpo_check_vnode_mmap

```
int mpo_check_vnode_mmap(cred, vp, label, prot);

struct ucred *cred;
struct vnode *vp;
struct label *label;
int prot;
```

Parameter	Description
	ter
cred	Subject credential
vp	Vnode to map
label	Policy label associated with *vp*
prot	Mmap protections (see mmap(2))

Determine whether the subject should be allowed to map the vnode *vp* with the protections specified in *prot*.

6.7.4.38. mpo_check_vnode_mmap_downgrade

```
void mpo_check_vnode_mmap_downgrade(cred, vp, label, prot);

struct ucred *cred;
struct vnode *vp;
struct label *label;
int *prot;
```

Parameter	Description
cred	See Section 6.7.4.37 "mpo_check_vnode_mmap".
vp	
label	
prot	Mmap protections to be downgraded

Downgrade the mmap protections based on the subject and object labels.

6.7.4.39. mpo_check_vnode_mprotect

```
int mpo_check_vnode_mprotect(cred, vp, label, prot);

struct ucred *cred;
struct vnode *vp;
struct label *label;
int prot;
```

Parameter	Description
cred	Subject credential
vp	Mapped vnode
label	
prot	Memory pro-

Parameter	Description
	ter
	tec-
	tions

Determine whether the subject should be allowed to set the specified memory protections on memory mapped from the vnode *vp*.

6.7.4.40. mpo_check_vnode_poll

```
int mpo_check_vnode_poll(active_cred, file_cred, vp, label);
```

```
struct ucred *active_cred;
struct ucred *file_cred;
struct vnode *vp;
struct label *label;
```

Parameter	Description
ter	
active_cred	Subject credential
file_cred	credential associated with the struct file
vp	Polled vnode
label	Policy label associated with *vp*

Determine whether the subject should be allowed to poll the vnode *vp*.

6.7.4.41. `mpo_check_vnode_rename_from`

```
int mpo_vnode_rename_from(cred, dvp, dlabel, vp, label, cnp);

struct ucred *cred;
struct vnode *dvp;
struct label *dlabel;
struct vnode *vp;
struct label *label;
struct componentname *cnp;
```

Parameter	Description
cred	Subject credential
dvp	Directory vnode
dlabel	Policy label associated with *dvp*
vp	Vnode to be renamed
label	Policy label associat-

Parameter	Description
	...enter ed with vp
cnp	Component name for vp

Determine whether the subject should be allowed to rename the vnode *vp* to something else.

6.7.4.42. mpo_check_vnode_rename_to

int **mpo_check_vnode_rename_to**(*cred, dvp, dlabel, vp, label, samedir, cnp*);

```
struct ucred *cred;
struct vnode *dvp;
struct label *dlabel;
struct vnode *vp;
struct label *label;
int samedir;
struct componentname *cnp;
```

Parameter	Description
cred	Subject credential
dvp	Directory vnode
dlabel	Policy label associated with dvp

156

Parameter	Description
vp	Overwritten vnode
label	Policy label associated with *vp*
samedir	Boolean; 1 if the source and destination directories are the same
cnp	Destination component name

Determine whether the subject should be allowed to rename to the vnode *vp*, into the directory *dvp*, or to the name represented by *cnp*. If there is no existing file to overwrite, *vp* and *label* will be NULL.

6.7.4.43. mpo_check_socket_listen

```
int mpo_check_socket_listen(cred, socket, socketlabel);

struct ucred *cred;
```

```
struct socket *socket;
struct label *socketlabel;
```

Parameter	Description
cred	Subject credential
socket	Object; socket
socketlabel	Policy label for socket

Determine whether the subject credential can listen on the passed socket. Return 0 for success, or an errno value for failure. Suggested failure: EACCES for label mismatch, or EPERM for lack of privilege.

6.7.4.44. mpo_check_vnode_lookup

```
int mpo_check_vnode_lookup( , , , cnp);

struct ucred *cred;
struct vnode *dvp;
struct label *dlabel;
struct componentname *cnp;
```

Parameter	Description
cred	Subject credential
dvp	Object; vnode
dlabel	Policy ... cy

Parameter	Description
dvp	...ter label for *dvp*
cnp	Component name being looked up

Determine whether the subject credential can perform a lookup in the passed directory vnode for the passed name. Return 0 for success, or an errno value for failure. Suggested failure: EACCES for label mismatch, or EPERM for lack of privilege.

6.7.4.45. mpo_check_vnode_open

```
int mpo_check_vnode_open(cred, vp, label, acc_mode);

struct ucred *cred;
struct vnode *vp;
struct label *label;
int acc_mode;
```

Parameter	Description
cred	Subject credential
vp	Object; vnode
label	Policy label for *vp*
acc_mode	open(2) access mode

Determine whether the subject credential can perform an open operation on the passed vnode with the passed access mode. Return 0 for success, or an errno value for failure. Suggested failure: EACCES for label mismatch, or EPERM for lack of privilege.

6.7.4.46. mpo_check_vnode_readdir

```
int mpo_check_vnode_readdir(, , );
```

```
struct ucred *cred;
struct vnode *dvp;
struct label *dlabel;
```

Parameter	Description	
Description		
cred	Subject credential	
dvp	Object; directory vnode	
dlabel	Policy label for *dvp*	

Determine whether the subject credential can perform a readdir operation on the passed directory vnode. Return 0 for success, or an errno value for failure. Suggested failure: EACCES for label mismatch, or EPERM for lack of privilege.

6.7.4.47. mpo_check_vnode_readlink

```
int mpo_check_vnode_readlink(cred, vp, label);
```

```
struct ucred *cred;
struct vnode *vp;
struct label *label;
```

Parameter	Description	
Description		
cred	Subject cre-	

Parameter	Description
cred	Subject credential
vp	Object; vnode
label	Policy label for vp

Determine whether the subject credential can perform a `readlink` operation on the passed symlink vnode. Return 0 for success, or an `errno` value for failure. Suggested failure: EACCES for label mismatch, or EPERM for lack of privilege. This call may be made in a number of situations, including an explicit `readlink` call by the user process, or as a result of an implicit `readlink` during a name lookup by the process.

6.7.4.48. mpo_check_vnode_revoke

```
int mpo_check_vnode_revoke(cred, vp, label);

struct ucred *cred;
struct vnode *vp;
struct label *label;
```

Parameter	Description
cred	Subject credential
vp	Object; vnode
label	Policy label for vp

Determine whether the subject credential can revoke access to the passed vnode. Return 0 for success, or an `errno` value for failure. Suggested failure: EACCES for label mismatch, or EPERM for lack of privilege.

6.7.4.49. `mpo_check_vnode_setacl`

```
int mpo_check_vnode_setacl(cred, vp, label, type, acl);
```

```
struct ucred *cred;
struct vnode *vp;
struct label *label;
acl_type_t type;
struct acl *acl;
```

Parameter	Description	Locking
cred	Subject credential	
vp	Object; vnode	
label	Policy label for vp	
type	ACL type	
acl	ACL	

Determine whether the subject credential can set the passed ACL of passed type on the passed vnode. Return 0 for success, or an `errno` value for failure. Suggested failure: EACCES for label mismatch, or EPERM for lack of privilege.

6.7.4.50. `mpo_check_vnode_setextattr`

```
int mpo_check_vnode_setextattr(cred, vp, label, attrnamespace, name, uio);
```

```
struct ucred *cred;
struct vnode *vp;
struct label *label;
int attrnamespace;
const char *name;
struct uio *uio;
```

Parameter	Description	Locking
cred	Subject	

162

Parameter	Description
cred	Subject credential
vp	Object; vnode
label	Policy label for *vp*
attrnamespace	Extended attribute namespace
name	Extended attribute name
uio	UIO structure pointer; see uio(9)

Determine whether the subject credential can set the extended attribute of passed name and passed namespace on the passed vnode. Policies implementing security labels backed into extended attributes may want to provide additional protections for those attributes. Additionally, policies should avoid making decisions based on the data referenced from *uio*, as there is a potential race condition between this check and the actual operation. The *uio* may also be NULL if a delete operation is being performed. Return 0 for success, or an errno value for failure. Suggested failure: EACCES for label mismatch, or EPERM for lack of privilege.

6.7.4.51. mpo_check_vnode_setflags

```
int mpo_check_vnode_setflags(cred, vp, label, flags);

struct ucred *cred;
struct vnode *vp;
struct label *label;
```

u_long *flags*;

Parameter	Description
cred	Subject credential
vp	Object; vnode
label	Policy label for *vp*
flags	Flags; see chflags(2)

Determine whether the subject credential can set the passed flags on the passed vnode. Return 0 for success, or an errno value for failure. Suggested failure: EACCES for label mismatch, or EPERM for lack of privilege.

6.7.4.52. mpo_check_vnode_setmode

int **mpo_check_vnode_setmode**(*cred*, *vp*, *label*, *mode*);

struct ucred *cred;
struct vnode *vp;
struct label *label;
mode_t mode;

Parameter	Description
cred	Subject credential
vp	Object; vnode

Parameter	Description	Locking
label	Policy label for vp	
mode	File mode; see chmod(2)	

Determine whether the subject credential can set the passed mode on the passed vnode. Return 0 for success, or an errno value for failure. Suggested failure: EACCES for label mismatch, or EPERM for lack of privilege.

6.7.4.53. mpo_check_vnode_setowner

```
int mpo_check_vnode_setowner(cred, vp, label, uid, gid);

struct ucred *cred;
struct vnode *vp;
struct label *label;
uid_t uid;
gid_t gid;
```

Parameter	Description	Locking
cred	Subject credential	
vp	Object; vnode	
label	Policy label for vp	
uid	User ID	
gid	Group ID	

Determine whether the subject credential can set the passed uid and passed gid as file uid and file gid on the passed vnode. The IDs may be set to (-1) to request no update. Return 0 for success, or an errno value for failure. Suggested failure: EACCES for label mismatch, or EPERM for lack of privilege.

6.7.4.54. mpo_check_vnode_setutimes

```
int mpo_check_vnode_setutimes(, , , , );

struct ucred *cred;
struct vnode *vp;
struct label *label;
struct timespec atime;
struct timespec mtime;
```

Description

Parameter	Description
cred	Subject credential
vp	Object; vp
label	Policy label for vp
atime	Access time; see utimes(2)
mtime	Modification time; see utimes(2)

Determine whether the subject credential can set the passed access timestamps on the passed vnode. Return 0 for success, or an errno value for failure. Suggested failure: EACCES for label mismatch, or EPERM for lack of privilege.

6.7.4.55. mpo_check_proc_sched

```
int mpo_check_proc_sched(ucred, proc);

struct ucred *ucred;
struct proc *proc;
```

Parameter	Description
cred	Subject credential
proc	Object; process

Determine whether the subject credential can change the scheduling parameters of the passed process. Return 0 for success, or an `errno` value for failure. Suggested failure: EACCES for label mismatch, EPERM for lack of privilege, or ESRCH to limit visibility.

See setpriority(2) for more information.

6.7.4.56. `mpo_check_proc_signal`

```
int mpo_check_proc_signal(cred, proc, signal);

struct ucred *cred;
struct proc *proc;
int signal;
```

Parameter	Description
cred	Subject credential
proc	Object; process
signal	Signal; see kill(2)

Determine whether the subject credential can deliver the passed signal to the passed process. Return 0 for success, or an `errno` value for failure. Suggested failure: EACCES for label mismatch, EPERM for lack of privilege, or ESRCH to limit visibility.

6.7.4.57. `mpo_check_vnode_stat`

```
int mpo_check_vnode_stat(cred, vp, label);

struct ucred *cred;
struct vnode *vp;
struct label *label;
```

Parameter	Description
cred	Subject credential
vp	Object; vnode
vnodelabel	Policy label for vp

Determine whether the subject credential can `stat` the passed vnode. Return 0 for success, or an `errno` value for failure. Suggested failure: EACCES for label mismatch, or EPERM for lack of privilege.

See stat(2) for more information.

6.7.4.58. mpo_check_ifnet_transmit

```
int mpo_check_ifnet_transmit(cred, ifnet, ifnetlabel, mbuf, mbuflabel);

struct ucred *cred;
struct ifnet *ifnet;
struct label *ifnetlabel;
struct mbuf *mbuf;
struct label *mbuflabel;
```

Parameter	Description
cred	Subject credential
ifnet	Network interface
ifnetlabel	Policy label

Parameter	Description
ifnet	... for *ifnet*
mbuf	object; mbuf to be sent
mbuflabel	label for *mbuf*

Determine whether the network interface can transmit the passed mbuf. Return 0 for success, or an `errno` value for failure. Suggested failure: EACCES for label mismatch, or EPERM for lack of privilege.

6.7.4.59. mpo_check_socket_deliver

```
int mpo_check_socket_deliver(cred, ifnet, ifnetlabel, mbuf, mbuflabel);

struct ucred *cred;
struct ifnet *ifnet;
struct label *ifnetlabel;
struct mbuf *mbuf;
struct label *mbuflabel;
```

Parameter	Description
cred	Subject credential
ifnet	Network interface
ifnetlabel	Policy label for *ifnet*

Parameter	Description
mbuf	mbuf object; mbuf to be delivered
mbuflabel	label for *mbuf*

Determine whether the socket may receive the datagram stored in the passed mbuf header. Return 0 for success, or an errno value for failure. Suggested failures: EACCES for label mismatch, or EPERM for lack of privilege.

6.7.4.60. mpo_check_socket_visible

```
int mpo_check_socket_visible(cred, so, socketlabel);

struct ucred *cred;
struct socket *so;
struct label *socketlabel;
```

Parameter	Description
cred	subject credential
so	socket object; socket
socketlabel	socket-type-label for *so*

Determine whether the subject credential cred can "see" the passed socket (*socket*) using system monitoring functions, such as those employed by netstat(8) and sockstat(1). Return 0 for success, or an errno value for failure. Suggested failure: EACCES for label mismatches, EPERM for lack of privilege, or ESRCH to hide visibility.

6.7.4.61. mpo_check_system_acct

```
int mpo_check_system_acct(ucred, vp, vlabel);

struct ucred *ucred;
struct vnode *vp;
struct label *vlabel;
```

Parameter	Description	Locking
ucred	Subject credential	
vp	Accounting file; acct(5)	
vlabel	Label associated with vp	

Determine whether the subject should be allowed to enable accounting, based on its label and the label of the accounting log file.

6.7.4.62. mpo_check_system_nfsd

```
int mpo_check_system_nfsd(cred);

struct ucred *cred;
```

Parameter	Description	Locking
cred	Subject credential	

Determine whether the subject should be allowed to call nfssvc(2).

6.7.4.63. mpo_check_system_reboot

```
int mpo_check_system_reboot(cred, howto);
```

```
struct ucred *cred;
int howto;
```

Parameter	Description	Locking
cred	Subject credential	
howto	howto parameter from reboot(2)	

Determine whether the subject should be allowed to reboot the system in the specified manner.

6.7.4.64. mpo_check_system_settime

```
int mpo_check_system_settime(cred);
```

```
struct ucred *cred;
```

Parameter	Description	Locking
cred	Subject credential	

Determine whether the user should be allowed to set the system clock.

6.7.4.65. mpo_check_system_swapon

```
int mpo_check_system_swapon(cred, vp, vlabel);
```

```
struct ucred *cred;
struct vnode *vp;
struct label *vlabel;
```

Parameter	Description	Locking
cred	Subject	

Parameter	Description
cred	Subject credential
vp	Swap device
vlabel	Label associated with vp

Determine whether the subject should be allowed to add *vp* as a swap device.

6.7.4.66. mpo_check_system_sysctl

```
int mpo_check_system_sysctl(cred, name, namelen, old, oldlenp, inkernel, new,
newlen);

struct ucred *cred;
int *name;
u_int *namelen;
void *old;
size_t *oldlenp;
int inkernel;
void *new;
size_t newlen;
```

Parameter	Description
cred	Subject credential
name	name sysctl(3)
namelen	name-len
old	old
oldlenp	oldlenp
inkernel	Boolean; true if

Pack-
ise-
tion
ter
called
from
ker-
nel

See
sysctl(3)
newlen

Determine whether the subject should be allowed to make the specified sysctl(3) transaction.

6.7.5. Label Management Calls

Relabel events occur when a user process has requested that the label on an object be modified. A two-phase update occurs: first, an access control check will be performed to determine if the update is both valid and permitted, and then the update itself is performed via a separate entry point. Relabel entry points typically accept the object, object label reference, and an update label submitted by the process. Memory allocation during relabel is discouraged, as relabel calls are not permitted to fail (failure should be reported earlier in the relabel check).

6.8. Userland Architecture

The TrustedBSD MAC Framework includes a number of policy-agnostic elements, including MAC library interfaces for abstractly managing labels, modifications to the system credential management and login libraries to support the assignment of MAC labels to users, and a set of tools to monitor and modify labels on processes, files, and network interfaces. More details on the user architecture will be added to this section in the near future.

6.8.1. APIs for Policy-Agnostic Label Management

The TrustedBSD MAC Framework provides a number of library and system calls permitting applications to manage MAC labels on objects using a policy-agnostic interface. This permits applications to manipulate labels for a variety of policies without being written to support specific policies. These interfaces are used by general-purpose tools such as ifconfig(8), ls(1) and ps(1) to view labels on network interfaces, files, and processes. The APIs also support MAC management tools including getfmac(8), getpmac(8), setfmac(8), setfsmac(8), and setpmac(8). The MAC APIs are documented in mac(3).

Applications handle MAC labels in two forms: an internalized form used to return and set labels on processes and objects (mac_t), and externalized form based on C strings appropriate for storage in configuration files, display to the user, or input from the user. Each MAC label contains a number of elements, each consisting of a name and value pair. Policy modules in the kernel bind to specific names and interpret the values in policy-specific ways. In the externalized string form, labels are represented by a comma-delimited list of name and value pairs separated by the / character. Labels may be directly converted to and from text using provided APIs; when retrieving labels from the kernel, internalized label storage must first be prepared for the desired label element set. Typically, this is done in one of two ways: using mac_prepare(3) and an arbitrary list of desired label elements, or one of the variants of the call that loads a default element set from the mac.conf(5) configuration file. Per-object defaults permit application writers to usefully display labels associated with objects without being aware of the policies present in the system.

Note

Currently, direct manipulation of label elements other than by conversion to a text string, string editing, and conversion back to an internalized label is not supported by the MAC library. Such interfaces may be added in the future if they prove necessary for application writers.

6.8.2. Binding of Labels to Users

The standard user context management interface, setusercontext(3), has been modified to retrieve MAC labels associated with a user's class from login.conf(5). These labels are then set along with other user context when either LOGIN_SETALL is specified, or when LOGIN_SETMAC is explicitly specified.

Note

It is expected that, in a future version of FreeBSD, the MAC label database will be separated from the login.conf user class abstraction, and be maintained in a separate database. However, the setusercontext(3) API should remain the same following such a change.

6.9. Conclusion

The TrustedBSD MAC framework permits kernel modules to augment the system security policy in a highly integrated manner. They may do this based on existing object properties, or based on label data that is maintained with the assistance of the MAC framework. The framework is sufficiently flexible to implement a variety of policy types, including information flow security policies such as MLS and Biba, as well as policies based on existing BSD credentials or file protections. Policy authors may wish to consult this documentation as well as existing security modules when implementing a new security service.

Chapter 7. Virtual Memory System

Contributed by Matthew Dillon.

7.1. Management of Physical Memory—vm_page_t

Physical memory is managed on a page-by-page basis through the vm_page_t structure. Pages of physical memory are categorized through the placement of their respective vm_page_t structures on one of several paging queues.

A page can be in a wired, active, inactive, cache, or free state. Except for the wired state, the page is typically placed in a doubly link list queue representing the state that it is in. Wired pages are not placed on any queue.

FreeBSD implements a more involved paging queue for cached and free pages in order to implement page coloring. Each of these states involves multiple queues arranged according to the size of the processor's L1 and L2 caches. When a new page needs to be allocated, FreeBSD attempts to obtain one that is reasonably well aligned from the point of view of the L1 and L2 caches relative to the VM object the page is being allocated for.

Additionally, a page may be held with a reference count or locked with a busy count. The VM system also implements an "ultimate locked" state for a page using the PG_BUSY bit in the page's flags.

In general terms, each of the paging queues operates in a LRU fashion. A page is typically placed in a wired or active state initially. When wired, the page is usually associated with a page table somewhere. The VM system ages the page by scanning pages in a more active paging queue (LRU) in order to move them to a less-active paging queue. Pages that get moved into the cache are still associated with a VM object but are candidates for immediate reuse. Pages in the free queue are truly free. FreeBSD attempts to minimize the number of pages in the free queue, but a certain minimum number of truly free pages must be maintained in order to accommodate page allocation at interrupt time.

If a process attempts to access a page that does not exist in its page table but does exist in one of the paging queues (such as the inactive or cache queues), a relatively inexpensive page reactivation fault occurs which causes the page to be reactivated. If the page does not exist in system memory at all, the process must block while the page is brought in from disk.

FreeBSD dynamically tunes its paging queues and attempts to maintain reasonable ratios of pages in the various queues as well as attempts to maintain a reasonable breakdown of clean versus dirty pages. The amount of rebalancing that occurs depends on the system's memory load. This rebalancing is implemented by the pageout daemon and involves laundering dirty pages (syncing them with their backing store), noticing when pages are activity referenced (resetting their position in the LRU queues or moving them between queues), migrating pages between queues when the queues are out of balance, and so forth. FreeBSD's VM system is willing to take a reasonable number of reactivation page faults to determine how active or how idle a page actually is. This leads to better decisions being made as to when to launder or swap-out a page.

7.2. The Unified Buffer Cache—vm_object_t

FreeBSD implements the idea of a generic "VM object". VM objects can be associated with backing store of various types—unbacked, swap-backed, physical device-backed, or file-backed storage. Since the filesystem uses the same VM objects to manage in-core data relating to files, the result is a unified buffer cache.

VM objects can be *shadowed*. That is, they can be stacked on top of each other. For example, you might have a swap-backed VM object stacked on top of a file-backed VM object in order to implement a MAP_PRIVATE mmap()ing. This stacking is also used to implement various sharing properties, including copy-on-write, for forked address spaces.

It should be noted that a vm_page_t can only be associated with one VM object at a time. The VM object shadowing implements the perceived sharing of the same page across multiple instances.

7.3. Filesystem I/O—struct buf

vnode-backed VM objects, such as file-backed objects, generally need to maintain their own clean/dirty info independent from the VM system's idea of clean/dirty. For example, when the VM system decides to synchronize a physical page to its backing store, the VM system needs to mark the page clean before the page is actually written to its backing store. Additionally, filesystems need to be able to map portions of a file or file metadata into KVM in order to operate on it.

The entities used to manage this are known as filesystem buffers, struct buf 's, or bp's. When a filesystem needs to operate on a portion of a VM object, it typically maps part of the object into a struct buf and then maps the pages in the struct buf into KVM. In the same manner, disk I/O is typically issued by mapping portions of objects into buffer structures and then issuing the I/O on the buffer structures. The underlying vm_page_t's are typically busied for the duration of the I/O. Filesystem buffers also have their own notion of being busy, which is useful to filesystem driver code which would rather operate on filesystem buffers instead of hard VM pages.

FreeBSD reserves a limited amount of KVM to hold mappings from struct bufs, but it should be made clear that this KVM is used solely to hold mappings and does not limit the ability to cache data. Physical data caching is strictly a function of vm_page_t 's, not filesystem buffers. However, since filesystem buffers are used to placehold I/O, they do inherently limit the amount of concurrent I/O possible. However, as there are usually a few thousand filesystem buffers available, this is not usually a problem.

7.4. Mapping Page Tables—vm_map_t, vm_entry_t

FreeBSD separates the physical page table topology from the VM system. All hard per-process page tables can be reconstructed on the fly and are usually considered throwaway. Special page tables such as those managing KVM are typically permanently preallocated. These page tables are not throwaway.

FreeBSD associates portions of vm_objects with address ranges in virtual memory through vm_map_t and vm_entry_t structures. Page tables are directly synthesized from the vm_map_t /vm_entry_t/ vm_object_t hierarchy. Recall that I mentioned that physical pages are only directly associated with a vm_object; that is not quite true. vm_page_t 's are also linked into page tables that they are actively associated with. One vm_page_t can be linked into several *pmaps*, as page tables are called. However, the hierarchical association holds, so all references to the same page in the same object reference the same vm_page_t and thus give us buffer cache unification across the board.

7.5. KVM Memory Mapping

FreeBSD uses KVM to hold various kernel structures. The single largest entity held in KVM is the filesystem buffer cache. That is, mappings relating to struct buf entities.

Unlike Linux, FreeBSD does *not* map all of physical memory into KVM. This means that FreeBSD can handle memory configurations up to 4G on 32 bit platforms. In fact, if the mmu were capable of it, FreeBSD could theoretically handle memory configurations up to 8TB on a 32 bit platform. However, since most 32 bit platforms are only capable of mapping 4GB of ram, this is a moot point.

KVM is managed through several mechanisms. The main mechanism used to manage KVM is the *zone allocator*. The zone allocator takes a chunk of KVM and splits it up into constant-sized blocks of memory in order to allocate a specific type of structure. You can use vmstat -m to get an overview of current KVM utilization broken down by zone.

7.6. Tuning the FreeBSD VM System

A concerted effort has been made to make the FreeBSD kernel dynamically tune itself. Typically you do not need to mess with anything beyond the maxusers and NMBCLUSTERS kernel config options. That is, kernel compilation options specified in (typically) /usr/src/sys/i386/conf/ *CONFIG_FILE*. A description of all available kernel configuration options can be found in /usr/src/sys/i386/conf/LINT .

In a large system configuration you may wish to increase maxusers . Values typically range from 10 to 128. Note that raising maxusers too high can cause the system to overflow available KVM resulting in unpredictable operation. It is better to leave maxusers at some reasonable number and add other options, such as NMBCLUSTERS, to increase specific resources.

If your system is going to use the network heavily, you may want to increase NMBCLUSTERS. Typical values range from 1024 to 4096.

The NBUF parameter is also traditionally used to scale the system. This parameter determines the amount of KVA the system can use to map filesystem buffers for I/O. Note that this parameter has nothing whatsoever to do with the unified buffer cache! This parameter is dynamically tuned in 3.0-CURRENT and later kernels and should generally not be adjusted manually. We recommend that you *not* try to specify an NBUF parameter. Let the system pick it. Too small a value can result in extremely inefficient filesystem operation while too large a value can starve the page queues by causing too many pages to become wired down.

By default, FreeBSD kernels are not optimized. You can set debugging and optimization flags with the makeoptions directive in the kernel configuration. Note that you should not use -g unless you can accommodate the large (typically 7 MB+) kernels that result.

```
makeoptions     DEBUG="-g"
makeoptions     COPTFLAGS="-O -pipe"
```

Sysctl provides a way to tune kernel parameters at run-time. You typically do not need to mess with any of the sysctl variables, especially the VM related ones.

Run time VM and system tuning is relatively straightforward. First, use Soft Updates on your UFS/FFS filesystems whenever possible. /usr/src/sys/ufs/ffs/README.softupdates contains instructions (and restrictions) on how to configure it.

Second, configure sufficient swap. You should have a swap partition configured on each physical disk, up to four, even on your "work" disks. You should have at least 2x the swap space as you have main memory, and possibly even more if you do not have a lot of memory. You should also size your swap partition based on the maximum memory configuration you ever intend to put on the machine so you do not have to repartition your disks later on. If you want to be able to accommodate a crash dump, your first swap partition must be at least as large as main memory and /var/crash must have sufficient free space to hold the dump.

NFS-based swap is perfectly acceptable on 4.X or later systems, but you must be aware that the NFS server will take the brunt of the paging load.

Chapter 8. SMPng Design Document

Written by John Baldwin and Robert Watson.

8.1. Introduction

This document presents the current design and implementation of the SMPng Architecture. First, the basic primitives and tools are introduced. Next, a general architecture for the FreeBSD kernel's synchronization and execution model is laid out. Then, locking strategies for specific subsystems are discussed, documenting the approaches taken to introduce fine-grained synchronization and parallelism for each subsystem. Finally, detailed implementation notes are provided to motivate design choices, and make the reader aware of important implications involving the use of specific primitives.

This document is a work-in-progress, and will be updated to reflect on-going design and implementation activities associated with the SMPng Project. Many sections currently exist only in outline form, but will be fleshed out as work proceeds. Updates or suggestions regarding the document may be directed to the document editors.

The goal of SMPng is to allow concurrency in the kernel. The kernel is basically one rather large and complex program. To make the kernel multi-threaded we use some of the same tools used to make other programs multi-threaded. These include mutexes, shared/exclusive locks, semaphores, and condition variables. For the definitions of these and other SMP-related terms, please see the Glossary section of this article.

8.2. Basic Tools and Locking Fundamentals

8.2.1. Atomic Instructions and Memory Barriers

There are several existing treatments of memory barriers and atomic instructions, so this section will not include a lot of detail. To put it simply, one can not go around reading variables without a lock if a lock is used to protect writes to that variable. This becomes obvious when you consider that memory barriers simply determine relative order of memory operations; they do not make any guarantee about timing of memory operations. That is, a memory barrier does not force the contents of a CPU's local cache or store buffer to flush. Instead, the memory barrier at lock release simply ensures that all writes to the protected data will be visible to other CPU's or devices if the write to release the lock is visible. The CPU is free to keep that data in its cache or store buffer as long as it wants. However, if another CPU performs an atomic instruction on the same datum, the first CPU must guarantee that the updated value is made visible to the second CPU along with any other operations that memory barriers may require.

For example, assuming a simple model where data is considered visible when it is in main memory (or a global cache), when an atomic instruction is triggered on one CPU, other CPU's store buffers and caches must flush any writes to that same cache line along with any pending operations behind a memory barrier.

This requires one to take special care when using an item protected by atomic instructions. For example, in the sleep mutex implementation, we have to use an `atomic_cmpset` rather than an `atomic_set` to turn on the MTX_CONTESTED bit. The reason is that we read the value of `mtx_lock` into a variable and then make a decision based on that read. However, the value we read may be stale, or it may change while we are making our decision. Thus, when the `atomic_set` executed, it may end up setting the bit on another value than the one we made the decision on. Thus, we have to use an `atomic_cmpset` to set the value only if the value we made the decision on is up-to-date and valid.

Finally, atomic instructions only allow one item to be updated or read. If one needs to atomically update several items, then a lock must be used instead. For example, if two counters must be read and have values that are consistent relative to each other, then those counters must be protected by a lock rather than by separate atomic instructions.

8.2.2. Read Locks Versus Write Locks

Read locks do not need to be as strong as write locks. Both types of locks need to ensure that the data they are accessing is not stale. However, only write access requires exclusive access. Multiple threads can safely read a value. Using different types of locks for reads and writes can be implemented in a number of ways.

First, sx locks can be used in this manner by using an exclusive lock when writing and a shared lock when reading. This method is quite straightforward.

A second method is a bit more obscure. You can protect a datum with multiple locks. Then for reading that data you simply need to have a read lock of one of the locks. However, to write to the data, you need to have a write lock of all of the locks. This can make writing rather expensive but can be useful when data is accessed in various ways. For example, the parent process pointer is protected by both the `proctree_lock` sx lock and the per-process mutex. Sometimes the proc lock is easier as we are just checking to see who a parent of a process is that we already have locked. However, other places such as `inferior` need to walk the tree of processes via parent pointers and locking each process would be prohibitive as well as a pain to guarantee that the condition you are checking remains valid for both the check and the actions taken as a result of the check.

8.2.3. Locking Conditions and Results

If you need a lock to check the state of a variable so that you can take an action based on the state you read, you can not just hold the lock while reading the variable and then drop the lock before you act on the value you read. Once you drop the lock, the variable can change rendering your decision invalid. Thus, you must hold the lock both while reading the variable and while performing the action as a result of the test.

8.3. General Architecture and Design

8.3.1. Interrupt Handling

Following the pattern of several other multi-threaded UNIX® kernels, FreeBSD deals with interrupt handlers by giving them their own thread context. Providing a context for interrupt handlers allows them to block on locks. To help avoid latency, however, interrupt threads run at real-time kernel priority. Thus, interrupt handlers should not execute for very long to avoid starving other kernel threads. In addition, since multiple handlers may share an interrupt thread, interrupt handlers should not sleep or use a sleepable lock to avoid starving another interrupt handler.

The interrupt threads currently in FreeBSD are referred to as heavyweight interrupt threads. They are called this because switching to an interrupt thread involves a full context switch. In the initial implementation, the kernel was not preemptive and thus interrupts that interrupted a kernel thread would have to wait until the kernel thread blocked or returned to userland before they would have an opportunity to run.

To deal with the latency problems, the kernel in FreeBSD has been made preemptive. Currently, we only preempt a kernel thread when we release a sleep mutex or when an interrupt comes in. However, the plan is to make the FreeBSD kernel fully preemptive as described below.

Not all interrupt handlers execute in a thread context. Instead, some handlers execute directly in primary interrupt context. These interrupt handlers are currently misnamed "fast" interrupt handlers since the `INTR_FAST` flag used in earlier versions of the kernel is used to mark these handlers. The only interrupts which currently use these types of interrupt handlers are clock interrupts and serial I/O device interrupts. Since these handlers do not have their own context, they may not acquire blocking locks and thus may only use spin mutexes.

Finally, there is one optional optimization that can be added in MD code called lightweight context switches. Since an interrupt thread executes in a kernel context, it can borrow the vmspace of any process. Thus, in a lightweight context switch, the switch to the interrupt thread does not switch vmspaces but borrows the vmspace of the interrupted thread. In order to ensure that the vmspace of the interrupted thread does not disappear out from under us, the interrupted thread is not allowed to execute until the interrupt thread is no longer borrowing its vmspace. This can happen when the interrupt thread either blocks or finishes. If an interrupt thread blocks, then it will use its own context when it is made runnable again. Thus, it can release the interrupted thread.

The cons of this optimization are that they are very machine specific and complex and thus only worth the effort if their is a large performance improvement. At this point it is probably too early to tell, and in fact, will probably hurt performance as almost all interrupt handlers will immediately block on Giant and require a thread fix-up when they block. Also, an alternative method of interrupt handling has been proposed by Mike Smith that works like so:

1. Each interrupt handler has two parts: a predicate which runs in primary interrupt context and a handler which runs in its own thread context.

2. If an interrupt handler has a predicate, then when an interrupt is triggered, the predicate is run. If the predicate returns true then the interrupt is assumed to be fully handled and the kernel returns from the interrupt. If the predicate returns false or there is no predicate, then the threaded handler is scheduled to run.

Fitting light weight context switches into this scheme might prove rather complicated. Since we may want to change to this scheme at some point in the future, it is probably best to defer work on light weight context switches until we have settled on the final interrupt handling architecture and determined how light weight context switches might or might not fit into it.

8.3.2. Kernel Preemption and Critical Sections

8.3.2.1. Kernel Preemption in a Nutshell

Kernel preemption is fairly simple. The basic idea is that a CPU should always be doing the highest priority work available. Well, that is the ideal at least. There are a couple of cases where the expense of achieving the ideal is not worth being perfect.

Implementing full kernel preemption is very straightforward: when you schedule a thread to be executed by putting it on a run queue, you check to see if its priority is higher than the currently executing thread. If so, you initiate a context switch to that thread.

While locks can protect most data in the case of a preemption, not all of the kernel is preemption safe. For example, if a thread holding a spin mutex preempted and the new thread attempts to grab the same spin mutex, the new thread may spin forever as the interrupted thread may never get a chance to execute. Also, some code such as the code to assign an address space number for a process during **exec** on the Alpha needs to not be preempted as it supports the actual context switch code. Preemption is disabled for these code sections by using a critical section.

8.3.2.2. Critical Sections

The responsibility of the critical section API is to prevent context switches inside of a critical section. With a fully preemptive kernel, every `setrunqueue` of a thread other than the current thread is a preemption point. One implementation is for `critical_enter` to set a per-thread flag that is cleared by its counterpart. If `setrunqueue` is called with this flag set, it does not preempt regardless of the priority of the new thread relative to the current thread. However, since critical sections are used in spin mutexes to prevent context switches and multiple spin mutexes can be acquired, the critical section API must support nesting. For this reason the current implementation uses a nesting count instead of a single per-thread flag.

In order to minimize latency, preemptions inside of a critical section are deferred rather than dropped. If a thread that would normally be preempted to is made runnable while the current thread is in a critical section, then a per-thread flag is set to indicate that there is a pending preemption. When the outermost critical section is exited, the flag is checked. If the flag is set, then the current thread is preempted to allow the higher priority thread to run.

Interrupts pose a problem with regards to spin mutexes. If a low-level interrupt handler needs a lock, it needs to not interrupt any code needing that lock to avoid possible data structure corruption. Currently, providing this mechanism is piggybacked onto critical section API by means of the `cpu_critical_enter` and `cpu_critical_exit` functions. Currently this API disables and re-enables interrupts on all of FreeBSD's current platforms. This approach may not be purely optimal, but it is simple to understand and simple to get right. Theoretically, this second API need only be used for spin mutexes that are used in primary interrupt context. However, to make the code simpler, it is used for all spin mutexes and even all critical sections. It may be desirable to split out the MD API from the MI API and only use it in conjunction with the MI API in the spin mutex implementation. If this approach is taken, then the MD API likely would need a rename to show that it is a separate API.

8.3.2.3. Design Tradeoffs

As mentioned earlier, a couple of trade-offs have been made to sacrifice cases where perfect preemption may not always provide the best performance.

The first trade-off is that the preemption code does not take other CPUs into account. Suppose we have a two CPU's A and B with the priority of A's thread as 4 and the priority of B's thread as 2. If CPU B makes a thread with priority 1 runnable, then in theory, we want CPU A to switch to the new thread so that we will be running the two highest priority runnable threads. However, the cost of determining which CPU to enforce a preemption on as well as actually signaling that CPU via an IPI along with the synchronization that would be required would be enormous. Thus, the current code would instead force CPU B to switch to the higher priority thread. Note that this still puts the system in a better position as CPU B is executing a thread of priority 1 rather than a thread of priority 2.

The second trade-off limits immediate kernel preemption to real-time priority kernel threads. In the simple case of preemption defined above, a thread is always preempted immediately (or as soon as a critical section is exited) if a higher priority thread is made runnable. However, many threads executing in the kernel only execute in a kernel context for a short time before either blocking or returning to userland. Thus, if the kernel preempts these threads to run another non-realtime kernel thread, the kernel may switch out the executing thread just before it is about to sleep or execute. The cache on the CPU must then adjust to the new thread. When the kernel returns to the preempted thread, it must refill all the cache information that was lost. In addition, two extra context switches are performed that could be avoided if the kernel deferred the preemption until the first thread blocked or returned to userland. Thus, by default, the preemption code will only preempt immediately if the higher priority thread is a real-time priority thread.

Turning on full kernel preemption for all kernel threads has value as a debugging aid since it exposes more race conditions. It is especially useful on UP systems were many races are hard to simulate otherwise. Thus, there is a kernel option `FULL_PREEMPTION` to enable preemption for all kernel threads that can be used for debugging purposes.

8.3.3. Thread Migration

Simply put, a thread migrates when it moves from one CPU to another. In a non-preemptive kernel this can only happen at well-defined points such as when calling `msleep` or returning to userland. However, in the preemptive kernel, an interrupt can force a preemption and possible migration at any time. This can have negative affects on per-CPU data since with the exception of `curthread` and `curpcb` the data can change whenever you migrate. Since you can potentially migrate at any time this renders unprotected per-CPU data access rather useless. Thus it is desirable to be able to disable migration for sections of code that need per-CPU data to be stable.

Critical sections currently prevent migration since they do not allow context switches. However, this may be too strong of a requirement to enforce in some cases since a critical section also effectively blocks interrupt threads on the current processor. As a result, another API has been provided to allow the current thread to indicate that if it preempted it should not migrate to another CPU.

This API is known as thread pinning and is provided by the scheduler. The API consists of two functions: `sched_pin` and `sched_unpin`. These functions manage a per-thread nesting count `td_pinned`. A thread is pinned when its nesting count is greater than zero and a thread starts off unpinned with a nesting count of zero. Each scheduler implementation is required to ensure that pinned threads are only executed on the CPU that they were executing on when the `sched_pin` was first called. Since the nesting count is only written to by the thread itself and is only read by other threads when the pinned thread is not executing but while `sched_lock` is held, then `td_pinned` does not need any locking. The `sched_pin` function increments the nesting count and `sched_unpin` decrements the nesting count. Note that these functions only operate on the current thread and bind the current thread to the CPU it is executing on at the time. To bind an arbitrary thread to a specific CPU, the `sched_bind` and `sched_unbind` functions should be used instead.

8.3.4. Callouts

The `timeout` kernel facility permits kernel services to register functions for execution as part of the `softclock` software interrupt. Events are scheduled based on a desired number of clock ticks, and callbacks to the consumer-provided function will occur at approximately the right time.

The global list of pending timeout events is protected by a global spin mutex, `callout_lock`; all access to the timeout list must be performed with this mutex held. When `softclock` is woken up, it scans the list of pending timeouts for those that should fire. In order to avoid lock order reversal, the `softclock` thread will release the `callout_lock` mutex when invoking the provided `timeout` callback function. If the `CALLOUT_MPSAFE` flag was not set during registration, then Giant will be grabbed before invoking the callout, and then released afterwards. The `callout_lock` mutex will be re-grabbed before proceeding. The `softclock` code is careful to leave the list in a consistent state while releasing the mutex. If `DIAGNOSTIC` is enabled, then the time taken to execute each function is measured, and a warning is generated if it exceeds a threshold.

8.4. Specific Locking Strategies

8.4.1. Credentials

`struct ucred` is the kernel's internal credential structure, and is generally used as the basis for process-driven access control within the kernel. BSD-derived systems use a "copy-on-write" model for credential data: multiple references may exist for a credential structure, and when a change needs to be made, the structure is duplicated, modified, and then the reference replaced. Due to wide-spread caching of the credential to implement access control on open, this results in substantial memory savings. With a move to fine-grained SMP, this model also saves substantially on locking operations by requiring that modification only occur on an unshared credential, avoiding the need for explicit synchronization when consuming a known-shared credential.

Credential structures with a single reference are considered mutable; shared credential structures must not be modified or a race condition is risked. A mutex, `cr_mtxp` protects the reference count of `struct ucred` so as to maintain consistency. Any use of the structure requires a valid reference for the duration of the use, or the structure may be released out from under the illegitimate consumer.

The `struct ucred` mutex is a leaf mutex and is implemented via a mutex pool for performance reasons.

Usually, credentials are used in a read-only manner for access control decisions, and in this case `td_ucred` is generally preferred because it requires no locking. When a process' credential is updated the `proc` lock must be held across the check and update operations thus avoid races. The process credential `p_ucred` must be used for check and update operations to prevent time-of-check, time-of-use races.

If system call invocations will perform access control after an update to the process credential, the value of `td_ucred` must also be refreshed to the current process value. This will prevent use of a stale credential following a change. The kernel automatically refreshes the `td_ucred` pointer in the thread structure from the process `p_ucred` whenever a process enters the kernel, permitting use of a fresh credential for kernel access control.

8.4.2. File Descriptors and File Descriptor Tables

Details to follow.

8.4.3. Jail Structures

`struct prison` stores administrative details pertinent to the maintenance of jails created using the jail(2) API. This includes the per-jail hostname, IP address, and related settings. This structure is reference-counted since pointers to instances of the structure are shared by many credential structures. A single mutex, `pr_mtx` protects read and write access to the reference count and all mutable variables inside the struct jail. Some variables are set only when the jail is created, and a valid reference to the `struct prison` is sufficient to read these values. The precise locking of each entry is documented via comments in `sys/jail.h` .

8.4.4. MAC Framework

The TrustedBSD MAC Framework maintains data in a variety of kernel objects, in the form of `struct label`. In general, labels in kernel objects are protected by the same lock as the remainder of the kernel object. For example, the `v_label` label in `struct vnode` is protected by the vnode lock on the vnode.

In addition to labels maintained in standard kernel objects, the MAC Framework also maintains a list of registered and active policies. The policy list is protected by a global mutex (`mac_policy_list_lock`) and a busy count (also protected by the mutex). Since many access control checks may occur in parallel, entry to the framework for a read-only access to the policy list requires holding the mutex while incrementing (and later decrementing) the busy count. The mutex need not be held for the duration of the MAC entry operation--some operations, such as label operations on file system objects--are long-lived. To modify the policy list, such as during policy registration and de-registration, the mutex must be held and the reference count must be zero, to prevent modification of the list while it is in use.

A condition variable, `mac_policy_list_not_busy`, is available to threads that need to wait for the list to become unbusy, but this condition variable must only be waited on if the caller is holding no other locks, or a lock order violation may be possible. The busy count, in effect, acts as a form of shared/exclusive lock over access to the framework: the difference is that, unlike with an sx lock, consumers waiting for the list to become unbusy may be starved, rather than permitting lock order problems with regards to the busy count and other locks that may be held on entry to (or inside) the MAC Framework.

8.4.5. Modules

For the module subsystem there exists a single lock that is used to protect the shared data. This lock is a shared/exclusive (SX) lock and has a good chance of needing to be acquired (shared or exclusively), therefore there are a few macros that have been added to make access to the lock more easy. These macros can be located in `sys/module.h` and are quite basic in terms of usage. The main structures protected under this lock are the `module_t` structures (when shared) and the global `modulelist_t` structure, modules. One should review the related source code in `kern/kern_module.c` to further understand the locking strategy.

8.4.6. Newbus Device Tree

The newbus system will have one sx lock. Readers will hold a shared (read) lock (sx_slock(9)) and writers will hold an exclusive (write) lock (sx_xlock(9)). Internal functions will not do locking at all. Externally visible ones will lock as needed. Those items that do not matter if the race is won or lost will not be locked, since they tend to be read all over the place (e.g., device_get_softc(9)). There will be relatively few changes to the newbus data structures, so a single lock should be sufficient and not impose a performance penalty.

8.4.7. Pipes

...

8.4.8. Processes and Threads

- process hierarchy

- proc locks, references

- thread-specific copies of proc entries to freeze during system calls, including td_ucred

- inter-process operations

- process groups and sessions

8.4.9. Scheduler

Lots of references to sched_lock and notes pointing at specific primitives and related magic elsewhere in the document.

8.4.10. Select and Poll

The select and poll functions permit threads to block waiting on events on file descriptors--most frequently, whether or not the file descriptors are readable or writable.

...

8.4.11. SIGIO

The SIGIO service permits processes to request the delivery of a SIGIO signal to its process group when the read/write status of specified file descriptors changes. At most one process or process group is permitted to register for SIGIO from any given kernel object, and that process or group is referred to as the owner. Each object supporting SIGIO registration contains pointer field that is NULL if the object is not registered, or points to a struct sigio describing the registration. This field is protected by a global mutex, sigio_lock. Callers to SIGIO maintenance functions must pass in this field "by reference" so that local register copies of the field are not made when unprotected by the lock.

One struct sigio is allocated for each registered object associated with any process or process group, and contains back-pointers to the object, owner, signal information, a credential, and the general disposition of the registration. Each process or progress group contains a list of registered struct sigio structures, p_sigiolst for processes, and pg_sigiolst for process groups. These lists are protected by the process or process group locks respectively. Most fields in each struct sigio are constant for the duration of the registration, with the exception of the sio_pgsigio field which links the struct sigio into the process or process group list. Developers implementing new kernel objects supporting SIGIO will, in general, want to avoid holding structure locks while invoking SIGIO supporting functions, such as fsetown or funsetown to avoid defining a lock order between structure locks and the global SIGIO lock. This is generally possible through use of an elevated reference count on the structure, such as reliance on a file descriptor reference to a pipe during a pipe operation.

8.4.12. Sysctl

The sysctl MIB service is invoked from both within the kernel and from userland applications using a system call. At least two issues are raised in locking: first, the protection of the structures maintaining the namespace, and second, interactions with kernel variables and functions that are accessed by the sysctl interface. Since sysctl permits the direct export (and modification) of kernel statistics and configuration parameters, the sysctl mechanism must become aware of appropriate locking semantics for those variables. Currently, sysctl makes use of a single global sx lock to serialize use of sysctl; however, it is assumed to operate under Giant and other protections are not provided. The remainder of this section speculates on locking and semantic changes to sysctl.

- Need to change the order of operations for sysctl's that update values from read old, copyin and copyout, write new to copyin, lock, read old and write new, unlock, copyout. Normal sysctl's that just copyout the old value and set a new value that they copyin may still be able to follow the old model. However, it may be cleaner to use the second model for all of the sysctl handlers to avoid lock operations.

- To allow for the common case, a sysctl could embed a pointer to a mutex in the SYSCTL_FOO macros and in the struct. This would work for most sysctl's. For values protected by sx locks, spin mutexes, or other locking strategies besides a single sleep mutex, SYSCTL_PROC nodes could be used to get the locking right.

8.4.13. Taskqueue

The taskqueue's interface has two basic locks associated with it in order to protect the related shared data. The taskqueue_queues_mutex is meant to serve as a lock to protect the taskqueue_queues TAILQ. The other mutex lock associated with this system is the one in the struct taskqueue data structure. The use of the synchronization primitive here is to protect the integrity of the data in the struct taskqueue . It should be noted that there are no separate macros to assist the user in locking down his/her own work since these locks are most likely not going to be used outside of kern/subr_taskqueue.c .

8.5. Implementation Notes

8.5.1. Sleep Queues

A sleep queue is a structure that holds the list of threads asleep on a wait channel. Each thread that is not asleep on a wait channel carries a sleep queue structure around with it. When a thread blocks on a wait channel, it donates its sleep queue structure to that wait channel. Sleep queues associated with a wait channel are stored in a hash table.

The sleep queue hash table holds sleep queues for wait channels that have at least one blocked thread. Each entry in the hash table is called a sleepqueue chain. The chain contains a linked list of sleep queues and a spin mutex. The spin mutex protects the list of sleep queues as well as the contents of the sleep queue structures on the list. Only one sleep queue is associated with a given wait channel. If multiple threads block on a wait channel than the sleep queues associated with all but the first thread are stored on a list of free sleep queues in the master sleep queue. When a thread is removed from the sleep queue it is given one of the sleep queue structures from the master queue's free list if it is not the only thread asleep on the queue. The last thread is given the master sleep queue when it is resumed. Since threads may be removed from the sleep queue in a different order than they are added, a thread may depart from a sleep queue with a different sleep queue structure than the one it arrived with.

The `sleepq_lock` function locks the spin mutex of the sleep queue chain that maps to a specific wait channel. The `sleepq_lookup` function looks in the hash table for the master sleep queue associated with a given wait channel. If no master sleep queue is found, it returns `NULL`. The `sleepq_release` function unlocks the spin mutex associated with a given wait channel.

A thread is added to a sleep queue via the `sleepq_add`. This function accepts the wait channel, a pointer to the mutex that protects the wait channel, a wait message description string, and a mask of flags. The sleep queue chain should be locked via `sleepq_lock` before this function is called. If no mutex protects the wait channel (or it is protected by Giant), then the mutex pointer argument should be `NULL`. The flags argument contains a type field that indicates the kind of sleep queue that the thread is being added to and a flag to indicate if the sleep is interruptible (`SLEEPQ_INTERRUPTIBLE`). Currently there are only two types of sleep queues: traditional sleep queues managed via the `msleep` and `wakeup` functions (`SLEEPQ_MSLEEP`) and condition variable sleep queues (`SLEEPQ_CONDVAR`). The sleep queue type and lock pointer argument are used solely for internal assertion checking. Code that calls `sleepq_add` should explicitly unlock any interlock protecting the wait channel after the associated sleepqueue chain has been locked via `sleepq_lock` and before blocking on the sleep queue via one of the waiting functions.

A timeout for a sleep is set by invoking `sleepq_set_timeout`. The function accepts the wait channel and the timeout time as a relative tick count as its arguments. If a sleep should be interrupted by arriving signals, the `sleepq_catch_signals` function should be called as well. This function accepts the wait channel as its only parameter. If there is already a signal pending for this thread, then `sleepq_catch_signals` will return a signal number; otherwise, it will return 0.

Once a thread has been added to a sleep queue, it blocks using one of the `sleepq_wait` functions. There are four wait functions depending on whether or not the caller wishes to use a timeout or have the sleep aborted by caught signals or an interrupt from the userland thread scheduler. The `sleepq_wait` function simply waits until the current thread is explicitly resumed by one of the wakeup functions. The `sleepq_timedwait` function waits until either the thread is explicitly resumed or the timeout set by an earlier call to `sleepq_set_timeout` expires. The `sleepq_wait_sig` function waits until either the thread is explicitly resumed or its sleep is aborted. The `sleepq_timedwait_sig` function waits until either the thread is explicitly resumed, the timeout set by an earlier call to `sleepq_set_timeout` expires, or the thread's sleep is aborted. All of the wait functions accept the wait channel as their first parameter. In addition, the `sleepq_timedwait_sig` function accepts a second boolean parameter to indicate if the earlier call to `sleepq_catch_signals` found a pending signal.

If the thread is explicitly resumed or is aborted by a signal, then a value of zero is returned by the wait function to indicate a successful sleep. If the thread is resumed by either a timeout or an interrupt from the userland thread scheduler then an appropriate errno value is returned instead. Note that since `sleepq_wait` can only return 0 it does not return anything and the caller should assume a successful sleep. Also, if a thread's sleep times out and is aborted simultaneously then `sleepq_timedwait_sig` will return an error indicating that a timeout occurred. If an error value of 0 is returned and either `sleepq_wait_sig` or `sleepq_timedwait_sig` was used to block, then the function `sleepq_calc_signal_retval` should be called to check for any pending signals and calculate an appropriate return value if any are found. The signal number returned by the earlier call to `sleepq_catch_signals` should be passed as the sole argument to `sleepq_calc_signal_retval`.

Threads asleep on a wait channel are explicitly resumed by the `sleepq_broadcast` and `sleepq_signal` functions. Both functions accept the wait channel from which to resume threads, a priority to raise resumed threads to, and a flags argument to indicate which type of sleep queue is being resumed. The priority argument is treated as a minimum priority. If a thread being resumed already has a higher priority (numerically lower) than the priority argument then its priority is not adjusted. The flags argument is used for internal assertions to ensure that sleep queues are not being treated as the wrong type. For example, the condition variable functions should not resume threads on a traditional sleep queue. The `sleepq_broadcast` function resumes all threads that are blocked on the specified wait channel while `sleepq_signal` only resumes the highest priority thread blocked on the wait channel. The sleep queue chain should first be locked via the `sleepq_lock` function before calling these functions.

A sleeping thread may have its sleep interrupted by calling the `sleepq_abort` function. This function must be called with `sched_lock` held and the thread must be queued on a sleep queue. A thread may also be removed from a specific sleep queue via the `sleepq_remove` function. This function accepts both a thread and a wait channel as an argument and only awakens the thread if it is on the sleep queue for the specified wait channel. If the thread is not on a sleep queue or it is on a sleep queue for a different wait channel, then this function does nothing.

8.5.2. Turnstiles

- Compare/contrast with sleep queues.

- Lookup/wait/release. - Describe TDF_TSNOBLOCK race.

- Priority propagation.

8.5.3. Details of the Mutex Implementation

- Should we require mutexes to be owned for mtx_destroy() since we can not safely assert that they are unowned by anyone else otherwise?

8.5.3.1. Spin Mutexes

- Use a critical section...

8.5.3.2. Sleep Mutexes

- Describe the races with contested mutexes

- Why it is safe to read mtx_lock of a contested mutex when holding the turnstile chain lock.

8.5.4. Witness

- What does it do

- How does it work

8.6. Miscellaneous Topics

8.6.1. Interrupt Source and ICU Abstractions

- struct isrc

- pic drivers

8.6.2. Other Random Questions/Topics

- Should we pass an interlock into `sema_wait`?

- Should we have non-sleepable sx locks?

- Add some info about proper use of reference counts.

Glossary

atomic	An operation is atomic if all of its effects are visible to other CPUs together when the proper access protocol is followed. In the degenerate case are atomic instructions provided directly by machine architectures. At a higher level, if several members of a structure are protected by a lock, then a set of operations are atomic if they are all performed while holding the lock without releasing the lock in between any of the operations. See Also operation.
block	A thread is blocked when it is waiting on a lock, resource, or condition. Unfortunately this term is a bit overloaded as a result. See Also sleep.
critical section	A section of code that is not allowed to be preempted. A critical section is entered and exited using the critical_enter(9) API.
MD	Machine dependent. See Also MI.
memory operation	A memory operation reads and/or writes to a memory location.
MI	Machine independent. See Also MD.
operation	See memory operation.
primary interrupt context	Primary interrupt context refers to the code that runs when an interrupt occurs. This code can either run an interrupt handler directly or schedule an asynchronous interrupt thread to execute the interrupt handlers for a given interrupt source.
realtime kernel thread	A high priority kernel thread. Currently, the only realtime priority kernel threads are interrupt threads. See Also thread.
sleep	A thread is asleep when it is blocked on a condition variable or a sleep queue via `msleep` or `tsleep`. See Also block.
sleepable lock	A sleepable lock is a lock that can be held by a thread which is asleep. Lockmgr locks and sx locks are currently the only sleepable locks in FreeBSD. Eventually, some sx locks such as the allproc and proctree locks may become non-sleepable locks. See Also sleep.
thread	A kernel thread represented by a struct thread. Threads own locks and hold a single execution context.
wait channel	A kernel virtual address that threads may sleep on.

Part II. Device Drivers

Table of Contents

Chapter 9. Writing FreeBSD Device Drivers

Written by Murray Stokely.
Based on intro(4) manual page by Jörg Wunsch.

9.1. Introduction

This chapter provides a brief introduction to writing device drivers for FreeBSD. A device in this context is a term used mostly for hardware-related stuff that belongs to the system, like disks, printers, or a graphics display with its keyboard. A device driver is the software component of the operating system that controls a specific device. There are also so-called pseudo-devices where a device driver emulates the behavior of a device in software without any particular underlying hardware. Device drivers can be compiled into the system statically or loaded on demand through the dynamic kernel linker facility `kld'.

Most devices in a UNIX®-like operating system are accessed through device-nodes, sometimes also called special files. These files are usually located under the directory /dev in the filesystem hierarchy.

Device drivers can roughly be broken down into two categories; character and network device drivers.

9.2. Dynamic Kernel Linker Facility - KLD

The kld interface allows system administrators to dynamically add and remove functionality from a running system. This allows device driver writers to load their new changes into a running kernel without constantly rebooting to test changes.

The kld interface is used through:

- kldload - loads a new kernel module

- kldunload - unloads a kernel module

- kldstat - lists loaded modules

Skeleton Layout of a kernel module

```
/*
 * KLD Skeleton
 * Inspired by Andrew Reiter's Daemonnews article
 */

#include <sys/types.h>
#include <sys/module.h>
#include <sys/systm.h>  /* uprintf */
#include <sys/errno.h>
#include <sys/param.h>  /* defines used in kernel.h */
#include <sys/kernel.h> /* types used in module initialization */

/*
 * Load handler that deals with the loading and unloading of a KLD.
 */

static int
skel_loader(struct module *m, int what, void *arg)
{
  int err = 0;
```

```
  switch (what) {
  case MOD_LOAD:                    /* kldload */
    uprintf("Skeleton KLD loaded.\n");
    break;
  case MOD_UNLOAD:
    uprintf("Skeleton KLD unloaded.\n");
    break;
  default:
    err = EOPNOTSUPP;
    break;
  }
  return(err);
}

/* Declare this module to the rest of the kernel */

static moduledata_t skel_mod = {
  "skel",
  skel_loader,
  NULL
};

DECLARE_MODULE(skeleton, skel_mod, SI_SUB_KLD, SI_ORDER_ANY);
```

9.2.1. Makefile

FreeBSD provides a system makefile to simplify compiling a kernel module.

```
SRCS=skeleton.c
KMOD=skeleton

.include <bsd.kmod.mk>
```

Running make with this makefile will create a file skeleton.ko that can be loaded into the kernel by typing:

```
# kldload -v ./skeleton.ko
```

9.3. Character Devices

A character device driver is one that transfers data directly to and from a user process. This is the most common type of device driver and there are plenty of simple examples in the source tree.

This simple example pseudo-device remembers whatever values are written to it and can then echo them back when read.

Example 9.1. Example of a Sample Echo Pseudo-Device Driver for FreeBSD 10.X

```
/*
 * Simple Echo pseudo-device KLD
 *
 * Murray Stokely
 * Søren (Xride) Straarup
 * Eitan Adler
 */

#include <sys/types.h>
#include <sys/module.h>
#include <sys/systm.h>  /* uprintf */
#include <sys/param.h>  /* defines used in kernel.h */
```

196

```
#include <sys/kernel.h> /* types used in module initialization */
#include <sys/conf.h>   /* cdevsw struct */
#include <sys/uio.h>    /* uio struct */
#include <sys/malloc.h>

#define BUFFERSIZE 255

/* Function prototypes */
static d_open_t     echo_open;
static d_close_t    echo_close;
static d_read_t     echo_read;
static d_write_t    echo_write;

/* Character device entry points */
static struct cdevsw echo_cdevsw = {
 .d_version = D_VERSION,
 .d_open = echo_open,
 .d_close = echo_close,
 .d_read = echo_read,
 .d_write = echo_write,
 .d_name = "echo",
};

struct s_echo {
 char msg[BUFFERSIZE + 1];
 int len;
};

/* vars */
static struct cdev *echo_dev;
static struct s_echo *echomsg;

MALLOC_DECLARE(M_ECHOBUF);
MALLOC_DEFINE(M_ECHOBUF, "echobuffer", "buffer for echo module");

/*
 * This function is called by the kld[un]load(2) system calls to
 * determine what actions to take when a module is loaded or unloaded.
 */
static int
echo_loader(struct module *m __unused, int what, void *arg __unused)
{
 int error = 0;

 switch (what) {
 case MOD_LOAD:                     /* kldload */
  error = make_dev_p(MAKEDEV_CHECKNAME | MAKEDEV_WAITOK,
      &echo_dev,
      &echo_cdevsw,
      0,
      UID_ROOT,
      GID_WHEEL,
      0600,
      "echo");
  if (error != 0)
   break;

  echomsg = malloc(sizeof(*echomsg), M_ECHOBUF, M_WAITOK |
      M_ZERO);
  printf("Echo device loaded.\n");
  break;
 case MOD_UNLOAD:
  destroy_dev(echo_dev);
  free(echomsg, M_ECHOBUF);
  printf("Echo device unloaded.\n");
  break;
```

```
   default:
    error = EOPNOTSUPP;
    break;
   }
   return (error);
 }

 static int
 echo_open(struct cdev *dev __unused, int oflags __unused, int devtype __unused,
     struct thread *td __unused)
 {
  int error = 0;

  uprintf("Opened device \"echo\" successfully.\n");
  return (error);
 }

 static int
 echo_close(struct cdev *dev __unused, int fflag __unused, int devtype __unused,
     struct thread *td __unused)
 {

  uprintf("Closing device \"echo\".\n");
  return (0);
 }

 /*
  * The read function just takes the buf that was saved via
  * echo_write() and returns it to userland for accessing.
  * uio(9)
  */
 static int
 echo_read(struct cdev *dev __unused, struct uio *uio, int ioflag __unused)
 {
  size_t amt;
  int error;

  /*
   * How big is this read operation?  Either as big as the user wants,
   * or as big as the remaining data.  Note that the 'len' does not
   * include the trailing null character.
   */
  amt = MIN(uio->uio_resid, uio->uio_offset >= echomsg->len + 1 ? 0 :
      echomsg->len + 1 - uio->uio_offset);

  if ((error = uiomove(echomsg->msg, amt, uio)) != 0)
   uprintf("uiomove failed!\n");

  return (error);
 }

 /*
  * echo_write takes in a character string and saves it
  * to buf for later accessing.
  */
 static int
 echo_write(struct cdev *dev __unused, struct uio *uio, int ioflag __unused)
 {
  size_t amt;
  int error;

  /*
   * We either write from the beginning or are appending -- do
   * not allow random access.
   */
  if (uio->uio_offset != 0 && (uio->uio_offset != echomsg->len))
```

```
      return (EINVAL);

    /* This is a new message, reset length */
    if (uio->uio_offset == 0)
      echomsg->len = 0;

    /* Copy the string in from user memory to kernel memory */
    amt = MIN(uio->uio_resid, (BUFFERSIZE - echomsg->len));

    error = uiomove(echomsg->msg + uio->uio_offset, amt, uio);

    /* Now we need to null terminate and record the length */
    echomsg->len = uio->uio_offset;
    echomsg->msg[echomsg->len] = 0;

    if (error != 0)
      uprintf("Write failed: bad address!\n");
    return (error);
  }

  DEV_MODULE(echo, echo_loader, NULL);
```

With this driver loaded try:

```
# echo -n "Test Data" > /dev/echo
# cat /dev/echo
Opened device "echo" successfully.
Test Data
Closing device "echo".
```

Real hardware devices are described in the next chapter.

9.4. Block Devices (Are Gone)

Other UNIX® systems may support a second type of disk device known as block devices. Block devices are disk devices for which the kernel provides caching. This caching makes block-devices almost unusable, or at least dangerously unreliable. The caching will reorder the sequence of write operations, depriving the application of the ability to know the exact disk contents at any one instant in time.

This makes predictable and reliable crash recovery of on-disk data structures (filesystems, databases, etc.) impossible. Since writes may be delayed, there is no way the kernel can report to the application which particular write operation encountered a write error, this further compounds the consistency problem.

For this reason, no serious applications rely on block devices, and in fact, almost all applications which access disks directly take great pains to specify that character (or "raw") devices should always be used. Because the implementation of the aliasing of each disk (partition) to two devices with different semantics significantly complicated the relevant kernel code FreeBSD dropped support for cached disk devices as part of the modernization of the disk I/O infrastructure.

9.5. Network Drivers

Drivers for network devices do not use device nodes in order to be accessed. Their selection is based on other decisions made inside the kernel and instead of calling open(), use of a network device is generally introduced by using the system call socket(2).

For more information see ifnet(9), the source of the loopback device, and Bill Paul's network drivers.

Chapter 10. ISA Device Drivers

Written by Sergey Babkin.
Modifications for Handbook made by Murray Stokely, Valentino Vaschetto and Wylie Stilwell.

10.1. Synopsis

This chapter introduces the issues relevant to writing a driver for an ISA device. The pseudo-code presented here is rather detailed and reminiscent of the real code but is still only pseudo-code. It avoids the details irrelevant to the subject of the discussion. The real-life examples can be found in the source code of real drivers. In particular the drivers ep and aha are good sources of information.

10.2. Basic Information

A typical ISA driver would need the following include files:

```
#include <sys/module.h>
#include <sys/bus.h>
#include <machine/bus.h>
#include <machine/resource.h>
#include <sys/rman.h>

#include <isa/isavar.h>
#include <isa/pnpvar.h>
```

They describe the things specific to the ISA and generic bus subsystem.

The bus subsystem is implemented in an object-oriented fashion, its main structures are accessed by associated method functions.

The list of bus methods implemented by an ISA driver is like one for any other bus. For a hypothetical driver named "xxx" they would be:

- `static void xxx_isa_identify (driver_t *, device_t);` Normally used for bus drivers, not device drivers. But for ISA devices this method may have special use: if the device provides some device-specific (non-PnP) way to auto-detect devices this routine may implement it.

- `static int xxx_isa_probe (device_t dev);` Probe for a device at a known (or PnP) location. This routine can also accommodate device-specific auto-detection of parameters for partially configured devices.

- `static int xxx_isa_attach (device_t dev);` Attach and initialize device.

- `static int xxx_isa_detach (device_t dev);` Detach device before unloading the driver module.

- `static int xxx_isa_shutdown (device_t dev);` Execute shutdown of the device before system shutdown.

- `static int xxx_isa_suspend (device_t dev);` Suspend the device before the system goes to the power-save state. May also abort transition to the power-save state.

- `static int xxx_isa_resume (device_t dev);` Resume the device activity after return from power-save state.

`xxx_isa_probe()` and `xxx_isa_attach()` are mandatory, the rest of the routines are optional, depending on the device's needs.

The driver is linked to the system with the following set of descriptions.

```
    /* table of supported bus methods */
```

```
    static device_method_t xxx_isa_methods[] = {
        /* list all the bus method functions supported by the driver */
        /* omit the unsupported methods */
        DEVMETHOD(device_identify,   xxx_isa_identify),
        DEVMETHOD(device_probe,      xxx_isa_probe),
        DEVMETHOD(device_attach,     xxx_isa_attach),
        DEVMETHOD(device_detach,     xxx_isa_detach),
        DEVMETHOD(device_shutdown,   xxx_isa_shutdown),
        DEVMETHOD(device_suspend,    xxx_isa_suspend),
        DEVMETHOD(device_resume,     xxx_isa_resume),

DEVMETHOD_END
    };

    static driver_t xxx_isa_driver = {
        "xxx",
        xxx_isa_methods,
        sizeof(struct xxx_softc),
    };


    static devclass_t xxx_devclass;

    DRIVER_MODULE(xxx, isa, xxx_isa_driver, xxx_devclass,
        load_function, load_argument);
```

Here struct **xxx_softc** is a device-specific structure that contains private driver data and descriptors for the driver's resources. The bus code automatically allocates one softc descriptor per device as needed.

If the driver is implemented as a loadable module then **load_function()** is called to do driver-specific initialization or clean-up when the driver is loaded or unloaded and load_argument is passed as one of its arguments. If the driver does not support dynamic loading (in other words it must always be linked into the kernel) then these values should be set to 0 and the last definition would look like:

```
    DRIVER_MODULE(xxx, isa, xxx_isa_driver,
        xxx_devclass, 0, 0);
```

If the driver is for a device which supports PnP then a table of supported PnP IDs must be defined. The table consists of a list of PnP IDs supported by this driver and human-readable descriptions of the hardware types and models having these IDs. It looks like:

```
    static struct isa_pnp_id xxx_pnp_ids[] = {
        /* a line for each supported PnP ID */
        { 0x12345678,   "Our device model 1234A" },
        { 0x12345679,   "Our device model 1234B" },
        { 0,          NULL }, /* end of table */
    };
```

If the driver does not support PnP devices it still needs an empty PnP ID table, like:

```
    static struct isa_pnp_id xxx_pnp_ids[] = {
        { 0,          NULL }, /* end of table */
    };
```

10.3. device_t **Pointer**

device_t is the pointer type for the device structure. Here we consider only the methods interesting from the device driver writer's standpoint. The methods to manipulate values in the device structure are:

- **device_t device_get_parent(dev)** Get the parent bus of a device.

- `driver_t device_get_driver(dev)` Get pointer to its driver structure.

- `char *device_get_name(dev)` Get the driver name, such as `"xxx"` for our example.

- `int device_get_unit(dev)` Get the unit number (units are numbered from 0 for the devices associated with each driver).

- `char *device_get_nameunit(dev)` Get the device name including the unit number, such as "xxx0", "xxx1" and so on.

- `char *device_get_desc(dev)` Get the device description. Normally it describes the exact model of device in human-readable form.

- `device_set_desc(dev, desc)` Set the description. This makes the device description point to the string desc which may not be deallocated or changed after that.

- `device_set_desc_copy(dev, desc)` Set the description. The description is copied into an internal dynamically allocated buffer, so the string desc may be changed afterwards without adverse effects.

- `void *device_get_softc(dev)` Get pointer to the device descriptor (struct `xxx_softc`) associated with this device.

- `u_int32_t device_get_flags(dev)` Get the flags specified for the device in the configuration file.

A convenience function `device_printf(dev, fmt, ...)` may be used to print the messages from the device driver. It automatically prepends the unitname and colon to the message.

The device_t methods are implemented in the file `kern/bus_subr.c`.

10.4. Configuration File and the Order of Identifying and Probing During Auto-Configuration

The ISA devices are described in the kernel configuration file like:

```
device xxx0 at isa? port 0x300 irq 10 drq 5
    iomem 0xd0000 flags 0x1 sensitive
```

The values of port, IRQ and so on are converted to the resource values associated with the device. They are optional, depending on the device's needs and abilities for auto-configuration. For example, some devices do not need DRQ at all and some allow the driver to read the IRQ setting from the device configuration ports. If a machine has multiple ISA buses the exact bus may be specified in the configuration line, like `isa0` or `isa1`, otherwise the device would be searched for on all the ISA buses.

`sensitive` is a resource requesting that this device must be probed before all non-sensitive devices. It is supported but does not seem to be used in any current driver.

For legacy ISA devices in many cases the drivers are still able to detect the configuration parameters. But each device to be configured in the system must have a config line. If two devices of some type are installed in the system but there is only one configuration line for the corresponding driver, ie:

```
device xxx0 at isa?
```

then only one device will be configured.

But for the devices supporting automatic identification by the means of Plug-n-Play or some proprietary protocol one configuration line is enough to configure all the devices in the system, like the one above or just simply:

```
device xxx at isa?
```

If a driver supports both auto-identified and legacy devices and both kinds are installed at once in one machine then it is enough to describe in the config file the legacy devices only. The auto-identified devices will be added automatically.

When an ISA bus is auto-configured the events happen as follows:

All the drivers' identify routines (including the PnP identify routine which identifies all the PnP devices) are called in random order. As they identify the devices they add them to the list on the ISA bus. Normally the drivers' identify routines associate their drivers with the new devices. The PnP identify routine does not know about the other drivers yet so it does not associate any with the new devices it adds.

The PnP devices are put to sleep using the PnP protocol to prevent them from being probed as legacy devices.

The probe routines of non-PnP devices marked as `sensitive` are called. If probe for a device went successfully, the attach routine is called for it.

The probe and attach routines of all non-PNP devices are called likewise.

The PnP devices are brought back from the sleep state and assigned the resources they request: I/O and memory address ranges, IRQs and DRQs, all of them not conflicting with the attached legacy devices.

Then for each PnP device the probe routines of all the present ISA drivers are called. The first one that claims the device gets attached. It is possible that multiple drivers would claim the device with different priority; in this case, the highest-priority driver wins. The probe routines must call `ISA_PNP_PROBE()` to compare the actual PnP ID with the list of the IDs supported by the driver and if the ID is not in the table return failure. That means that absolutely every driver, even the ones not supporting any PnP devices must call `ISA_PNP_PROBE()`, at least with an empty PnP ID table to return failure on unknown PnP devices.

The probe routine returns a positive value (the error code) on error, zero or negative value on success.

The negative return values are used when a PnP device supports multiple interfaces. For example, an older compatibility interface and a newer advanced interface which are supported by different drivers. Then both drivers would detect the device. The driver which returns a higher value in the probe routine takes precedence (in other words, the driver returning 0 has highest precedence, returning -1 is next, returning -2 is after it and so on). In result the devices which support only the old interface will be handled by the old driver (which should return -1 from the probe routine) while the devices supporting the new interface as well will be handled by the new driver (which should return 0 from the probe routine). If multiple drivers return the same value then the one called first wins. So if a driver returns value 0 it may be sure that it won the priority arbitration.

The device-specific identify routines can also assign not a driver but a class of drivers to the device. Then all the drivers in the class are probed for this device, like the case with PnP. This feature is not implemented in any existing driver and is not considered further in this document.

Because the PnP devices are disabled when probing the legacy devices they will not be attached twice (once as legacy and once as PnP). But in case of device-dependent identify routines it is the responsibility of the driver to make sure that the same device will not be attached by the driver twice: once as legacy user-configured and once as auto-identified.

Another practical consequence for the auto-identified devices (both PnP and device-specific) is that the flags can not be passed to them from the kernel configuration file. So they must either not use the flags at all or use the flags from the device unit 0 for all the auto-identified devices or use the sysctl interface instead of flags.

Other unusual configurations may be accommodated by accessing the configuration resources directly with functions of families `resource_query_*()` and `resource_*_value()`. Their implementations are located in `kern/subr_bus.c`. The old IDE disk driver `i386/isa/wd.c` contains examples of such use. But the standard means of configuration must always be preferred. Leave parsing the configuration resources to the bus configuration code.

10.5. Resources

The information that a user enters into the kernel configuration file is processed and passed to the kernel as configuration resources. This information is parsed by the bus configuration code and transformed into a value of structure device_t and the bus resources associated with it. The drivers may access the configuration resources directly using functions resource_* for more complex cases of configuration. However, generally this is neither needed nor recommended, so this issue is not discussed further here.

The bus resources are associated with each device. They are identified by type and number within the type. For the ISA bus the following types are defined:

- *SYS_RES_IRQ* - interrupt number

- *SYS_RES_DRQ* - ISA DMA channel number

- *SYS_RES_MEMORY* - range of device memory mapped into the system memory space

- *SYS_RES_IOPORT* - range of device I/O registers

The enumeration within types starts from 0, so if a device has two memory regions it would have resources of type SYS_RES_MEMORY numbered 0 and 1. The resource type has nothing to do with the C language type, all the resource values have the C language type unsigned long and must be cast as necessary. The resource numbers do not have to be contiguous, although for ISA they normally would be. The permitted resource numbers for ISA devices are:

```
IRQ: 0-1
DRQ: 0-1
MEMORY: 0-3
IOPORT: 0-7
```

All the resources are represented as ranges, with a start value and count. For IRQ and DRQ resources the count would normally be equal to 1. The values for memory refer to the physical addresses.

Three types of activities can be performed on resources:

- set/get

- allocate/release

- activate/deactivate

Setting sets the range used by the resource. Allocation reserves the requested range that no other driver would be able to reserve it (and checking that no other driver reserved this range already). Activation makes the resource accessible to the driver by doing whatever is necessary for that (for example, for memory it would be mapping into the kernel virtual address space).

The functions to manipulate resources are:

- int bus_set_resource(device_t dev, int type, int rid, u_long start, u_long count)

  Set a range for a resource. Returns 0 if successful, error code otherwise. Normally, this function will return an error only if one of type, rid, start or count has a value that falls out of the permitted range.

  - dev - driver's device

  - type - type of resource, SYS_RES_*

  - rid - resource number (ID) within type

- start, count - resource range

- `int bus_get_resource(device_t dev, int type, int rid, u_long *startp, u_long *countp)`

  Get the range of resource. Returns 0 if successful, error code if the resource is not defined yet.

- `u_long bus_get_resource_start(device_t dev, int type, int rid) u_long bus_get_resource_count (device_t dev, int type, int rid)`

  Convenience functions to get only the start or count. Return 0 in case of error, so if the resource start has 0 among the legitimate values it would be impossible to tell if the value is 0 or an error occurred. Luckily, no ISA resources for add-on drivers may have a start value equal to 0.

- `void bus_delete_resource(device_t dev, int type, int rid)`

  Delete a resource, make it undefined.

- `struct resource * bus_alloc_resource(device_t dev, int type, int *rid, u_long start, u_long end, u_long count, u_int flags)`

  Allocate a resource as a range of count values not allocated by anyone else, somewhere between start and end. Alas, alignment is not supported. If the resource was not set yet it is automatically created. The special values of start 0 and end ~0 (all ones) means that the fixed values previously set by bus_set_resource() must be used instead: start and count as themselves and end=(start+count), in this case if the resource was not defined before then an error is returned. Although rid is passed by reference it is not set anywhere by the resource allocation code of the ISA bus. (The other buses may use a different approach and modify it).

Flags are a bitmap, the flags interesting for the caller are:

- *RF_ACTIVE* - causes the resource to be automatically activated after allocation.

- *RF_SHAREABLE* - resource may be shared at the same time by multiple drivers.

- *RF_TIMESHARE* - resource may be time-shared by multiple drivers, i.e., allocated at the same time by many but activated only by one at any given moment of time.

- Returns 0 on error. The allocated values may be obtained from the returned handle using methods rhand_*() .

- `int bus_release_resource(device_t dev, int type, int rid, struct resource *r)`

- Release the resource, r is the handle returned by bus_alloc_resource(). Returns 0 on success, error code otherwise.

- `int bus_activate_resource(device_t dev, int type, int rid, struct resource *r)  int bus_deactivate_resource(device_t dev, int type, int rid, struct resource *r)`

- Activate or deactivate resource. Return 0 on success, error code otherwise. If the resource is time-shared and currently activated by another driver then EBUSY is returned.

- `int bus_setup_intr(device_t dev, struct resource *r, int flags, driver_intr_t *handler, void *arg, void **cookiep) int bus_teardown_intr(device_t dev, struct resource *r, void *cookie)`

- Associate or de-associate the interrupt handler with a device. Return 0 on success, error code otherwise.

- r - the activated resource handler describing the IRQ

  flags - the interrupt priority level, one of:

  - INTR_TYPE_TTY - terminals and other likewise character-type devices. To mask them use spltty().

- (INTR_TYPE_TTY | INTR_TYPE_FAST) - terminal type devices with small input buffer, critical to the data loss on input (such as the old-fashioned serial ports). To mask them use `spltty()`.

- INTR_TYPE_BIO - block-type devices, except those on the CAM controllers. To mask them use `splbio()`.

- INTR_TYPE_CAM - CAM (Common Access Method) bus controllers. To mask them use `splcam()`.

- INTR_TYPE_NET - network interface controllers. To mask them use `splimp()`.

- INTR_TYPE_MISC - miscellaneous devices. There is no other way to mask them than by `splhigh()` which masks all interrupts.

When an interrupt handler executes all the other interrupts matching its priority level will be masked. The only exception is the MISC level for which no other interrupts are masked and which is not masked by any other interrupt.

- *handler* - pointer to the handler function, the type driver_intr_t is defined as `void driver_intr_t(void *)`

- *arg* - the argument passed to the handler to identify this particular device. It is cast from void* to any real type by the handler. The old convention for the ISA interrupt handlers was to use the unit number as argument, the new (recommended) convention is using a pointer to the device softc structure.

- *cookie[p]* - the value received from `setup()` is used to identify the handler when passed to `teardown()`

A number of methods are defined to operate on the resource handlers (struct resource *). Those of interest to the device driver writers are:

- `u_long rman_get_start(r) u_long rman_get_end(r)` Get the start and end of allocated resource range.

- `void *rman_get_virtual(r)` Get the virtual address of activated memory resource.

10.6. Bus Memory Mapping

In many cases data is exchanged between the driver and the device through the memory. Two variants are possible:

(a) memory is located on the device card

(b) memory is the main memory of the computer

In case (a) the driver always copies the data back and forth between the on-card memory and the main memory as necessary. To map the on-card memory into the kernel virtual address space the physical address and length of the on-card memory must be defined as a SYS_RES_MEMORY resource. That resource can then be allocated and activated, and its virtual address obtained using `rman_get_virtual()`. The older drivers used the function `pmap_mapdev()` for this purpose, which should not be used directly any more. Now it is one of the internal steps of resource activation.

Most of the ISA cards will have their memory configured for physical location somewhere in range 640KB-1MB. Some of the ISA cards require larger memory ranges which should be placed somewhere under 16MB (because of the 24-bit address limitation on the ISA bus). In that case if the machine has more memory than the start address of the device memory (in other words, they overlap) a memory hole must be configured at the address range used by devices. Many BIOSes allow configuration of a memory hole of 1MB starting at 14MB or 15MB. FreeBSD can handle the memory holes properly if the BIOS reports them properly (this feature may be broken on old BIOSes).

In case (b) just the address of the data is sent to the device, and the device uses DMA to actually access the data in the main memory. Two limitations are present: First, ISA cards can only access memory below 16MB. Second, the contiguous pages in virtual address space may not be contiguous in physical address space, so the device may have to do scatter/gather operations. The bus subsystem provides ready solutions for some of these problems, the rest has to be done by the drivers themselves.

Two structures are used for DMA memory allocation, bus_dma_tag_t and bus_dmamap_t. Tag describes the properties required for the DMA memory. Map represents a memory block allocated according to these properties. Multiple maps may be associated with the same tag.

Tags are organized into a tree-like hierarchy with inheritance of the properties. A child tag inherits all the requirements of its parent tag, and may make them more strict but never more loose.

Normally one top-level tag (with no parent) is created for each device unit. If multiple memory areas with different requirements are needed for each device then a tag for each of them may be created as a child of the parent tag.

The tags can be used to create a map in two ways.

First, a chunk of contiguous memory conformant with the tag requirements may be allocated (and later may be freed). This is normally used to allocate relatively long-living areas of memory for communication with the device. Loading of such memory into a map is trivial: it is always considered as one chunk in the appropriate physical memory range.

Second, an arbitrary area of virtual memory may be loaded into a map. Each page of this memory will be checked for conformance to the map requirement. If it conforms then it is left at its original location. If it is not then a fresh conformant "bounce page" is allocated and used as intermediate storage. When writing the data from the non-conformant original pages they will be copied to their bounce pages first and then transferred from the bounce pages to the device. When reading the data would go from the device to the bounce pages and then copied to their non-conformant original pages. The process of copying between the original and bounce pages is called synchronization. This is normally used on a per-transfer basis: buffer for each transfer would be loaded, transfer done and buffer unloaded.

The functions working on the DMA memory are:

- int bus_dma_tag_create(bus_dma_tag_t parent, bus_size_t alignment, bus_size_t boundary, bus_addr_t lowaddr, bus_addr_t highaddr, bus_dma_filter_t *filter, void *filterarg, bus_size_t maxsize, int nsegments, bus_size_t maxsegsz, int flags, bus_dma_tag_t *dmat)

Create a new tag. Returns 0 on success, the error code otherwise.

- *parent* - parent tag, or NULL to create a top-level tag.

- *alignment* - required physical alignment of the memory area to be allocated for this tag. Use value 1 for "no specific alignment". Applies only to the future bus_dmamem_alloc() but not bus_dmamap_create() calls.

- *boundary* - physical address boundary that must not be crossed when allocating the memory. Use value 0 for "no boundary". Applies only to the future bus_dmamem_alloc() but not bus_dmamap_create() calls. Must be power of 2. If the memory is planned to be used in non-cascaded DMA mode (i.e., the DMA addresses will be supplied not by the device itself but by the ISA DMA controller) then the boundary must be no larger than 64KB (64*1024) due to the limitations of the DMA hardware.

- *lowaddr, highaddr* - the names are slightly misleading; these values are used to limit the permitted range of physical addresses used to allocate the memory. The exact meaning varies depending on the planned future use:

  - For bus_dmamem_alloc() all the addresses from 0 to lowaddr-1 are considered permitted, the higher ones are forbidden.

  - For bus_dmamap_create() all the addresses outside the inclusive range [lowaddr; highaddr] are considered accessible. The addresses of pages inside the range are passed to the filter function which decides if they are accessible. If no filter function is supplied then all the range is considered unaccessible.

  - For the ISA devices the normal values (with no filter function) are:

  lowaddr = BUS_SPACE_MAXADDR_24BIT

highaddr = BUS_SPACE_MAXADDR

- *filter, filterarg* - the filter function and its argument. If NULL is passed for filter then the whole range [lowaddr, highaddr] is considered unaccessible when doing `bus_dmamap_create()`. Otherwise the physical address of each attempted page in range [lowaddr; highaddr] is passed to the filter function which decides if it is accessible. The prototype of the filter function is: `int filterfunc(void *arg, bus_addr_t paddr)`. It must return 0 if the page is accessible, non-zero otherwise.

- *maxsize* - the maximal size of memory (in bytes) that may be allocated through this tag. In case it is difficult to estimate or could be arbitrarily big, the value for ISA devices would be `BUS_SPACE_MAXSIZE_24BIT`.

- *nsegments* - maximal number of scatter-gather segments supported by the device. If unrestricted then the value `BUS_SPACE_UNRESTRICTED` should be used. This value is recommended for the parent tags, the actual restrictions would then be specified for the descendant tags. Tags with nsegments equal to `BUS_SPACE_UN-RESTRICTED` may not be used to actually load maps, they may be used only as parent tags. The practical limit for nsegments seems to be about 250-300, higher values will cause kernel stack overflow (the hardware can not normally support that many scatter-gather buffers anyway).

- *maxsegsz* - maximal size of a scatter-gather segment supported by the device. The maximal value for ISA device would be `BUS_SPACE_MAXSIZE_24BIT`.

- *flags* - a bitmap of flags. The only interesting flags are:

  - *BUS_DMA_ALLOCNOW* - requests to allocate all the potentially needed bounce pages when creating the tag.

  - *BUS_DMA_ISA* - mysterious flag used only on Alpha machines. It is not defined for the i386 machines. Probably it should be used by all the ISA drivers for Alpha machines but it looks like there are no such drivers yet.

- *dmat* - pointer to the storage for the new tag to be returned.

- `int bus_dma_tag_destroy(bus_dma_tag_t dmat)`

  Destroy a tag. Returns 0 on success, the error code otherwise.

  dmat - the tag to be destroyed.

- `int bus_dmamem_alloc(bus_dma_tag_t dmat, void** vaddr, int flags, bus_dmamap_t *mapp)`

  Allocate an area of contiguous memory described by the tag. The size of memory to be allocated is tag's maxsize. Returns 0 on success, the error code otherwise. The result still has to be loaded by `bus_dmamap_load()` before being used to get the physical address of the memory.

  - *dmat* - the tag

  - *vaddr* - pointer to the storage for the kernel virtual address of the allocated area to be returned.

  - flags - a bitmap of flags. The only interesting flag is:

    - *BUS_DMA_NOWAIT* - if the memory is not immediately available return the error. If this flag is not set then the routine is allowed to sleep until the memory becomes available.

  - *mapp* - pointer to the storage for the new map to be returned.

- `void bus_dmamem_free(bus_dma_tag_t dmat, void *vaddr, bus_dmamap_t map)`

  Free the memory allocated by `bus_dmamem_alloc()`. At present, freeing of the memory allocated with ISA restrictions is not implemented. Because of this the recommended model of use is to keep and re-use the allocated areas for as long as possible. Do not lightly free some area and then shortly allocate it again. That does not mean that `bus_dmamem_free()` should not be used at all: hopefully it will be properly implemented soon.

- *dmat* - the tag

- *vaddr* - the kernel virtual address of the memory

- *map* - the map of the memory (as returned from `bus_dmamem_alloc()`)

- int bus_dmamap_create(`bus_dma_tag_t dmat, int flags, bus_dmamap_t *mapp`)

Create a map for the tag, to be used in `bus_dmamap_load()` later. Returns 0 on success, the error code otherwise.

- *dmat* - the tag

- *flags* - theoretically, a bit map of flags. But no flags are defined yet, so at present it will be always 0.

- *mapp* - pointer to the storage for the new map to be returned

- int bus_dmamap_destroy(`bus_dma_tag_t dmat, bus_dmamap_t map`)

Destroy a map. Returns 0 on success, the error code otherwise.

- dmat - the tag to which the map is associated

- map - the map to be destroyed

- int bus_dmamap_load(`bus_dma_tag_t dmat, bus_dmamap_t map, void *buf, bus_size_t buflen, bus_dmamap_callback_t *callback, void *callback_arg, int flags`)

Load a buffer into the map (the map must be previously created by `bus_dmamap_create()` or `bus_dmamem_alloc()`). All the pages of the buffer are checked for conformance to the tag requirements and for those not conformant the bounce pages are allocated. An array of physical segment descriptors is built and passed to the callback routine. This callback routine is then expected to handle it in some way. The number of bounce buffers in the system is limited, so if the bounce buffers are needed but not immediately available the request will be queued and the callback will be called when the bounce buffers will become available. Returns 0 if the callback was executed immediately or EINPROGRESS if the request was queued for future execution. In the latter case the synchronization with queued callback routine is the responsibility of the driver.

- *dmat* - the tag

- *map* - the map

- *buf* - kernel virtual address of the buffer

- *buflen* - length of the buffer

- *callback*, `callback_arg` - the callback function and its argument

The prototype of callback function is:

```
void callback(void *arg, bus_dma_segment_t *seg, int nseg, int error)
```

- *arg* - the same as callback_arg passed to `bus_dmamap_load()`

- *seg* - array of the segment descriptors

- *nseg* - number of descriptors in array

- *error* - indication of the segment number overflow: if it is set to EFBIG then the buffer did not fit into the maximal number of segments permitted by the tag. In this case only the permitted number of descriptors will be in the array. Handling of this situation is up to the driver: depending on the desired semantics it can either consider this an error or split the buffer in two and handle the second part separately

Each entry in the segments array contains the fields:

- *ds_addr* - physical bus address of the segment

- *ds_len* - length of the segment

- `void bus_dmamap_unload(bus_dma_tag_t dmat, bus_dmamap_t map)`

unload the map.

- *dmat* - tag

- *map* - loaded map

- `void bus_dmamap_sync (bus_dma_tag_t dmat, bus_dmamap_t map, bus_dmasync_op_t op)`

Synchronise a loaded buffer with its bounce pages before and after physical transfer to or from device. This is the function that does all the necessary copying of data between the original buffer and its mapped version. The buffers must be synchronized both before and after doing the transfer.

- *dmat* - tag

- *map* - loaded map

- *op* - type of synchronization operation to perform:

- `BUS_DMASYNC_PREREAD` - before reading from device into buffer

- `BUS_DMASYNC_POSTREAD` - after reading from device into buffer

- `BUS_DMASYNC_PREWRITE` - before writing the buffer to device

- `BUS_DMASYNC_POSTWRITE` - after writing the buffer to device

As of now PREREAD and POSTWRITE are null operations but that may change in the future, so they must not be ignored in the driver. Synchronization is not needed for the memory obtained from `bus_dmamem_alloc()`.

Before calling the callback function from `bus_dmamap_load()` the segment array is stored in the stack. And it gets pre-allocated for the maximal number of segments allowed by the tag. Because of this the practical limit for the number of segments on i386 architecture is about 250-300 (the kernel stack is 4KB minus the size of the user structure, size of a segment array entry is 8 bytes, and some space must be left). Because the array is allocated based on the maximal number this value must not be set higher than really needed. Fortunately, for most of hardware the maximal supported number of segments is much lower. But if the driver wants to handle buffers with a very large number of scatter-gather segments it should do that in portions: load part of the buffer, transfer it to the device, load next part of the buffer, and so on.

Another practical consequence is that the number of segments may limit the size of the buffer. If all the pages in the buffer happen to be physically non-contiguous then the maximal supported buffer size for that fragmented case would be (nsegments * page_size). For example, if a maximal number of 10 segments is supported then on i386 maximal guaranteed supported buffer size would be 40K. If a higher size is desired then special tricks should be used in the driver.

If the hardware does not support scatter-gather at all or the driver wants to support some buffer size even if it is heavily fragmented then the solution is to allocate a contiguous buffer in the driver and use it as intermediate storage if the original buffer does not fit.

Below are the typical call sequences when using a map depend on the use of the map. The characters -> are used to show the flow of time.

For a buffer which stays practically fixed during all the time between attachment and detachment of a device:

bus_dmamem_alloc -> bus_dmamap_load -> ...use buffer... -> -> bus_dmamap_unload -> bus_dmamem_free

For a buffer that changes frequently and is passed from outside the driver:

```
bus_dmamap_create ->
-> bus_dmamap_load -> bus_dmamap_sync(PRE...) -> do transfer ->
-> bus_dmamap_sync(POST...) -> bus_dmamap_unload ->
...
-> bus_dmamap_load -> bus_dmamap_sync(PRE...) -> do transfer ->
-> bus_dmamap_sync(POST...) -> bus_dmamap_unload ->
-> bus_dmamap_destroy
```

When loading a map created by bus_dmamem_alloc() the passed address and size of the buffer must be the same as used in bus_dmamem_alloc(). In this case it is guaranteed that the whole buffer will be mapped as one segment (so the callback may be based on this assumption) and the request will be executed immediately (EINPROGRESS will never be returned). All the callback needs to do in this case is to save the physical address.

A typical example would be:

```
static void
alloc_callback(void *arg, bus_dma_segment_t *seg, int nseg, int error)
{
  *(bus_addr_t *)arg = seg[0].ds_addr;
}


...
int error;
struct somedata {
  ....
};
struct somedata *vsomedata; /* virtual address */
bus_addr_t psomedata; /* physical bus-relative address */
bus_dma_tag_t tag_somedata;
bus_dmamap_t map_somedata;
...

error=bus_dma_tag_create(parent_tag, alignment,
  boundary, lowaddr, highaddr, /*filter*/ NULL, /*filterarg*/ NULL,
  /*maxsize*/ sizeof(struct somedata), /*nsegments*/ 1,
  /*maxsegsz*/ sizeof(struct somedata), /*flags*/ 0,
  &tag_somedata);
if(error)
return error;

error = bus_dmamem_alloc(tag_somedata, &vsomedata, /* flags*/ 0,
    &map_somedata);
if(error)
    return error;

bus_dmamap_load(tag_somedata, map_somedata, (void *)vsomedata,
    sizeof (struct somedata), alloc_callback,
    (void *) &psomedata, /*flags*/0);
```

Looks a bit long and complicated but that is the way to do it. The practical consequence is: if multiple memory areas are allocated always together it would be a really good idea to combine them all into one structure and allocate as one (if the alignment and boundary limitations permit).

When loading an arbitrary buffer into the map created by bus_dmamap_create() special measures must be taken to synchronize with the callback in case it would be delayed. The code would look like:

```
{
  int s;
  int error;

  s = splsoftvm();
```

```
        error = bus_dmamap_load(
            dmat,
            dmamap,
            buffer_ptr,
            buffer_len,
            callback,
            /*callback_arg*/ buffer_descriptor,
            /*flags*/0);
        if (error == EINPROGRESS) {
            /*
             * Do whatever is needed to ensure synchronization
             * with callback. Callback is guaranteed not to be started
             * until we do splx() or tsleep().
             */
        }
    splx(s);
}
```

Two possible approaches for the processing of requests are:

1. If requests are completed by marking them explicitly as done (such as the CAM requests) then it would be simpler to put all the further processing into the callback driver which would mark the request when it is done. Then not much extra synchronization is needed. For the flow control reasons it may be a good idea to freeze the request queue until this request gets completed.

2. If requests are completed when the function returns (such as classic read or write requests on character devices) then a synchronization flag should be set in the buffer descriptor and `tsleep()` called. Later when the callback gets called it will do its processing and check this synchronization flag. If it is set then the callback should issue a wakeup. In this approach the callback function could either do all the needed processing (just like the previous case) or simply save the segments array in the buffer descriptor. Then after callback completes the calling function could use this saved segments array and do all the processing.

10.7. DMA

The Direct Memory Access (DMA) is implemented in the ISA bus through the DMA controller (actually, two of them but that is an irrelevant detail). To make the early ISA devices simple and cheap the logic of the bus control and address generation was concentrated in the DMA controller. Fortunately, FreeBSD provides a set of functions that mostly hide the annoying details of the DMA controller from the device drivers.

The simplest case is for the fairly intelligent devices. Like the bus master devices on PCI they can generate the bus cycles and memory addresses all by themselves. The only thing they really need from the DMA controller is bus arbitration. So for this purpose they pretend to be cascaded slave DMA controllers. And the only thing needed from the system DMA controller is to enable the cascaded mode on a DMA channel by calling the following function when attaching the driver:

`void isa_dmacascade(int channel_number)`

All the further activity is done by programming the device. When detaching the driver no DMA-related functions need to be called.

For the simpler devices things get more complicated. The functions used are:

- `int isa_dma_acquire(int chanel_number)`

  Reserve a DMA channel. Returns 0 on success or EBUSY if the channel was already reserved by this or a different driver. Most of the ISA devices are not able to share DMA channels anyway, so normally this function is called when attaching a device. This reservation was made redundant by the modern interface of bus resources but still must be used in addition to the latter. If not used then later, other DMA routines will panic.

- `int isa_dma_release(int chanel_number)`

Release a previously reserved DMA channel. No transfers must be in progress when the channel is released (in addition the device must not try to initiate transfer after the channel is released).

- `void isa_dmainit(int chan, u_int bouncebufsize)`

Allocate a bounce buffer for use with the specified channel. The requested size of the buffer can not exceed 64KB. This bounce buffer will be automatically used later if a transfer buffer happens to be not physically contiguous or outside of the memory accessible by the ISA bus or crossing the 64KB boundary. If the transfers will be always done from buffers which conform to these conditions (such as those allocated by `bus_dmamem_alloc()` with proper limitations) then `isa_dmainit()` does not have to be called. But it is quite convenient to transfer arbitrary data using the DMA controller. The bounce buffer will automatically care of the scatter-gather issues.

  - *chan* - channel number

  - *bouncebufsize* - size of the bounce buffer in bytes

- `void isa_dmastart(int flags, caddr_t addr, u_int nbytes, int chan)`

Prepare to start a DMA transfer. This function must be called to set up the DMA controller before actually starting transfer on the device. It checks that the buffer is contiguous and falls into the ISA memory range, if not then the bounce buffer is automatically used. If bounce buffer is required but not set up by `isa_dmainit()` or too small for the requested transfer size then the system will panic. In case of a write request with bounce buffer the data will be automatically copied to the bounce buffer.

- flags - a bitmask determining the type of operation to be done. The direction bits B_READ and B_WRITE are mutually exclusive.

  - B_READ - read from the ISA bus into memory

  - B_WRITE - write from the memory to the ISA bus

  - B_RAW - if set then the DMA controller will remember the buffer and after the end of transfer will automatically re-initialize itself to repeat transfer of the same buffer again (of course, the driver may change the data in the buffer before initiating another transfer in the device). If not set then the parameters will work only for one transfer, and `isa_dmastart()` will have to be called again before initiating the next transfer. Using B_RAW makes sense only if the bounce buffer is not used.

- addr - virtual address of the buffer

- nbytes - length of the buffer. Must be less or equal to 64KB. Length of 0 is not allowed: the DMA controller will understand it as 64KB while the kernel code will understand it as 0 and that would cause unpredictable effects. For channels number 4 and higher the length must be even because these channels transfer 2 bytes at a time. In case of an odd length the last byte will not be transferred.

- chan - channel number

- `void isa_dmadone(int flags, caddr_t addr, int nbytes, int chan)`

Synchronize the memory after device reports that transfer is done. If that was a read operation with a bounce buffer then the data will be copied from the bounce buffer to the original buffer. Arguments are the same as for `isa_dmastart()`. Flag B_RAW is permitted but it does not affect `isa_dmadone()` in any way.

- `int isa_dmastatus(int channel_number)`

Returns the number of bytes left in the current transfer to be transferred. In case the flag B_READ was set in `isa_dmastart()` the number returned will never be equal to zero. At the end of transfer it will be automatically reset back to the length of buffer. The normal use is to check the number of bytes left after the device signals that the transfer is completed. If the number of bytes is not 0 then something probably went wrong with that transfer.

- `int isa_dmastop(int channel_number)`

Aborts the current transfer and returns the number of bytes left untransferred.

10.8. xxx_isa_probe

This function probes if a device is present. If the driver supports auto-detection of some part of device configuration (such as interrupt vector or memory address) this auto-detection must be done in this routine.

As for any other bus, if the device cannot be detected or is detected but failed the self-test or some other problem happened then it returns a positive value of error. The value ENXIO must be returned if the device is not present. Other error values may mean other conditions. Zero or negative values mean success. Most of the drivers return zero as success.

The negative return values are used when a PnP device supports multiple interfaces. For example, an older compatibility interface and a newer advanced interface which are supported by different drivers. Then both drivers would detect the device. The driver which returns a higher value in the probe routine takes precedence (in other words, the driver returning 0 has highest precedence, one returning -1 is next, one returning -2 is after it and so on). In result the devices which support only the old interface will be handled by the old driver (which should return -1 from the probe routine) while the devices supporting the new interface as well will be handled by the new driver (which should return 0 from the probe routine).

The device descriptor struct xxx_softc is allocated by the system before calling the probe routine. If the probe routine returns an error the descriptor will be automatically deallocated by the system. So if a probing error occurs the driver must make sure that all the resources it used during probe are deallocated and that nothing keeps the descriptor from being safely deallocated. If the probe completes successfully the descriptor will be preserved by the system and later passed to the routine **xxx_isa_attach()**. If a driver returns a negative value it can not be sure that it will have the highest priority and its attach routine will be called. So in this case it also must release all the resources before returning and if necessary allocate them again in the attach routine. When **xxx_isa_probe()** returns 0 releasing the resources before returning is also a good idea and a well-behaved driver should do so. But in cases where there is some problem with releasing the resources the driver is allowed to keep resources between returning 0 from the probe routine and execution of the attach routine.

A typical probe routine starts with getting the device descriptor and unit:

```
struct xxx_softc *sc = device_get_softc(dev);
int unit = device_get_unit(dev);
int pnperror;
int error = 0;

sc->dev = dev; /* link it back */
sc->unit = unit;
```

Then check for the PnP devices. The check is carried out by a table containing the list of PnP IDs supported by this driver and human-readable descriptions of the device models corresponding to these IDs.

```
pnperror=ISA_PNP_PROBE(device_get_parent(dev), dev,
xxx_pnp_ids); if(pnperror == ENXIO) return ENXIO;
```

The logic of ISA_PNP_PROBE is the following: If this card (device unit) was not detected as PnP then ENOENT will be returned. If it was detected as PnP but its detected ID does not match any of the IDs in the table then ENXIO is returned. Finally, if it has PnP support and it matches on of the IDs in the table, 0 is returned and the appropriate description from the table is set by **device_set_desc()**.

If a driver supports only PnP devices then the condition would look like:

```
if(pnperror != 0)
```

```
                return pnperror;
```

No special treatment is required for the drivers which do not support PnP because they pass an empty PnP ID table and will always get ENXIO if called on a PnP card.

The probe routine normally needs at least some minimal set of resources, such as I/O port number to find the card and probe it. Depending on the hardware the driver may be able to discover the other necessary resources automatically. The PnP devices have all the resources pre-set by the PnP subsystem, so the driver does not need to discover them by itself.

Typically the minimal information required to get access to the device is the I/O port number. Then some devices allow to get the rest of information from the device configuration registers (though not all devices do that). So first we try to get the port start value:

```
sc->port0 = bus_get_resource_start(dev,
        SYS_RES_IOPORT, 0 /*rid*/); if(sc->port0 == 0) return ENXIO;
```

The base port address is saved in the structure softc for future use. If it will be used very often then calling the resource function each time would be prohibitively slow. If we do not get a port we just return an error. Some device drivers can instead be clever and try to probe all the possible ports, like this:

```
        /* table of all possible base I/O port addresses for this device */
        static struct xxx_allports {
            u_short port; /* port address */
            short used; /* flag: if this port is already used by some unit */
        } xxx_allports = {
            { 0x300, 0 },
            { 0x320, 0 },
            { 0x340, 0 },
            { 0, 0 } /* end of table */
        };

        ...
        int port, i;
        ...

        port = bus_get_resource_start(dev, SYS_RES_IOPORT, 0 /*rid*/);
        if(port !=0 ) {
            for(i=0; xxx_allports[i].port!=0; i++) {
                if(xxx_allports[i].used || xxx_allports[i].port != port)
                    continue;

                /* found it */
                xxx_allports[i].used = 1;
                /* do probe on a known port */
                return xxx_really_probe(dev, port);
            }
            return ENXIO; /* port is unknown or already used */
        }

        /* we get here only if we need to guess the port */
        for(i=0; xxx_allports[i].port!=0; i++) {
            if(xxx_allports[i].used)
                continue;

            /* mark as used - even if we find nothing at this port
             * at least we won't probe it in future
             */
            xxx_allports[i].used = 1;

            error = xxx_really_probe(dev, xxx_allports[i].port);
            if(error == 0) /* found a device at that port */
```

216

```
            return 0;
    }
    /* probed all possible addresses, none worked */
    return ENXIO;
```

Of course, normally the driver's `identify()` routine should be used for such things. But there may be one valid reason why it may be better to be done in `probe()`: if this probe would drive some other sensitive device crazy. The probe routines are ordered with consideration of the **sensitive** flag: the sensitive devices get probed first and the rest of the devices later. But the `identify()` routines are called before any probes, so they show no respect to the sensitive devices and may upset them.

Now, after we got the starting port we need to set the port count (except for PnP devices) because the kernel does not have this information in the configuration file.

```
    if(pnperror /* only for non-PnP devices */
    && bus_set_resource(dev, SYS_RES_IOPORT, 0, sc->port0,
    XXX_PORT_COUNT)<0)
        return ENXIO;
```

Finally allocate and activate a piece of port address space (special values of start and end mean "use those we set by `bus_set_resource()`"):

```
    sc->port0_rid = 0;
    sc->port0_r = bus_alloc_resource(dev, SYS_RES_IOPORT,
    &sc->port0_rid,
        /*start*/ 0, /*end*/ ~0, /*count*/ 0, RF_ACTIVE);

    if(sc->port0_r == NULL)
        return ENXIO;
```

Now having access to the port-mapped registers we can poke the device in some way and check if it reacts like it is expected to. If it does not then there is probably some other device or no device at all at this address.

Normally drivers do not set up the interrupt handlers until the attach routine. Instead they do probes in the polling mode using the `DELAY()` function for timeout. The probe routine must never hang forever, all the waits for the device must be done with timeouts. If the device does not respond within the time it is probably broken or misconfigured and the driver must return error. When determining the timeout interval give the device some extra time to be on the safe side: although `DELAY()` is supposed to delay for the same amount of time on any machine it has some margin of error, depending on the exact CPU.

If the probe routine really wants to check that the interrupts really work it may configure and probe the interrupts too. But that is not recommended.

```
    /* implemented in some very device-specific way */
    if(error = xxx_probe_ports(sc))
        goto bad; /* will deallocate the resources before returning */
```

The function `xxx_probe_ports()` may also set the device description depending on the exact model of device it discovers. But if there is only one supported device model this can be as well done in a hardcoded way. Of course, for the PnP devices the PnP support sets the description from the table automatically.

```
    if(pnperror)
        device_set_desc(dev, "Our device model 1234");
```

Then the probe routine should either discover the ranges of all the resources by reading the device configuration registers or make sure that they were set explicitly by the user. We will consider it with an example of on-board memory. The probe routine should be as non-intrusive as possible, so allocation and check of functionality of the rest of resources (besides the ports) would be better left to the attach routine.

The memory address may be specified in the kernel configuration file or on some devices it may be pre-configured in non-volatile configuration registers. If both sources are available and different, which one should be used? Probably if the user bothered to set the address explicitly in the kernel configuration file they know what they are doing and this one should take precedence. An example of implementation could be:

```
/* try to find out the config address first */
sc->mem0_p = bus_get_resource_start(dev, SYS_RES_MEMORY, 0 /*rid*/);
if(sc->mem0_p == 0) { /* nope, not specified by user */
    sc->mem0_p = xxx_read_mem0_from_device_config(sc);


if(sc->mem0_p == 0)
        /* can't get it from device config registers either */
        goto bad;
} else {
    if(xxx_set_mem0_address_on_device(sc) < 0)
        goto bad; /* device does not support that address */
}

/* just like the port, set the memory size,
 * for some devices the memory size would not be constant
 * but should be read from the device configuration registers instead
 * to accommodate different models of devices. Another option would
 * be to let the user set the memory size as "msize" configuration
 * resource which will be automatically handled by the ISA bus.
 */
if(pnperror) { /* only for non-PnP devices */
    sc->mem0_size = bus_get_resource_count(dev, SYS_RES_MEMORY, 0 /*rid*/);
    if(sc->mem0_size == 0) /* not specified by user */
        sc->mem0_size = xxx_read_mem0_size_from_device_config(sc);

    if(sc->mem0_size == 0) {
        /* suppose this is a very old model of device without
         * auto-configuration features and the user gave no preference,
         * so assume the minimalistic case
         * (of course, the real value will vary with the driver)
         */
        sc->mem0_size = 8*1024;
    }

    if(xxx_set_mem0_size_on_device(sc) < 0)
        goto bad; /* device does not support that size */

    if(bus_set_resource(dev, SYS_RES_MEMORY, /*rid*/0,
            sc->mem0_p, sc->mem0_size)<0)
        goto bad;
} else {
    sc->mem0_size = bus_get_resource_count(dev, SYS_RES_MEMORY, 0 /*rid*/);
}
```

Resources for IRQ and DRQ are easy to check by analogy.

If all went well then release all the resources and return success.

```
xxx_free_resources(sc);
return 0;
```

Finally, handle the troublesome situations. All the resources should be deallocated before returning. We make use of the fact that before the structure softc is passed to us it gets zeroed out, so we can find out if some resource was allocated: then its descriptor is non-zero.

```
bad:
```

```
xxx_free_resources(sc);
if(error)
        return error;
else /* exact error is unknown */
    return ENXIO;
```

That would be all for the probe routine. Freeing of resources is done from multiple places, so it is moved to a function which may look like:

```
static void
        xxx_free_resources(sc)
            struct xxx_softc *sc;
    {
        /* check every resource and free if not zero */

        /* interrupt handler */
        if(sc->intr_r) {
            bus_teardown_intr(sc->dev, sc->intr_r, sc->intr_cookie);
            bus_release_resource(sc->dev, SYS_RES_IRQ, sc->intr_rid,
                sc->intr_r);
            sc->intr_r = 0;
        }

        /* all kinds of memory maps we could have allocated */
        if(sc->data_p) {
            bus_dmamap_unload(sc->data_tag, sc->data_map);
            sc->data_p = 0;
        }
         if(sc->data) { /* sc->data_map may be legitimately equal to 0 */
            /* the map will also be freed */
            bus_dmamem_free(sc->data_tag, sc->data, sc->data_map);
            sc->data = 0;
        }
        if(sc->data_tag) {
            bus_dma_tag_destroy(sc->data_tag);
            sc->data_tag = 0;
        }

        ... free other maps and tags if we have them ...

        if(sc->parent_tag) {
            bus_dma_tag_destroy(sc->parent_tag);
            sc->parent_tag = 0;
        }

        /* release all the bus resources */
        if(sc->mem0_r) {
            bus_release_resource(sc->dev, SYS_RES_MEMORY, sc->mem0_rid,
                sc->mem0_r);
            sc->mem0_r = 0;
        }
        ...
        if(sc->port0_r) {
            bus_release_resource(sc->dev, SYS_RES_IOPORT, sc->port0_rid,
                sc->port0_r);
            sc->port0_r = 0;
        }
    }
```

10.9. xxx_isa_attach

The attach routine actually connects the driver to the system if the probe routine returned success and the system had chosen to attach that driver. If the probe routine returned 0 then the attach routine may expect to receive the device structure softc intact, as it was set by the probe routine. Also if the probe routine returns 0 it may expect that the attach routine for this device shall be called at some point in the future. If the probe routine returns a negative value then the driver may make none of these assumptions.

The attach routine returns 0 if it completed successfully or error code otherwise.

The attach routine starts just like the probe routine, with getting some frequently used data into more accessible variables.

```
struct xxx_softc *sc = device_get_softc(dev);
int unit = device_get_unit(dev);
int error = 0;
```

Then allocate and activate all the necessary resources. Because normally the port range will be released before returning from probe, it has to be allocated again. We expect that the probe routine had properly set all the resource ranges, as well as saved them in the structure softc. If the probe routine had left some resource allocated then it does not need to be allocated again (which would be considered an error).

```
sc->port0_rid = 0;
sc->port0_r = bus_alloc_resource(dev, SYS_RES_IOPORT,  &sc->port0_rid,
    /*start*/ 0, /*end*/ ~0, /*count*/ 0, RF_ACTIVE);

if(sc->port0_r == NULL)
    return ENXIO;

/* on-board memory */
sc->mem0_rid = 0;
sc->mem0_r = bus_alloc_resource(dev, SYS_RES_MEMORY,  &sc->mem0_rid,
    /*start*/ 0, /*end*/ ~0, /*count*/ 0, RF_ACTIVE);

if(sc->mem0_r == NULL)
    goto bad;

/* get its virtual address */
sc->mem0_v = rman_get_virtual(sc->mem0_r);
```

The DMA request channel (DRQ) is allocated likewise. To initialize it use functions of the **isa_dma*()** family. For example:

```
isa_dmacascade(sc->drq0);
```

The interrupt request line (IRQ) is a bit special. Besides allocation the driver's interrupt handler should be associated with it. Historically in the old ISA drivers the argument passed by the system to the interrupt handler was the device unit number. But in modern drivers the convention suggests passing the pointer to structure softc. The important reason is that when the structures softc are allocated dynamically then getting the unit number from softc is easy while getting softc from the unit number is difficult. Also this convention makes the drivers for different buses look more uniform and allows them to share the code: each bus gets its own probe, attach, detach and other bus-specific routines while the bulk of the driver code may be shared among them.

```
sc->intr_rid = 0;
sc->intr_r = bus_alloc_resource(dev, SYS_RES_MEMORY, &sc->intr_rid,
    /*start*/ 0, /*end*/ ~0, /*count*/ 0, RF_ACTIVE);

if(sc->intr_r == NULL)
    goto bad;

/*
 * XXX_INTR_TYPE is supposed to be defined depending on the type of
 * the driver, for example as INTR_TYPE_CAM for a CAM driver
 */
error = bus_setup_intr(dev, sc->intr_r, XXX_INTR_TYPE,
    (driver_intr_t *) xxx_intr, (void *) sc, &sc->intr_cookie);
```

```
                if(error)
                    goto bad;
```

If the device needs to make DMA to the main memory then this memory should be allocated like described before:

```
        error=bus_dma_tag_create(NULL, /*alignment*/ 4,
            /*boundary*/ 0, /*lowaddr*/ BUS_SPACE_MAXADDR_24BIT,
            /*highaddr*/ BUS_SPACE_MAXADDR, /*filter*/ NULL, /*filterarg*/ NULL,
            /*maxsize*/ BUS_SPACE_MAXSIZE_24BIT,
            /*nsegments*/ BUS_SPACE_UNRESTRICTED,
            /*maxsegsz*/ BUS_SPACE_MAXSIZE_24BIT, /*flags*/ 0,
            &sc->parent_tag);
        if(error)
            goto bad;

        /* many things get inherited from the parent tag
         * sc->data is supposed to point to the structure with the shared data,
         * for example for a ring buffer it could be:
         * struct {
         *   u_short rd_pos;
         *   u_short wr_pos;
         *   char    bf[XXX_RING_BUFFER_SIZE]
         * } *data;
         */
        error=bus_dma_tag_create(sc->parent_tag, 1,
            0, BUS_SPACE_MAXADDR, 0, /*filter*/ NULL, /*filterarg*/ NULL,
            /*maxsize*/ sizeof(* sc->data), /*nsegments*/ 1,
            /*maxsegsz*/ sizeof(* sc->data), /*flags*/ 0,
            &sc->data_tag);
        if(error)
            goto bad;

        error = bus_dmamem_alloc(sc->data_tag, &sc->data, /* flags*/ 0,
            &sc->data_map);
        if(error)
             goto bad;

        /* xxx_alloc_callback() just saves the physical address at
         * the pointer passed as its argument, in this case &sc->data_p.
         * See details in the section on bus memory mapping.
         * It can be implemented like:
         *
         * static void
         * xxx_alloc_callback(void *arg, bus_dma_segment_t *seg,
         *     int nseg, int error)
         * {
         *     *(bus_addr_t *)arg = seg[0].ds_addr;
         * }
         */
        bus_dmamap_load(sc->data_tag, sc->data_map, (void *)sc->data,
            sizeof (* sc->data), xxx_alloc_callback, (void *) &sc->data_p,
            /*flags*/0);
```

After all the necessary resources are allocated the device should be initialized. The initialization may include testing that all the expected features are functional.

```
        if(xxx_initialize(sc) < 0)
            goto bad;
```

The bus subsystem will automatically print on the console the device description set by probe. But if the driver wants to print some extra information about the device it may do so, for example:

```
        device_printf(dev, "has on-card FIFO buffer of %d bytes\n", sc->fifosize);
```

If the initialization routine experiences any problems then printing messages about them before returning error is also recommended.

The final step of the attach routine is attaching the device to its functional subsystem in the kernel. The exact way to do it depends on the type of the driver: a character device, a block device, a network device, a CAM SCSI bus device and so on.

If all went well then return success.

```
error = xxx_attach_subsystem(sc);
if(error)
    goto bad;

return 0;
```

Finally, handle the troublesome situations. All the resources should be deallocated before returning an error. We make use of the fact that before the structure softc is passed to us it gets zeroed out, so we can find out if some resource was allocated: then its descriptor is non-zero.

```
bad:

xxx_free_resources(sc);
if(error)
    return error;
else /* exact error is unknown */
    return ENXIO;
```

That would be all for the attach routine.

10.10. xxx_isa_detach

If this function is present in the driver and the driver is compiled as a loadable module then the driver gets the ability to be unloaded. This is an important feature if the hardware supports hot plug. But the ISA bus does not support hot plug, so this feature is not particularly important for the ISA devices. The ability to unload a driver may be useful when debugging it, but in many cases installation of the new version of the driver would be required only after the old version somehow wedges the system and a reboot will be needed anyway, so the efforts spent on writing the detach routine may not be worth it. Another argument that unloading would allow upgrading the drivers on a production machine seems to be mostly theoretical. Installing a new version of a driver is a dangerous operation which should never be performed on a production machine (and which is not permitted when the system is running in secure mode). Still, the detach routine may be provided for the sake of completeness.

The detach routine returns 0 if the driver was successfully detached or the error code otherwise.

The logic of detach is a mirror of the attach. The first thing to do is to detach the driver from its kernel subsystem. If the device is currently open then the driver has two choices: refuse to be detached or forcibly close and proceed with detach. The choice used depends on the ability of the particular kernel subsystem to do a forced close and on the preferences of the driver's author. Generally the forced close seems to be the preferred alternative.

```
struct xxx_softc *sc = device_get_softc(dev);
int error;

error = xxx_detach_subsystem(sc);
if(error)
    return error;
```

Next the driver may want to reset the hardware to some consistent state. That includes stopping any ongoing transfers, disabling the DMA channels and interrupts to avoid memory corruption by the device. For most of the drivers this is exactly what the shutdown routine does, so if it is included in the driver we can just call it.

```
xxx_isa_shutdown(dev);
```

And finally release all the resources and return success.

```
xxx_free_resources(sc);
return 0;
```

10.11. xxx_isa_shutdown

This routine is called when the system is about to be shut down. It is expected to bring the hardware to some consistent state. For most of the ISA devices no special action is required, so the function is not really necessary because the device will be re-initialized on reboot anyway. But some devices have to be shut down with a special procedure, to make sure that they will be properly detected after soft reboot (this is especially true for many devices with proprietary identification protocols). In any case disabling DMA and interrupts in the device registers and stopping any ongoing transfers is a good idea. The exact action depends on the hardware, so we do not consider it here in any detail.

10.12. xxx_intr

The interrupt handler is called when an interrupt is received which may be from this particular device. The ISA bus does not support interrupt sharing (except in some special cases) so in practice if the interrupt handler is called then the interrupt almost for sure came from its device. Still, the interrupt handler must poll the device registers and make sure that the interrupt was generated by its device. If not it should just return.

The old convention for the ISA drivers was getting the device unit number as an argument. This is obsolete, and the new drivers receive whatever argument was specified for them in the attach routine when calling bus_setup_intr(). By the new convention it should be the pointer to the structure softc. So the interrupt handler commonly starts as:

```
static void
xxx_intr(struct xxx_softc *sc)
{
```

It runs at the interrupt priority level specified by the interrupt type parameter of bus_setup_intr(). That means that all the other interrupts of the same type as well as all the software interrupts are disabled.

To avoid races it is commonly written as a loop:

```
while(xxx_interrupt_pending(sc)) {
    xxx_process_interrupt(sc);
    xxx_acknowledge_interrupt(sc);
}
```

The interrupt handler has to acknowledge interrupt to the device only but not to the interrupt controller, the system takes care of the latter.

Chapter 11. PCI Devices

This chapter will talk about the FreeBSD mechanisms for writing a device driver for a device on a PCI bus.

11.1. Probe and Attach

Information here about how the PCI bus code iterates through the unattached devices and see if a newly loaded kld will attach to any of them.

11.1.1. Sample Driver Source (`mypci.c`)

```
/*
 * Simple KLD to play with the PCI functions.
 *
 * Murray Stokely
 */

#include <sys/param.h>  /* defines used in kernel.h */
#include <sys/module.h>
#include <sys/systm.h>
#include <sys/errno.h>
#include <sys/kernel.h>  /* types used in module initialization */
#include <sys/conf.h>  /* cdevsw struct */
#include <sys/uio.h>  /* uio struct */
#include <sys/malloc.h>
#include <sys/bus.h>  /* structs, prototypes for pci bus stuff and DEVMETHOD macros! */

#include <machine/bus.h>
#include <sys/rman.h>
#include <machine/resource.h>

#include <dev/pci/pcivar.h> /* For pci_get macros! */
#include <dev/pci/pcireg.h>

/* The softc holds our per-instance data. */
struct mypci_softc {
  device_t my_dev;
  struct cdev *my_cdev;
};

/* Function prototypes */
static d_open_t  mypci_open;
static d_close_t mypci_close;
static d_read_t  mypci_read;
static d_write_t mypci_write;

/* Character device entry points */

static struct cdevsw mypci_cdevsw = {
  .d_version = D_VERSION,
  .d_open = mypci_open,
  .d_close = mypci_close,
  .d_read = mypci_read,
  .d_write = mypci_write,
  .d_name = "mypci",
};

/*
 * In the cdevsw routines, we find our softc by using the si_drv1 member
 * of struct cdev.  We set this variable to point to our softc in our
 * attach routine when we create the /dev entry.
 */
```

```
int
mypci_open(struct cdev *dev, int oflags, int devtype, struct thread *td)
{
 struct mypci_softc *sc;

 /* Look up our softc. */
 sc = dev->si_drv1;
 device_printf(sc->my_dev, "Opened successfully.\n");
 return (0);
}

int
mypci_close(struct cdev *dev, int fflag, int devtype, struct thread *td)
{
 struct mypci_softc *sc;

 /* Look up our softc. */
 sc = dev->si_drv1;
 device_printf(sc->my_dev, "Closed.\n");
 return (0);
}

int
mypci_read(struct cdev *dev, struct uio *uio, int ioflag)
{
 struct mypci_softc *sc;

 /* Look up our softc. */
 sc = dev->si_drv1;
 device_printf(sc->my_dev, "Asked to read %d bytes.\n", uio->uio_resid);
 return (0);
}

int
mypci_write(struct cdev *dev, struct uio *uio, int ioflag)
{
 struct mypci_softc *sc;

 /* Look up our softc. */
 sc = dev->si_drv1;
 device_printf(sc->my_dev, "Asked to write %d bytes.\n", uio->uio_resid);
 return (0);
}

/* PCI Support Functions */

/*
 * Compare the device ID of this device against the IDs that this driver
 * supports.  If there is a match, set the description and return success.
 */
static int
mypci_probe(device_t dev)
{

 device_printf(dev, "MyPCI Probe\nVendor ID : 0x%x\nDevice ID : 0x%x\n",
     pci_get_vendor(dev), pci_get_device(dev));

 if (pci_get_vendor(dev) == 0x11c1) {
  printf("We've got the Winmodem, probe successful!\n");
  device_set_desc(dev, "WinModem");
  return (BUS_PROBE_DEFAULT);
 }
 return (ENXIO);
}
```

```
/* Attach function is only called if the probe is successful. */

static int
mypci_attach(device_t dev)
{
 struct mypci_softc *sc;

 printf("MyPCI Attach for : deviceID : 0x%x\n", pci_get_devid(dev));

 /* Look up our softc and initialize its fields. */
 sc = device_get_softc(dev);
 sc->my_dev = dev;

 /*
  * Create a /dev entry for this device.  The kernel will assign us
  * a major number automatically.  We use the unit number of this
  * device as the minor number and name the character device
  * "mypci<unit>".
  */
 sc->my_cdev = make_dev(&mypci_cdevsw, device_get_unit(dev),
     UID_ROOT, GID_WHEEL, 0600, "mypci%u", device_get_unit(dev));
 sc->my_cdev->si_drv1 = sc;
 printf("Mypci device loaded.\n");
 return (0);
}

/* Detach device. */

static int
mypci_detach(device_t dev)
{
 struct mypci_softc *sc;

 /* Teardown the state in our softc created in our attach routine. */
 sc = device_get_softc(dev);
 destroy_dev(sc->my_cdev);
 printf("Mypci detach!\n");
 return (0);
}

/* Called during system shutdown after sync. */

static int
mypci_shutdown(device_t dev)
{

 printf("Mypci shutdown!\n");
 return (0);
}

/*
 * Device suspend routine.
 */
static int
mypci_suspend(device_t dev)
{

 printf("Mypci suspend!\n");
 return (0);
}

/*
 * Device resume routine.
 */
static int
mypci_resume(device_t dev)
```

```
{
  printf("Mypci resume!\n");
  return (0);
}

static device_method_t mypci_methods[] = {
  /* Device interface */
  DEVMETHOD(device_probe,    mypci_probe),
  DEVMETHOD(device_attach,   mypci_attach),
  DEVMETHOD(device_detach,   mypci_detach),
  DEVMETHOD(device_shutdown, mypci_shutdown),
  DEVMETHOD(device_suspend,  mypci_suspend),
  DEVMETHOD(device_resume,   mypci_resume),

  DEVMETHOD_END
};

static devclass_t mypci_devclass;

DEFINE_CLASS_0(mypci, mypci_driver, mypci_methods, sizeof(struct mypci_softc));
DRIVER_MODULE(mypci, pci, mypci_driver, mypci_devclass, 0, 0);
```

11.1.2. Makefile for Sample Driver

```
# Makefile for mypci driver

KMOD= mypci
SRCS= mypci.c
SRCS+= device_if.h bus_if.h pci_if.h

.include <bsd.kmod.mk>
```

If you place the above source file and `Makefile` into a directory, you may run `make` to compile the sample driver. Additionally, you may run `make load` to load the driver into the currently running kernel and `make unload` to unload the driver after it is loaded.

11.1.3. Additional Resources

• PCI Special Interest Group

• PCI System Architecture, Fourth Edition by Tom Shanley, et al.

11.2. Bus Resources

FreeBSD provides an object-oriented mechanism for requesting resources from a parent bus. Almost all devices will be a child member of some sort of bus (PCI, ISA, USB, SCSI, etc) and these devices need to acquire resources from their parent bus (such as memory segments, interrupt lines, or DMA channels).

11.2.1. Base Address Registers

To do anything particularly useful with a PCI device you will need to obtain the *Base Address Registers* (BARs) from the PCI Configuration space. The PCI-specific details of obtaining the BAR are abstracted in the `bus_alloc_resource()` function.

For example, a typical driver might have something similar to this in the `attach()` function:

```
    sc->bar0id = PCIR_BAR(0);
    sc->bar0res = bus_alloc_resource(dev, SYS_RES_MEMORY, &sc->bar0id,
      0, ~0, 1, RF_ACTIVE);
    if (sc->bar0res == NULL) {
```

```
        printf("Memory allocation of PCI base register 0 failed!\n");
        error = ENXIO;
        goto fail1;
    }

    sc->bar1id = PCIR_BAR(1);
    sc->bar1res = bus_alloc_resource(dev, SYS_RES_MEMORY, &sc->bar1id,
       0, ~0, 1, RF_ACTIVE);
    if (sc->bar1res == NULL) {
        printf("Memory allocation of PCI base register 1 failed!\n");
        error =  ENXIO;
        goto fail2;
    }
    sc->bar0_bt = rman_get_bustag(sc->bar0res);
    sc->bar0_bh = rman_get_bushandle(sc->bar0res);
    sc->bar1_bt = rman_get_bustag(sc->bar1res);
    sc->bar1_bh = rman_get_bushandle(sc->bar1res);
```

Handles for each base address register are kept in the **softc** structure so that they can be used to write to the device later.

These handles can then be used to read or write from the device registers with the **bus_space_*** functions. For example, a driver might contain a shorthand function to read from a board specific register like this:

```
uint16_t
board_read(struct ni_softc *sc, uint16_t address)
{
    return bus_space_read_2(sc->bar1_bt, sc->bar1_bh, address);
}
```

Similarly, one could write to the registers with:

```
void
board_write(struct ni_softc *sc, uint16_t address, uint16_t value)
{
    bus_space_write_2(sc->bar1_bt, sc->bar1_bh, address, value);
}
```

These functions exist in 8bit, 16bit, and 32bit versions and you should use **bus_space_{read|write}_{1|2|4}** accordingly.

> **Note**
>
> In FreeBSD 7.0 and later, you can use the **bus_*** functions instead of **bus_space_*** . The **bus_*** functions take a struct resource * pointer instead of a bus tag and handle. Thus, you could drop the bus tag and bus handle members from the **softc** and rewrite the **board_read()** function as:
>
> ```
> uint16_t
> board_read(struct ni_softc *sc, uint16_t address)
> {
>   return (bus_read(sc->bar1res, address));
> }
> ```

11.2.2. Interrupts

Interrupts are allocated from the object-oriented bus code in a way similar to the memory resources. First an IRQ resource must be allocated from the parent bus, and then the interrupt handler must be set up to deal with this IRQ.

Again, a sample from a device **attach()** function says more than words.

```
/* Get the IRQ resource */

    sc->irqid = 0x0;
    sc->irqres = bus_alloc_resource(dev, SYS_RES_IRQ, &(sc->irqid),
      0, ~0, 1, RF_SHAREABLE | RF_ACTIVE);
    if (sc->irqres == NULL) {
printf("IRQ allocation failed!\n");
error = ENXIO;
goto fail3;
    }

    /* Now we should set up the interrupt handler */

    error = bus_setup_intr(dev, sc->irqres, INTR_TYPE_MISC,
      my_handler, sc, &(sc->handler));
    if (error) {
printf("Couldn't set up irq\n");
goto fail4;
    }
```

Some care must be taken in the detach routine of the driver. You must quiesce the device's interrupt stream, and remove the interrupt handler. Once `bus_teardown_intr()` has returned, you know that your interrupt handler will no longer be called and that all threads that might have been executing this interrupt handler have returned. Since this function can sleep, you must not hold any mutexes when calling this function.

11.2.3. DMA

This section is obsolete, and present only for historical reasons. The proper methods for dealing with these issues is to use the **bus_space_dma*()** functions instead. This paragraph can be removed when this section is updated to reflect that usage. However, at the moment, the API is in a bit of flux, so once that settles down, it would be good to update this section to reflect that.

On the PC, peripherals that want to do bus-mastering DMA must deal with physical addresses. This is a problem since FreeBSD uses virtual memory and deals almost exclusively with virtual addresses. Fortunately, there is a function, **vtophys()** to help.

```
#include <vm/vm.h>
#include <vm/pmap.h>

#define vtophys(virtual_address) (...)
```

The solution is a bit different on the alpha however, and what we really want is a function called **vtobus()**.

```
#if defined(__alpha__)
#define vtobus(va)        alpha_XXX_dmamap((vm_offset_t)va)
#else
#define vtobus(va)        vtophys(va)
#endif
```

11.2.4. Deallocating Resources

It is very important to deallocate all of the resources that were allocated during **attach()**. Care must be taken to deallocate the correct stuff even on a failure condition so that the system will remain usable while your driver dies.

Chapter 12. Common Access Method SCSI Controllers

Written by Sergey Babkin.
Modifications for Handbook made by Murray Stokely.

12.1. Synopsis

This document assumes that the reader has a general understanding of device drivers in FreeBSD and of the SCSI protocol. Much of the information in this document was extracted from the drivers:

- ncr (/sys/pci/ncr.c) by Wolfgang Stanglmeier and Stefan Esser

- sym (/sys/dev/sym/sym_hipd.c) by Gerard Roudier

- aic7xxx (/sys/dev/aic7xxx/aic7xxx.c) by Justin T. Gibbs

and from the CAM code itself (by Justin T. Gibbs, see /sys/cam/*). When some solution looked the most logical and was essentially verbatim extracted from the code by Justin T. Gibbs, I marked it as "recommended".

The document is illustrated with examples in pseudo-code. Although sometimes the examples have many details and look like real code, it is still pseudo-code. It was written to demonstrate the concepts in an understandable way. For a real driver other approaches may be more modular and efficient. It also abstracts from the hardware details, as well as issues that would cloud the demonstrated concepts or that are supposed to be described in the other chapters of the developers handbook. Such details are commonly shown as calls to functions with descriptive names, comments or pseudo-statements. Fortunately real life full-size examples with all the details can be found in the real drivers.

12.2. General Architecture

CAM stands for Common Access Method. It is a generic way to address the I/O buses in a SCSI-like way. This allows a separation of the generic device drivers from the drivers controlling the I/O bus: for example the disk driver becomes able to control disks on both SCSI, IDE, and/or any other bus so the disk driver portion does not have to be rewritten (or copied and modified) for every new I/O bus. Thus the two most important active entities are:

- *Peripheral Modules* - a driver for peripheral devices (disk, tape, CD-ROM, etc.)

- *SCSI Interface Modules* (SIM) - a Host Bus Adapter drivers for connecting to an I/O bus such as SCSI or IDE.

A peripheral driver receives requests from the OS, converts them to a sequence of SCSI commands and passes these SCSI commands to a SCSI Interface Module. The SCSI Interface Module is responsible for passing these commands to the actual hardware (or if the actual hardware is not SCSI but, for example, IDE then also converting the SCSI commands to the native commands of the hardware).

Because we are interested in writing a SCSI adapter driver here, from this point on we will consider everything from the SIM standpoint.

A typical SIM driver needs to include the following CAM-related header files:

```
#include <cam/cam.h>
#include <cam/cam_ccb.h>
#include <cam/cam_sim.h>
#include <cam/cam_xpt_sim.h>
#include <cam/cam_debug.h>
```

```
#include <cam/scsi/scsi_all.h>
```

The first thing each SIM driver must do is register itself with the CAM subsystem. This is done during the driver's **xxx_attach()** function (here and further xxx_ is used to denote the unique driver name prefix). The **xxx_attach()** function itself is called by the system bus auto-configuration code which we do not describe here.

This is achieved in multiple steps: first it is necessary to allocate the queue of requests associated with this SIM:

```
struct cam_devq *devq;

if(( devq = cam_simq_alloc(SIZE) )==NULL) {
    error; /* some code to handle the error */
}
```

Here **SIZE** is the size of the queue to be allocated, maximal number of requests it could contain. It is the number of requests that the SIM driver can handle in parallel on one SCSI card. Commonly it can be calculated as:

```
SIZE = NUMBER_OF_SUPPORTED_TARGETS * MAX_SIMULTANEOUS_COMMANDS_PER_TARGET
```

Next we create a descriptor of our SIM:

```
struct cam_sim *sim;

if(( sim = cam_sim_alloc(action_func, poll_func, driver_name,
        softc, unit, mtx, max_dev_transactions,
        max_tagged_dev_transactions, devq) )==NULL) {
    cam_simq_free(devq);
    error; /* some code to handle the error */
}
```

Note that if we are not able to create a SIM descriptor we free the **devq** also because we can do nothing else with it and we want to conserve memory.

If a SCSI card has multiple SCSI buses on it then each bus requires its own **cam_sim** structure.

An interesting question is what to do if a SCSI card has more than one SCSI bus, do we need one **devq** structure per card or per SCSI bus? The answer given in the comments to the CAM code is: either way, as the driver's author prefers.

The arguments are:

- action_func - pointer to the driver's **xxx_action** function.

  static void **xxx_action** (*struct cam_sim *sim, union ccb *ccb*);

  *struct cam_sim *sim, , union ccb *ccb* ;

- poll_func - pointer to the driver's **xxx_poll()**

  static void **xxx_poll** (*struct cam_sim *sim*);

  *struct cam_sim *sim* ;

- driver_name - the name of the actual driver, such as "ncr" or "wds".

- softc - pointer to the driver's internal descriptor for this SCSI card. This pointer will be used by the driver in future to get private data.

- unit - the controller unit number, for example for controller "mps0" this number will be 0

- mtx - Lock associated with this SIM. For SIMs that don't know about locking, pass in Giant. For SIMs that do, pass in the lock used to guard this SIM's data structures. This lock will be held when xxx_action and xxx_poll are called.

- max_dev_transactions - maximal number of simultaneous transactions per SCSI target in the non-tagged mode. This value will be almost universally equal to 1, with possible exceptions only for the non-SCSI cards. Also the drivers that hope to take advantage by preparing one transaction while another one is executed may set it to 2 but this does not seem to be worth the complexity.

- max_tagged_dev_transactions - the same thing, but in the tagged mode. Tags are the SCSI way to initiate multiple transactions on a device: each transaction is assigned a unique tag and the transaction is sent to the device. When the device completes some transaction it sends back the result together with the tag so that the SCSI adapter (and the driver) can tell which transaction was completed. This argument is also known as the maximal tag depth. It depends on the abilities of the SCSI adapter.

Finally we register the SCSI buses associated with our SCSI adapter:

```
if(xpt_bus_register(sim, softc, bus_number) != CAM_SUCCESS) {
    cam_sim_free(sim, /*free_devq*/ TRUE);
    error; /* some code to handle the error */
}
```

If there is one **devq** structure per SCSI bus (i.e., we consider a card with multiple buses as multiple cards with one bus each) then the bus number will always be 0, otherwise each bus on the SCSI card should be get a distinct number. Each bus needs its own separate structure cam_sim.

After that our controller is completely hooked to the CAM system. The value of **devq** can be discarded now: sim will be passed as an argument in all further calls from CAM and devq can be derived from it.

CAM provides the framework for such asynchronous events. Some events originate from the lower levels (the SIM drivers), some events originate from the peripheral drivers, some events originate from the CAM subsystem itself. Any driver can register callbacks for some types of the asynchronous events, so that it would be notified if these events occur.

A typical example of such an event is a device reset. Each transaction and event identifies the devices to which it applies by the means of "path". The target-specific events normally occur during a transaction with this device. So the path from that transaction may be re-used to report this event (this is safe because the event path is copied in the event reporting routine but not deallocated nor passed anywhere further). Also it is safe to allocate paths dynamically at any time including the interrupt routines, although that incurs certain overhead, and a possible problem with this approach is that there may be no free memory at that time. For a bus reset event we need to define a wildcard path including all devices on the bus. So we can create the path for the future bus reset events in advance and avoid problems with the future memory shortage:

```
struct cam_path *path;

if(xpt_create_path(&path, /*periph*/NULL,
            cam_sim_path(sim), CAM_TARGET_WILDCARD,
            CAM_LUN_WILDCARD) != CAM_REQ_CMP) {
    xpt_bus_deregister(cam_sim_path(sim));
    cam_sim_free(sim, /*free_devq*/TRUE);
    error; /* some code to handle the error */
}

softc->wpath = path;
softc->sim = sim;
```

As you can see the path includes:

- ID of the peripheral driver (NULL here because we have none)

- ID of the SIM driver (cam_sim_path(sim))

- SCSI target number of the device (CAM_TARGET_WILDCARD means "all devices")

- SCSI LUN number of the subdevice (CAM_LUN_WILDCARD means "all LUNs")

If the driver can not allocate this path it will not be able to work normally, so in that case we dismantle that SCSI bus.

And we save the path pointer in the softc structure for future use. After that we save the value of sim (or we can also discard it on the exit from xxx_probe() if we wish).

That is all for a minimalistic initialization. To do things right there is one more issue left.

For a SIM driver there is one particularly interesting event: when a target device is considered lost. In this case resetting the SCSI negotiations with this device may be a good idea. So we register a callback for this event with CAM. The request is passed to CAM by requesting CAM action on a CAM control block for this type of request:

```
struct ccb_setasync csa;

xpt_setup_ccb(&csa.ccb_h, path, /*priority*/5);
csa.ccb_h.func_code = XPT_SASYNC_CB;
csa.event_enable = AC_LOST_DEVICE;
csa.callback = xxx_async;
csa.callback_arg = sim;
xpt_action((union ccb *)&csa);
```

Now we take a look at the xxx_action() and xxx_poll() driver entry points.

static void **xxx_action** (*struct cam_sim *sim, union ccb *ccb*);

*struct cam_sim *sim, , union ccb *ccb ;*

Do some action on request of the CAM subsystem. Sim describes the SIM for the request, CCB is the request itself. CCB stands for "CAM Control Block". It is a union of many specific instances, each describing arguments for some type of transactions. All of these instances share the CCB header where the common part of arguments is stored.

CAM supports the SCSI controllers working in both initiator ("normal") mode and target (simulating a SCSI device) mode. Here we only consider the part relevant to the initiator mode.

There are a few function and macros (in other words, methods) defined to access the public data in the struct sim:

- cam_sim_path(sim) - the path ID (see above)

- cam_sim_name(sim) - the name of the sim

- cam_sim_softc(sim) - the pointer to the softc (driver private data) structure

- cam_sim_unit(sim) - the unit number

- cam_sim_bus(sim) - the bus ID

To identify the device, xxx_action() can get the unit number and pointer to its structure softc using these functions.

The type of request is stored in ccb->ccb_h.func_code . So generally xxx_action() consists of a big switch:

```
struct xxx_softc *softc = (struct xxx_softc *) cam_sim_softc(sim);
struct ccb_hdr *ccb_h = &ccb->ccb_h;
int unit = cam_sim_unit(sim);
int bus = cam_sim_bus(sim);

switch(ccb_h->func_code) {
case ...:
    ...
default:
    ccb_h->status = CAM_REQ_INVALID;
    xpt_done(ccb);
    break;
}
```

As can be seen from the default case (if an unknown command was received) the return code of the command is set into ccb->ccb_h.status and the completed CCB is returned back to CAM by calling xpt_done(ccb).

xpt_done() does not have to be called from xxx_action(): For example an I/O request may be enqueued inside the SIM driver and/or its SCSI controller. Then when the device would post an interrupt signaling that the processing of this request is complete xpt_done() may be called from the interrupt handling routine.

Actually, the CCB status is not only assigned as a return code but a CCB has some status all the time. Before CCB is passed to the xxx_action() routine it gets the status CCB_REQ_INPROG meaning that it is in progress. There are a surprising number of status values defined in /sys/cam/cam.h which should be able to represent the status of a request in great detail. More interesting yet, the status is in fact a "bitwise or" of an enumerated status value (the lower 6 bits) and possible additional flag-like bits (the upper bits). The enumerated values will be discussed later in more detail. The summary of them can be found in the Errors Summary section. The possible status flags are:

- *CAM_DEV_QFRZN* - if the SIM driver gets a serious error (for example, the device does not respond to the selection or breaks the SCSI protocol) when processing a CCB it should freeze the request queue by calling xpt_freeze_simq(), return the other enqueued but not processed yet CCBs for this device back to the CAM queue, then set this flag for the troublesome CCB and call xpt_done(). This flag causes the CAM subsystem to unfreeze the queue after it handles the error.

- *CAM_AUTOSNS_VALID* - if the device returned an error condition and the flag CAM_DIS_AUTOSENSE is not set in CCB the SIM driver must execute the REQUEST SENSE command automatically to extract the sense (extended error information) data from the device. If this attempt was successful the sense data should be saved in the CCB and this flag set.

- *CAM_RELEASE_SIMQ* - like CAM_DEV_QFRZN but used in case there is some problem (or resource shortage) with the SCSI controller itself. Then all the future requests to the controller should be stopped by xpt_freeze_simq(). The controller queue will be restarted after the SIM driver overcomes the shortage and informs CAM by returning some CCB with this flag set.

- *CAM_SIM_QUEUED* - when SIM puts a CCB into its request queue this flag should be set (and removed when this CCB gets dequeued before being returned back to CAM). This flag is not used anywhere in the CAM code now, so its purpose is purely diagnostic.

- *CAM_QOS_VALID* - The QOS data is now valid.

The function xxx_action() is not allowed to sleep, so all the synchronization for resource access must be done using SIM or device queue freezing. Besides the aforementioned flags the CAM subsystem provides functions xpt_release_simq() and xpt_release_devq() to unfreeze the queues directly, without passing a CCB to CAM.

The CCB header contains the following fields:

- *path* - path ID for the request

- *target_id* - target device ID for the request

- *target_lun* - LUN ID of the target device

- *timeout* - timeout interval for this command, in milliseconds

- *timeout_ch* - a convenience place for the SIM driver to store the timeout handle (the CAM subsystem itself does not make any assumptions about it)

- *flags* - various bits of information about the request spriv_ptr0, spriv_ptr1 - fields reserved for private use by the SIM driver (such as linking to the SIM queues or SIM private control blocks); actually, they exist as unions: spriv_ptr0 and spriv_ptr1 have the type (void *), spriv_field0 and spriv_field1 have the type unsigned long, sim_priv.entries[0].bytes and sim_priv.entries[1].bytes are byte arrays of the size consistent with the other incarnations of the union and sim_priv.bytes is one array, twice bigger.

The recommended way of using the SIM private fields of CCB is to define some meaningful names for them and use these meaningful names in the driver, like:

```
#define ccb_some_meaningful_name    sim_priv.entries[0].bytes
#define ccb_hcb spriv_ptr1 /* for hardware control block */
```

The most common initiator mode requests are:

• *XPT_SCSI_IO* - execute an I/O transaction

The instance "struct ccb_scsiio csio" of the union ccb is used to transfer the arguments. They are:

• *cdb_io* - pointer to the SCSI command buffer or the buffer itself

• *cdb_len* - SCSI command length

• *data_ptr* - pointer to the data buffer (gets a bit complicated if scatter/gather is used)

• *dxfer_len* - length of the data to transfer

• *sglist_cnt* - counter of the scatter/gather segments

• *scsi_status* - place to return the SCSI status

• *sense_data* - buffer for the SCSI sense information if the command returns an error (the SIM driver is supposed to run the REQUEST SENSE command automatically in this case if the CCB flag CAM_DIS_AUTOSENSE is not set)

• *sense_len* - the length of that buffer (if it happens to be higher than size of sense_data the SIM driver must silently assume the smaller value) resid, sense_resid - if the transfer of data or SCSI sense returned an error these are the returned counters of the residual (not transferred) data. They do not seem to be especially meaningful, so in a case when they are difficult to compute (say, counting bytes in the SCSI controller's FIFO buffer) an approximate value will do as well. For a successfully completed transfer they must be set to zero.

• *tag_action* - the kind of tag to use:

  • CAM_TAG_ACTION_NONE - do not use tags for this transaction

  • MSG_SIMPLE_Q_TAG, MSG_HEAD_OF_Q_TAG, MSG_ORDERED_Q_TAG - value equal to the appropriate tag message (see /sys/cam/scsi/scsi_message.h); this gives only the tag type, the SIM driver must assign the tag value itself

The general logic of handling this request is the following:

The first thing to do is to check for possible races, to make sure that the command did not get aborted when it was sitting in the queue:

```
struct ccb_scsiio *csio = &ccb->csio;

if ((ccb_h->status & CAM_STATUS_MASK) != CAM_REQ_INPROG) {
    xpt_done(ccb);
    return;
}
```

Also we check that the device is supported at all by our controller:

```
if(ccb_h->target_id > OUR_MAX_SUPPORTED_TARGET_ID
|| cch_h->target_id == OUR_SCSI_CONTROLLERS_OWN_ID) {
    ccb_h->status = CAM_TID_INVALID;
    xpt_done(ccb);
    return;
}
if(ccb_h->target_lun > OUR_MAX_SUPPORTED_LUN) {
```

```
        ccb_h->status = CAM_LUN_INVALID;
        xpt_done(ccb);
        return;
    }
```

Then allocate whatever data structures (such as card-dependent hardware control block) we need to process this request. If we can not then freeze the SIM queue and remember that we have a pending operation, return the CCB back and ask CAM to re-queue it. Later when the resources become available the SIM queue must be unfrozen by returning a ccb with the CAM_SIMQ_RELEASE bit set in its status. Otherwise, if all went well, link the CCB with the hardware control block (HCB) and mark it as queued.

```
    struct xxx_hcb *hcb = allocate_hcb(softc, unit, bus);

    if(hcb == NULL) {
        softc->flags |= RESOURCE_SHORTAGE;
        xpt_freeze_simq(sim, /*count*/1);
        ccb_h->status = CAM_REQUEUE_REQ;
        xpt_done(ccb);
        return;
    }

    hcb->ccb = ccb; ccb_h->ccb_hcb = (void *)hcb;
    ccb_h->status |= CAM_SIM_QUEUED;
```

Extract the target data from CCB into the hardware control block. Check if we are asked to assign a tag and if yes then generate an unique tag and build the SCSI tag messages. The SIM driver is also responsible for negotiations with the devices to set the maximal mutually supported bus width, synchronous rate and offset.

```
    hcb->target = ccb_h->target_id; hcb->lun = ccb_h->target_lun;
    generate_identify_message(hcb);
    if( ccb_h->tag_action != CAM_TAG_ACTION_NONE )
        generate_unique_tag_message(hcb, ccb_h->tag_action);
    if( !target_negotiated(hcb) )
        generate_negotiation_messages(hcb);
```

Then set up the SCSI command. The command storage may be specified in the CCB in many interesting ways, specified by the CCB flags. The command buffer can be contained in CCB or pointed to, in the latter case the pointer may be physical or virtual. Since the hardware commonly needs physical address we always convert the address to the physical one, typically using the busdma API.

In case if a physical address is requested it is OK to return the CCB with the status CAM_REQ_INVALID, the current drivers do that. If necessary a physical address can be also converted or mapped back to a virtual address but with big pain, so we do not do that.

```
    if(ccb_h->flags & CAM_CDB_POINTER) {
        /* CDB is a pointer */
        if(!(ccb_h->flags & CAM_CDB_PHYS)) {
            /* CDB pointer is virtual */
            hcb->cmd = vtobus(csio->cdb_io.cdb_ptr);
        } else {
            /* CDB pointer is physical */
            hcb->cmd = csio->cdb_io.cdb_ptr -;
        }
    } else {
        /* CDB is in the ccb (buffer) */
        hcb->cmd = vtobus(csio->cdb_io.cdb_bytes);
    }
    hcb->cmdlen = csio->cdb_len;
```

Now it is time to set up the data. Again, the data storage may be specified in the CCB in many interesting ways, specified by the CCB flags. First we get the direction of the data transfer. The simplest case is if there is no data to transfer:

```
int dir = (ccb_h->flags & CAM_DIR_MASK);

if (dir == CAM_DIR_NONE)
    goto end_data;
```

Then we check if the data is in one chunk or in a scatter-gather list, and the addresses are physical or virtual. The SCSI controller may be able to handle only a limited number of chunks of limited length. If the request hits this limitation we return an error. We use a special function to return the CCB to handle in one place the HCB resource shortages. The functions to add chunks are driver-dependent, and here we leave them without detailed implementation. See description of the SCSI command (CDB) handling for the details on the address-translation issues. If some variation is too difficult or impossible to implement with a particular card it is OK to return the status CAM_REQ_INVALID. Actually, it seems like the scatter-gather ability is not used anywhere in the CAM code now. But at least the case for a single non-scattered virtual buffer must be implemented, it is actively used by CAM.

```
int rv;

initialize_hcb_for_data(hcb);

if((!(ccb_h->flags & CAM_SCATTER_VALID)) {
    /* single buffer */
    if(!(ccb_h->flags & CAM_DATA_PHYS)) {
        rv = add_virtual_chunk(hcb, csio->data_ptr, csio->dxfer_len, dir);
        }
    } else {
        rv = add_physical_chunk(hcb, csio->data_ptr, csio->dxfer_len, dir);
    }
} else {
    int i;
    struct bus_dma_segment *segs;
    segs = (struct bus_dma_segment *)csio->data_ptr;

    if ((ccb_h->flags & CAM_SG_LIST_PHYS) != 0) {
        /* The SG list pointer is physical */
        rv = setup_hcb_for_physical_sg_list(hcb, segs, csio->sglist_cnt);
    } else if (!(ccb_h->flags & CAM_DATA_PHYS)) {
        /* SG buffer pointers are virtual */
        for (i = 0; i < csio->sglist_cnt; i++) {
            rv = add_virtual_chunk(hcb, segs[i].ds_addr,
                segs[i].ds_len, dir);
            if (rv != CAM_REQ_CMP)
                break;
        }
    } else {
        /* SG buffer pointers are physical */
        for (i = 0; i < csio->sglist_cnt; i++) {
            rv = add_physical_chunk(hcb, segs[i].ds_addr,
                segs[i].ds_len, dir);
            if (rv != CAM_REQ_CMP)
                break;
        }
    }
}
if(rv != CAM_REQ_CMP) {
    /* we expect that add_*_chunk() functions return CAM_REQ_CMP
     * if they added a chunk successfully, CAM_REQ_TOO_BIG if
     * the request is too big (too many bytes or too many chunks),
     * CAM_REQ_INVALID in case of other troubles
     */
    free_hcb_and_ccb_done(hcb, ccb, rv);
    return;
}
end_data:
```

If disconnection is disabled for this CCB we pass this information to the hcb:

```
if(ccb_h->flags & CAM_DIS_DISCONNECT)
    hcb_disable_disconnect(hcb);
```

If the controller is able to run REQUEST SENSE command all by itself then the value of the flag CAM_DIS_AU-TOSENSE should also be passed to it, to prevent automatic REQUEST SENSE if the CAM subsystem does not want it.

The only thing left is to set up the timeout, pass our hcb to the hardware and return, the rest will be done by the interrupt handler (or timeout handler).

```
ccb_h->timeout_ch = timeout(xxx_timeout, (caddr_t) hcb,
    (ccb_h->timeout * hz) / 1000); /* convert milliseconds to ticks */
put_hcb_into_hardware_queue(hcb);
return;
```

And here is a possible implementation of the function returning CCB:

```
static void
free_hcb_and_ccb_done(struct xxx_hcb *hcb, union ccb *ccb, u_int32_t status)
{
    struct xxx_softc *softc = hcb->softc;

    ccb->ccb_h.ccb_hcb = 0;
    if(hcb != NULL) {
        untimeout(xxx_timeout, (caddr_t) hcb, ccb->ccb_h.timeout_ch);
        /* we're about to free a hcb, so the shortage has ended */
        if(softc->flags & RESOURCE_SHORTAGE) {
            softc->flags &= ~RESOURCE_SHORTAGE;
            status |= CAM_RELEASE_SIMQ;
        }
        free_hcb(hcb); /* also removes hcb from any internal lists */
    }
    ccb->ccb_h.status = status |
        (ccb->ccb_h.status & ~(CAM_STATUS_MASK|CAM_SIM_QUEUED));
    xpt_done(ccb);
}
```

- *XPT_RESET_DEV* - send the SCSI "BUS DEVICE RESET" message to a device

There is no data transferred in CCB except the header and the most interesting argument of it is target_id. Depending on the controller hardware a hardware control block just like for the XPT_SCSI_IO request may be constructed (see XPT_SCSI_IO request description) and sent to the controller or the SCSI controller may be immediately programmed to send this RESET message to the device or this request may be just not supported (and return the status CAM_REQ_INVALID). Also on completion of the request all the disconnected transactions for this target must be aborted (probably in the interrupt routine).

Also all the current negotiations for the target are lost on reset, so they might be cleaned too. Or they clearing may be deferred, because anyway the target would request re-negotiation on the next transaction.

- *XPT_RESET_BUS* - send the RESET signal to the SCSI bus

No arguments are passed in the CCB, the only interesting argument is the SCSI bus indicated by the struct sim pointer.

A minimalistic implementation would forget the SCSI negotiations for all the devices on the bus and return the status CAM_REQ_CMP.

The proper implementation would in addition actually reset the SCSI bus (possible also reset the SCSI controller) and mark all the CCBs being processed, both those in the hardware queue and those being disconnected, as done with the status CAM_SCSI_BUS_RESET. Like:

```
int targ, lun;
struct xxx_hcb *h, *hh;
struct ccb_trans_settings neg;
struct cam_path *path;

/* The SCSI bus reset may take a long time, in this case its completion
 * should be checked by interrupt or timeout. But for simplicity
 * we assume here that it is really fast.
 */
reset_scsi_bus(softc);

/* drop all enqueued CCBs */
for(h = softc->first_queued_hcb; h != NULL; h = hh) {
    hh = h->next;
    free_hcb_and_ccb_done(h, h->ccb, CAM_SCSI_BUS_RESET);
}

/* the clean values of negotiations to report */
neg.bus_width = 8;
neg.sync_period = neg.sync_offset = 0;
neg.valid = (CCB_TRANS_BUS_WIDTH_VALID
    | CCB_TRANS_SYNC_RATE_VALID | CCB_TRANS_SYNC_OFFSET_VALID);

/* drop all disconnected CCBs and clean negotiations  */
for(targ=0; targ <= OUR_MAX_SUPPORTED_TARGET; targ++) {
    clean_negotiations(softc, targ);

    /* report the event if possible */
    if(xpt_create_path(&path, /*periph*/NULL,
            cam_sim_path(sim), targ,
            CAM_LUN_WILDCARD) == CAM_REQ_CMP) {
        xpt_async(AC_TRANSFER_NEG, path, &neg);
        xpt_free_path(path);
    }

    for(lun=0; lun <= OUR_MAX_SUPPORTED_LUN; lun++)
        for(h = softc->first_discon_hcb[targ][lun]; h != NULL; h = hh) {
            hh=h->next;
            free_hcb_and_ccb_done(h, h->ccb, CAM_SCSI_BUS_RESET);
        }
}

ccb->ccb_h.status = CAM_REQ_CMP;
xpt_done(ccb);

/* report the event */
xpt_async(AC_BUS_RESET, softc->wpath, NULL);
return;
```

Implementing the SCSI bus reset as a function may be a good idea because it would be re-used by the timeout function as a last resort if the things go wrong.

• *XPT_ABORT* - abort the specified CCB

The arguments are transferred in the instance "struct ccb_abort cab" of the union ccb. The only argument field in it is:

abort_ccb - pointer to the CCB to be aborted

If the abort is not supported just return the status CAM_UA_ABORT. This is also the easy way to minimally implement this call, return CAM_UA_ABORT in any case.

The hard way is to implement this request honestly. First check that abort applies to a SCSI transaction:

```
struct ccb *abort_ccb;
abort_ccb = ccb->cab.abort_ccb;

if(abort_ccb->ccb_h.func_code != XPT_SCSI_IO) {
    ccb->ccb_h.status = CAM_UA_ABORT;
    xpt_done(ccb);
    return;
}
```

Then it is necessary to find this CCB in our queue. This can be done by walking the list of all our hardware control blocks in search for one associated with this CCB:

```
struct xxx_hcb *hcb, *h;

hcb = NULL;

/* We assume that softc->first_hcb is the head of the list of all
 * HCBs associated with this bus, including those enqueued for
 * processing, being processed by hardware and disconnected ones.
 */
for(h = softc->first_hcb; h != NULL; h = h->next) {
    if(h->ccb == abort_ccb) {
        hcb = h;
        break;
    }
}

if(hcb == NULL) {
    /* no such CCB in our queue */
    ccb->ccb_h.status = CAM_PATH_INVALID;
    xpt_done(ccb);
    return;
}

hcb=found_hcb;
```

Now we look at the current processing status of the HCB. It may be either sitting in the queue waiting to be sent to the SCSI bus, being transferred right now, or disconnected and waiting for the result of the command, or actually completed by hardware but not yet marked as done by software. To make sure that we do not get in any races with hardware we mark the HCB as being aborted, so that if this HCB is about to be sent to the SCSI bus the SCSI controller will see this flag and skip it.

```
int hstatus;

/* shown as a function, in case special action is needed to make
 * this flag visible to hardware
 */
set_hcb_flags(hcb, HCB_BEING_ABORTED);

abort_again:

hstatus = get_hcb_status(hcb);
switch(hstatus) {
case HCB_SITTING_IN_QUEUE:
    remove_hcb_from_hardware_queue(hcb);
    /* FALLTHROUGH */
case HCB_COMPLETED:
    /* this is an easy case */
    free_hcb_and_ccb_done(hcb, abort_ccb, CAM_REQ_ABORTED);
```

```
        break;
```

If the CCB is being transferred right now we would like to signal to the SCSI controller in some hardware-dependent way that we want to abort the current transfer. The SCSI controller would set the SCSI ATTENTION signal and when the target responds to it send an ABORT message. We also reset the timeout to make sure that the target is not sleeping forever. If the command would not get aborted in some reasonable time like 10 seconds the timeout routine would go ahead and reset the whole SCSI bus. Because the command will be aborted in some reasonable time we can just return the abort request now as successfully completed, and mark the aborted CCB as aborted (but not mark it as done yet).

```
case HCB_BEING_TRANSFERRED:
    untimeout(xxx_timeout, (caddr_t) hcb, abort_ccb->ccb_h.timeout_ch);
    abort_ccb->ccb_h.timeout_ch =
        timeout(xxx_timeout, (caddr_t) hcb, 10 * hz);
    abort_ccb->ccb_h.status = CAM_REQ_ABORTED;
    /* ask the controller to abort that HCB, then generate
     * an interrupt and stop
     */
    if(signal_hardware_to_abort_hcb_and_stop(hcb) < 0) {
        /* oops, we missed the race with hardware, this transaction
         * got off the bus before we aborted it, try again */
        goto abort_again;
    }

    break;
```

If the CCB is in the list of disconnected then set it up as an abort request and re-queue it at the front of hardware queue. Reset the timeout and report the abort request to be completed.

```
case HCB_DISCONNECTED:
    untimeout(xxx_timeout, (caddr_t) hcb, abort_ccb->ccb_h.timeout_ch);
    abort_ccb->ccb_h.timeout_ch =
        timeout(xxx_timeout, (caddr_t) hcb, 10 * hz);
    put_abort_message_into_hcb(hcb);
    put_hcb_at_the_front_of_hardware_queue(hcb);
    break;
}
ccb->ccb_h.status = CAM_REQ_CMP;
xpt_done(ccb);
return;
```

That is all for the ABORT request, although there is one more issue. Because the ABORT message cleans all the ongoing transactions on a LUN we have to mark all the other active transactions on this LUN as aborted. That should be done in the interrupt routine, after the transaction gets aborted.

Implementing the CCB abort as a function may be quite a good idea, this function can be re-used if an I/O transaction times out. The only difference would be that the timed out transaction would return the status CAM_CMD_TIMEOUT for the timed out request. Then the case XPT_ABORT would be small, like that:

```
case XPT_ABORT:
    struct ccb *abort_ccb;
    abort_ccb = ccb->cab.abort_ccb;

    if(abort_ccb->ccb_h.func_code != XPT_SCSI_IO) {
        ccb->ccb_h.status = CAM_UA_ABORT;
        xpt_done(ccb);
        return;
    }
    if(xxx_abort_ccb(abort_ccb, CAM_REQ_ABORTED) < 0)
        /* no such CCB in our queue */
        ccb->ccb_h.status = CAM_PATH_INVALID;
    else
        ccb->ccb_h.status = CAM_REQ_CMP;
    xpt_done(ccb);
```

Chapter 12. Common Access Method SCSI Controllers

```
        return;
```

- *XPT_SET_TRAN_SETTINGS* - explicitly set values of SCSI transfer settings

  The arguments are transferred in the instance "struct ccb_trans_setting cts" of the union ccb:

  - *valid* - a bitmask showing which settings should be updated:

  - *CCB_TRANS_SYNC_RATE_VALID* - synchronous transfer rate

  - *CCB_TRANS_SYNC_OFFSET_VALID* - synchronous offset

  - *CCB_TRANS_BUS_WIDTH_VALID* - bus width

  - *CCB_TRANS_DISC_VALID* - set enable/disable disconnection

  - *CCB_TRANS_TQ_VALID* - set enable/disable tagged queuing

  - *flags* - consists of two parts, binary arguments and identification of sub-operations. The binary arguments are:

    - *CCB_TRANS_DISC_ENB* - enable disconnection

    - *CCB_TRANS_TAG_ENB* - enable tagged queuing

  - the sub-operations are:

    - *CCB_TRANS_CURRENT_SETTINGS* - change the current negotiations

    - *CCB_TRANS_USER_SETTINGS* - remember the desired user values sync_period, sync_offset - self-explanatory, if sync_offset==0 then the asynchronous mode is requested bus_width - bus width, in bits (not bytes)

Two sets of negotiated parameters are supported, the user settings and the current settings. The user settings are not really used much in the SIM drivers, this is mostly just a piece of memory where the upper levels can store (and later recall) its ideas about the parameters. Setting the user parameters does not cause re-negotiation of the transfer rates. But when the SCSI controller does a negotiation it must never set the values higher than the user parameters, so it is essentially the top boundary.

The current settings are, as the name says, current. Changing them means that the parameters must be re-negotiated on the next transfer. Again, these "new current settings" are not supposed to be forced on the device, just they are used as the initial step of negotiations. Also they must be limited by actual capabilities of the SCSI controller: for example, if the SCSI controller has 8-bit bus and the request asks to set 16-bit wide transfers this parameter must be silently truncated to 8-bit transfers before sending it to the device.

One caveat is that the bus width and synchronous parameters are per target while the disconnection and tag enabling parameters are per lun.

The recommended implementation is to keep 3 sets of negotiated (bus width and synchronous transfer) parameters:

- *user* - the user set, as above

- *current* - those actually in effect

- *goal* - those requested by setting of the "current" parameters

The code looks like:

```
    struct ccb_trans_settings *cts;
    int targ, lun;
    int flags;
```

```
        cts = &ccb->cts;
        targ = ccb_h->target_id;
        lun = ccb_h->target_lun;
        flags = cts->flags;
        if(flags & CCB_TRANS_USER_SETTINGS) {
            if(flags & CCB_TRANS_SYNC_RATE_VALID)
                softc->user_sync_period[targ] = cts->sync_period;
            if(flags & CCB_TRANS_SYNC_OFFSET_VALID)
                softc->user_sync_offset[targ] = cts->sync_offset;
            if(flags & CCB_TRANS_BUS_WIDTH_VALID)
                softc->user_bus_width[targ] = cts->bus_width;

            if(flags & CCB_TRANS_DISC_VALID) {
                softc->user_tflags[targ][lun] &= ~CCB_TRANS_DISC_ENB;
                softc->user_tflags[targ][lun] |= flags & CCB_TRANS_DISC_ENB;
            }
            if(flags & CCB_TRANS_TQ_VALID) {
                softc->user_tflags[targ][lun] &= ~CCB_TRANS_TQ_ENB;
                softc->user_tflags[targ][lun] |= flags & CCB_TRANS_TQ_ENB;
            }
        }
        if(flags & CCB_TRANS_CURRENT_SETTINGS) {
            if(flags & CCB_TRANS_SYNC_RATE_VALID)
                softc->goal_sync_period[targ] =
                    max(cts->sync_period, OUR_MIN_SUPPORTED_PERIOD);
            if(flags & CCB_TRANS_SYNC_OFFSET_VALID)
                softc->goal_sync_offset[targ] =
                    min(cts->sync_offset, OUR_MAX_SUPPORTED_OFFSET);
            if(flags & CCB_TRANS_BUS_WIDTH_VALID)
                softc->goal_bus_width[targ] = min(cts->bus_width, OUR_BUS_WIDTH);

            if(flags & CCB_TRANS_DISC_VALID) {
                softc->current_tflags[targ][lun] &= ~CCB_TRANS_DISC_ENB;
                softc->current_tflags[targ][lun] |= flags & CCB_TRANS_DISC_ENB;
            }
            if(flags & CCB_TRANS_TQ_VALID) {
                softc->current_tflags[targ][lun] &= ~CCB_TRANS_TQ_ENB;
                softc->current_tflags[targ][lun] |= flags & CCB_TRANS_TQ_ENB;
            }
        }
        ccb->ccb_h.status = CAM_REQ_CMP;
        xpt_done(ccb);
        return;
```

Then when the next I/O request will be processed it will check if it has to re-negotiate, for example by calling the function target_negotiated(hcb). It can be implemented like this:

```
int
target_negotiated(struct xxx_hcb *hcb)
{
    struct softc *softc = hcb->softc;
    int targ = hcb->targ;

    if( softc->current_sync_period[targ] != softc->goal_sync_period[targ]
     || softc->current_sync_offset[targ] != softc->goal_sync_offset[targ]
     || softc->current_bus_width[targ] != softc->goal_bus_width[targ] )
        return 0; /* FALSE */
    else
        return 1; /* TRUE */
}
```

After the values are re-negotiated the resulting values must be assigned to both current and goal parameters, so for future I/O transactions the current and goal parameters would be the same and target_negotiated() would return TRUE. When the card is initialized (in xxx_attach()) the current negotiation values must be initialized to narrow asynchronous mode, the goal and current values must be initialized to the maximal values supported by controller.

XPT_GET_TRAN_SETTINGS - get values of SCSI transfer settings

This operations is the reverse of XPT_SET_TRAN_SETTINGS. Fill up the CCB instance "struct ccb_trans_setting cts" with data as requested by the flags CCB_TRANS_CURRENT_SETTINGS or CCB_TRANS_USER_SETTINGS (if both are set then the existing drivers return the current settings). Set all the bits in the valid field.

XPT_CALC_GEOMETRY - calculate logical (BIOS) geometry of the disk

The arguments are transferred in the instance "struct ccb_calc_geometry ccg" of the union ccb:

- *block_size* - input, block (A.K.A sector) size in bytes

- *volume_size* - input, volume size in bytes

- *cylinders* - output, logical cylinders

- *heads* - output, logical heads

- *secs_per_track* - output, logical sectors per track

If the returned geometry differs much enough from what the SCSI controller BIOS thinks and a disk on this SCSI controller is used as bootable the system may not be able to boot. The typical calculation example taken from the aic7xxx driver is:

```
struct     ccb_calc_geometry *ccg;
u_int32_t size_mb;
u_int32_t secs_per_cylinder;
int    extended;

ccg = &ccb->ccg;
size_mb = ccg->volume_size
    / ((1024L * 1024L) / ccg->block_size);
extended = check_cards_EEPROM_for_extended_geometry(softc);

if (size_mb > 1024 && extended) {
    ccg->heads = 255;
    ccg->secs_per_track = 63;
} else {
    ccg->heads = 64;
    ccg->secs_per_track = 32;
}
secs_per_cylinder = ccg->heads * ccg->secs_per_track;
ccg->cylinders = ccg->volume_size / secs_per_cylinder;
ccb->ccb_h.status = CAM_REQ_CMP;
xpt_done(ccb);
return;
```

This gives the general idea, the exact calculation depends on the quirks of the particular BIOS. If BIOS provides no way set the "extended translation" flag in EEPROM this flag should normally be assumed equal to 1. Other popular geometries are:

```
128 heads, 63 sectors - Symbios controllers
16 heads, 63 sectors - old controllers
```

Some system BIOSes and SCSI BIOSes fight with each other with variable success, for example a combination of Symbios 875/895 SCSI and Phoenix BIOS can give geometry 128/63 after power up and 255/63 after a hard reset or soft reboot.

- *XPT_PATH_INQ* - path inquiry, in other words get the SIM driver and SCSI controller (also known as HBA - Host Bus Adapter) properties

The properties are returned in the instance "struct ccb_pathinq cpi" of the union ccb:

- version_num - the SIM driver version number, now all drivers use 1

- hba_inquiry - bitmask of features supported by the controller:

- PI_MDP_ABLE - supports MDP message (something from SCSI3?)

- PI_WIDE_32 - supports 32 bit wide SCSI

- PI_WIDE_16 - supports 16 bit wide SCSI

- PI_SDTR_ABLE - can negotiate synchronous transfer rate

- PI_LINKED_CDB - supports linked commands

- PI_TAG_ABLE - supports tagged commands

- PI_SOFT_RST - supports soft reset alternative (hard reset and soft reset are mutually exclusive within a SCSI bus)

- target_sprt - flags for target mode support, 0 if unsupported

- hba_misc - miscellaneous controller features:

- PIM_SCANHILO - bus scans from high ID to low ID

- PIM_NOREMOVE - removable devices not included in scan

- PIM_NOINITIATOR - initiator role not supported

- PIM_NOBUSRESET - user has disabled initial BUS RESET

- hba_eng_cnt - mysterious HBA engine count, something related to compression, now is always set to 0

- vuhba_flags - vendor-unique flags, unused now

- max_target - maximal supported target ID (7 for 8-bit bus, 15 for 16-bit bus, 127 for Fibre Channel)

- max_lun - maximal supported LUN ID (7 for older SCSI controllers, 63 for newer ones)

- async_flags - bitmask of installed Async handler, unused now

- hpath_id - highest Path ID in the subsystem, unused now

- unit_number - the controller unit number, cam_sim_unit(sim)

- bus_id - the bus number, cam_sim_bus(sim)

- initiator_id - the SCSI ID of the controller itself

- base_transfer_speed - nominal transfer speed in KB/s for asynchronous narrow transfers, equals to 3300 for SCSI

- sim_vid - SIM driver's vendor id, a zero-terminated string of maximal length SIM_IDLEN including the terminating zero

- hba_vid - SCSI controller's vendor id, a zero-terminated string of maximal length HBA_IDLEN including the terminating zero

- dev_name - device driver name, a zero-terminated string of maximal length DEV_IDLEN including the terminating zero, equal to cam_sim_name(sim)

The recommended way of setting the string fields is using strncpy, like:

```
strncpy(cpi->dev_name, cam_sim_name(sim), DEV_IDLEN);
```

After setting the values set the status to CAM_REQ_CMP and mark the CCB as done.

12.3. Polling

```
static void xxx_poll (struct cam_sim *sim);

struct cam_sim *sim ;
```

The poll function is used to simulate the interrupts when the interrupt subsystem is not functioning (for example, when the system has crashed and is creating the system dump). The CAM subsystem sets the proper interrupt level before calling the poll routine. So all it needs to do is to call the interrupt routine (or the other way around, the poll routine may be doing the real action and the interrupt routine would just call the poll routine). Why bother about a separate function then? Because of different calling conventions. The xxx_poll routine gets the struct cam_sim pointer as its argument when the PCI interrupt routine by common convention gets pointer to the struct xxx_softc and the ISA interrupt routine gets just the device unit number. So the poll routine would normally look as:

```
static void
xxx_poll(struct cam_sim *sim)
{
    xxx_intr((struct xxx_softc *)cam_sim_softc(sim)); /* for PCI device */
}
```

or

```
static void
xxx_poll(struct cam_sim *sim)
{
    xxx_intr(cam_sim_unit(sim)); /* for ISA device */
}
```

12.4. Asynchronous Events

If an asynchronous event callback has been set up then the callback function should be defined.

```
static void
ahc_async(void *callback_arg, u_int32_t code, struct cam_path *path, void *arg)
```

- callback_arg - the value supplied when registering the callback

- code - identifies the type of event

- path - identifies the devices to which the event applies

- arg - event-specific argument

Implementation for a single type of event, AC_LOST_DEVICE, looks like:

```
struct xxx_softc *softc;
```

```
struct cam_sim *sim;
int targ;
struct ccb_trans_settings neg;

sim = (struct cam_sim *)callback_arg;
softc = (struct xxx_softc *)cam_sim_softc(sim);
switch (code) {
case AC_LOST_DEVICE:
    targ = xpt_path_target_id(path);
    if(targ <= OUR_MAX_SUPPORTED_TARGET) {
        clean_negotiations(softc, targ);
        /* send indication to CAM */
        neg.bus_width = 8;
        neg.sync_period = neg.sync_offset = 0;
        neg.valid = (CCB_TRANS_BUS_WIDTH_VALID
            | CCB_TRANS_SYNC_RATE_VALID | CCB_TRANS_SYNC_OFFSET_VALID);
        xpt_async(AC_TRANSFER_NEG, path, &neg);
    }
    break;
default:
    break;
}
```

12.5. Interrupts

The exact type of the interrupt routine depends on the type of the peripheral bus (PCI, ISA and so on) to which the SCSI controller is connected.

The interrupt routines of the SIM drivers run at the interrupt level splcam. So `splcam()` should be used in the driver to synchronize activity between the interrupt routine and the rest of the driver (for a multiprocessor-aware driver things get yet more interesting but we ignore this case here). The pseudo-code in this document happily ignores the problems of synchronization. The real code must not ignore them. A simple-minded approach is to set `splcam()` on the entry to the other routines and reset it on return thus protecting them by one big critical section. To make sure that the interrupt level will be always restored a wrapper function can be defined, like:

```
static void
xxx_action(struct cam_sim *sim, union ccb *ccb)
{
    int s;
    s = splcam();
    xxx_action1(sim, ccb);
    splx(s);
}

static void
xxx_action1(struct cam_sim *sim, union ccb *ccb)
{
    ... process the request ...
}
```

This approach is simple and robust but the problem with it is that interrupts may get blocked for a relatively long time and this would negatively affect the system's performance. On the other hand the functions of the `spl()` family have rather high overhead, so vast amount of tiny critical sections may not be good either.

The conditions handled by the interrupt routine and the details depend very much on the hardware. We consider the set of "typical" conditions.

First, we check if a SCSI reset was encountered on the bus (probably caused by another SCSI controller on the same SCSI bus). If so we drop all the enqueued and disconnected requests, report the events and re-initialize our SCSI controller. It is important that during this initialization the controller will not issue another reset or else two controllers on the same SCSI bus could ping-pong resets forever. The case of fatal controller error/hang could be handled in the same place, but it will probably need also sending RESET signal to the SCSI bus to reset the status of the connections with the SCSI devices.

```
    int fatal=0;
    struct ccb_trans_settings neg;
    struct cam_path *path;

    if( detected_scsi_reset(softc)
    || (fatal = detected_fatal_controller_error(softc)) ) {
        int targ, lun;
        struct xxx_hcb *h, *hh;

        /* drop all enqueued CCBs */
        for(h = softc->first_queued_hcb; h != NULL; h = hh) {
            hh = h->next;
            free_hcb_and_ccb_done(h, h->ccb, CAM_SCSI_BUS_RESET);
        }

        /* the clean values of negotiations to report */
        neg.bus_width = 8;
        neg.sync_period = neg.sync_offset = 0;
        neg.valid = (CCB_TRANS_BUS_WIDTH_VALID
            | CCB_TRANS_SYNC_RATE_VALID | CCB_TRANS_SYNC_OFFSET_VALID);

        /* drop all disconnected CCBs and clean negotiations  */
        for(targ=0; targ <= OUR_MAX_SUPPORTED_TARGET; targ++) {
            clean_negotiations(softc, targ);

            /* report the event if possible */
            if(xpt_create_path(&path, /*periph*/NULL,
                    cam_sim_path(sim), targ,
                    CAM_LUN_WILDCARD) == CAM_REQ_CMP) {
                xpt_async(AC_TRANSFER_NEG, path, &neg);
                xpt_free_path(path);
            }

            for(lun=0; lun <= OUR_MAX_SUPPORTED_LUN; lun++)
                for(h = softc->first_discon_hcb[targ][lun]; h != NULL; h = hh) {
                    hh=h->next;
                    if(fatal)
                        free_hcb_and_ccb_done(h, h->ccb, CAM_UNREC_HBA_ERROR);
                    else
                        free_hcb_and_ccb_done(h, h->ccb, CAM_SCSI_BUS_RESET);
                }
        }

        /* report the event */
        xpt_async(AC_BUS_RESET, softc->wpath, NULL);

        /* re-initialization may take a lot of time, in such case
         * its completion should be signaled by another interrupt or
         * checked on timeout - but for simplicity we assume here that
         * it is really fast
         */
        if(!fatal) {
            reinitialize_controller_without_scsi_reset(softc);
        } else {
            reinitialize_controller_with_scsi_reset(softc);
        }
        schedule_next_hcb(softc);
        return;
    }
```

If interrupt is not caused by a controller-wide condition then probably something has happened to the current hardware control block. Depending on the hardware there may be other non-HCB-related events, we just do not consider them here. Then we analyze what happened to this HCB:

```
struct xxx_hcb *hcb, *h, *hh;
int hcb_status, scsi_status;
int ccb_status;
int targ;
int lun_to_freeze;

hcb = get_current_hcb(softc);
if(hcb == NULL) {
    /* either stray interrupt or something went very wrong
     * or this is something hardware-dependent
     */
    handle as necessary;
    return;
}

targ = hcb->target;
hcb_status = get_status_of_current_hcb(softc);
```

First we check if the HCB has completed and if so we check the returned SCSI status.

```
if(hcb_status == COMPLETED) {
    scsi_status = get_completion_status(hcb);
```

Then look if this status is related to the REQUEST SENSE command and if so handle it in a simple way.

```
    if(hcb->flags & DOING_AUTOSENSE) {
        if(scsi_status == GOOD) { /* autosense was successful */
            hcb->ccb->ccb_h.status |= CAM_AUTOSNS_VALID;
            free_hcb_and_ccb_done(hcb, hcb->ccb, CAM_SCSI_STATUS_ERROR);
        } else {
autosense_failed:
            free_hcb_and_ccb_done(hcb, hcb->ccb, CAM_AUTOSENSE_FAIL);
        }
        schedule_next_hcb(softc);
        return;
    }
```

Else the command itself has completed, pay more attention to details. If auto-sense is not disabled for this CCB and the command has failed with sense data then run REQUEST SENSE command to receive that data.

```
    hcb->ccb->csio.scsi_status = scsi_status;
    calculate_residue(hcb);

    if( (hcb->ccb->ccb_h.flags & CAM_DIS_AUTOSENSE)==0
    && ( scsi_status == CHECK_CONDITION
            || scsi_status == COMMAND_TERMINATED) ) {
        /* start auto-SENSE */
        hcb->flags |= DOING_AUTOSENSE;
        setup_autosense_command_in_hcb(hcb);
        restart_current_hcb(softc);
        return;
    }
    if(scsi_status == GOOD)
        free_hcb_and_ccb_done(hcb, hcb->ccb, CAM_REQ_CMP);
    else
        free_hcb_and_ccb_done(hcb, hcb->ccb, CAM_SCSI_STATUS_ERROR);
    schedule_next_hcb(softc);
    return;
}
```

One typical thing would be negotiation events: negotiation messages received from a SCSI target (in answer to our negotiation attempt or by target's initiative) or the target is unable to negotiate (rejects our negotiation messages or does not answer them).

```
switch(hcb_status) {
case TARGET_REJECTED_WIDE_NEG:
```

```
            /* revert to 8-bit bus */
            softc->current_bus_width[targ] = softc->goal_bus_width[targ] = 8;
            /* report the event */
            neg.bus_width = 8;
            neg.valid = CCB_TRANS_BUS_WIDTH_VALID;
            xpt_async(AC_TRANSFER_NEG, hcb->ccb.ccb_h.path_id, &neg);
            continue_current_hcb(softc);
            return;
    case TARGET_ANSWERED_WIDE_NEG:
        {
            int wd;

            wd = get_target_bus_width_request(softc);
            if(wd <= softc->goal_bus_width[targ]) {
                /* answer is acceptable */
                softc->current_bus_width[targ] =
                softc->goal_bus_width[targ] = neg.bus_width = wd;

                /* report the event */
                neg.valid = CCB_TRANS_BUS_WIDTH_VALID;
                xpt_async(AC_TRANSFER_NEG, hcb->ccb.ccb_h.path_id, &neg);
            } else {
                prepare_reject_message(hcb);
            }
        }
        continue_current_hcb(softc);
        return;
    case TARGET_REQUESTED_WIDE_NEG:
        {
            int wd;

            wd = get_target_bus_width_request(softc);
            wd = min (wd, OUR_BUS_WIDTH);
            wd = min (wd, softc->user_bus_width[targ]);

            if(wd != softc->current_bus_width[targ]) {
                /* the bus width has changed */
                softc->current_bus_width[targ] =
                softc->goal_bus_width[targ] = neg.bus_width = wd;

                /* report the event */
                neg.valid = CCB_TRANS_BUS_WIDTH_VALID;
                xpt_async(AC_TRANSFER_NEG, hcb->ccb.ccb_h.path_id, &neg);
            }
            prepare_width_nego_rsponse(hcb, wd);
        }
        continue_current_hcb(softc);
        return;
}
```

Then we handle any errors that could have happened during auto-sense in the same simple-minded way as before. Otherwise we look closer at the details again.

```
if(hcb->flags & DOING_AUTOSENSE)
    goto autosense_failed;

switch(hcb_status) {
```

The next event we consider is unexpected disconnect. Which is considered normal after an ABORT or BUS DEVICE RESET message and abnormal in other cases.

```
case UNEXPECTED_DISCONNECT:
    if(requested_abort(hcb)) {
        /* abort affects all commands on that target+LUN, so
         * mark all disconnected HCBs on that target+LUN as aborted too
         */
```

```
                    for(h = softc->first_discon_hcb[hcb->target][hcb->lun];
                            h != NULL; h = hh) {
                        hh=h->next;
                        free_hcb_and_ccb_done(h, h->ccb, CAM_REQ_ABORTED);
                    }
                    ccb_status = CAM_REQ_ABORTED;
            } else if(requested_bus_device_reset(hcb)) {
                    int lun;

                    /* reset affects all commands on that target, so
                     * mark all disconnected HCBs on that target+LUN as reset
                     */

                    for(lun=0; lun <= OUR_MAX_SUPPORTED_LUN; lun++)
                        for(h = softc->first_discon_hcb[hcb->target][lun];
                                h != NULL; h = hh) {
                            hh=h->next;
                            free_hcb_and_ccb_done(h, h->ccb, CAM_SCSI_BUS_RESET);
                        }

                    /* send event */
                    xpt_async(AC_SENT_BDR, hcb->ccb->ccb_h.path_id, NULL);

                    /* this was the CAM_RESET_DEV request itself, it is completed */
                    ccb_status = CAM_REQ_CMP;
            } else {
                    calculate_residue(hcb);
                    ccb_status = CAM_UNEXP_BUSFREE;
                    /* request the further code to freeze the queue */
                    hcb->ccb->ccb_h.status |= CAM_DEV_QFRZN;
                    lun_to_freeze = hcb->lun;
            }
            break;
```

If the target refuses to accept tags we notify CAM about that and return back all commands for this LUN:

```
        case TAGS_REJECTED:
            /* report the event */
            neg.flags = 0 & ~CCB_TRANS_TAG_ENB;
            neg.valid = CCB_TRANS_TQ_VALID;
            xpt_async(AC_TRANSFER_NEG, hcb->ccb.ccb_h.path_id, &neg);

            ccb_status = CAM_MSG_REJECT_REC;
            /* request the further code to freeze the queue */
            hcb->ccb->ccb_h.status |= CAM_DEV_QFRZN;
            lun_to_freeze = hcb->lun;
            break;
```

Then we check a number of other conditions, with processing basically limited to setting the CCB status:

```
        case SELECTION_TIMEOUT:
            ccb_status = CAM_SEL_TIMEOUT;
            /* request the further code to freeze the queue */
            hcb->ccb->ccb_h.status |= CAM_DEV_QFRZN;
            lun_to_freeze = CAM_LUN_WILDCARD;
            break;
        case PARITY_ERROR:
            ccb_status = CAM_UNCOR_PARITY;
            break;
        case DATA_OVERRUN:
        case ODD_WIDE_TRANSFER:
            ccb_status = CAM_DATA_RUN_ERR;
            break;
        default:
            /* all other errors are handled in a generic way */
            ccb_status = CAM_REQ_CMP_ERR;
            /* request the further code to freeze the queue */
```

```
            hcb->ccb->ccb_h.status |= CAM_DEV_QFRZN;
            lun_to_freeze = CAM_LUN_WILDCARD;
            break;
    }
```

Then we check if the error was serious enough to freeze the input queue until it gets proceeded and do so if it is:

```
if(hcb->ccb->ccb_h.status & CAM_DEV_QFRZN) {
    /* freeze the queue */
    xpt_freeze_devq(ccb->ccb_h.path, /*count*/1);

    /* re-queue all commands for this target/LUN back to CAM */

    for(h = softc->first_queued_hcb; h != NULL; h = hh) {
        hh = h->next;

        if(targ == h->targ
        && (lun_to_freeze == CAM_LUN_WILDCARD || lun_to_freeze == h->lun) )
            free_hcb_and_ccb_done(h, h->ccb, CAM_REQUEUE_REQ);
    }
}
free_hcb_and_ccb_done(hcb, hcb->ccb, ccb_status);
schedule_next_hcb(softc);
return;
```

This concludes the generic interrupt handling although specific controllers may require some additions.

12.6. Errors Summary

When executing an I/O request many things may go wrong. The reason of error can be reported in the CCB status with great detail. Examples of use are spread throughout this document. For completeness here is the summary of recommended responses for the typical error conditions:

- *CAM_RESRC_UNAVAIL* - some resource is temporarily unavailable and the SIM driver cannot generate an event when it will become available. An example of this resource would be some intra-controller hardware resource for which the controller does not generate an interrupt when it becomes available.

- *CAM_UNCOR_PARITY* - unrecovered parity error occurred

- *CAM_DATA_RUN_ERR* - data overrun or unexpected data phase (going in other direction than specified in CAM_DIR_MASK) or odd transfer length for wide transfer

- *CAM_SEL_TIMEOUT* - selection timeout occurred (target does not respond)

- *CAM_CMD_TIMEOUT* - command timeout occurred (the timeout function ran)

- *CAM_SCSI_STATUS_ERROR* - the device returned error

- *CAM_AUTOSENSE_FAIL* - the device returned error and the REQUEST SENSE COMMAND failed

- *CAM_MSG_REJECT_REC* - MESSAGE REJECT message was received

- *CAM_SCSI_BUS_RESET* - received SCSI bus reset

- *CAM_REQ_CMP_ERR* - "impossible" SCSI phase occurred or something else as weird or just a generic error if further detail is not available

- *CAM_UNEXP_BUSFREE* - unexpected disconnect occurred

- *CAM_BDR_SENT* - BUS DEVICE RESET message was sent to the target

- *CAM_UNREC_HBA_ERROR* - unrecoverable Host Bus Adapter Error

- *CAM_REQ_TOO_BIG* - the request was too large for this controller

- *CAM_REQUEUE_REQ* - this request should be re-queued to preserve transaction ordering. This typically occurs when the SIM recognizes an error that should freeze the queue and must place other queued requests for the target at the sim level back into the XPT queue. Typical cases of such errors are selection timeouts, command timeouts and other like conditions. In such cases the troublesome command returns the status indicating the error, the and the other commands which have not be sent to the bus yet get re-queued.

- *CAM_LUN_INVALID* - the LUN ID in the request is not supported by the SCSI controller

- *CAM_TID_INVALID* - the target ID in the request is not supported by the SCSI controller

12.7. Timeout Handling

When the timeout for an HCB expires that request should be aborted, just like with an XPT_ABORT request. The only difference is that the returned status of aborted request should be CAM_CMD_TIMEOUT instead of CAM_REQ_ABORTED (that is why implementation of the abort better be done as a function). But there is one more possible problem: what if the abort request itself will get stuck? In this case the SCSI bus should be reset, just like with an XPT_RESET_BUS request (and the idea about implementing it as a function called from both places applies here too). Also we should reset the whole SCSI bus if a device reset request got stuck. So after all the timeout function would look like:

```
static void
xxx_timeout(void *arg)
{
    struct xxx_hcb *hcb = (struct xxx_hcb *)arg;
    struct xxx_softc *softc;
    struct ccb_hdr *ccb_h;

    softc = hcb->softc;
    ccb_h = &hcb->ccb->ccb_h;

    if(hcb->flags & HCB_BEING_ABORTED
    || ccb_h->func_code == XPT_RESET_DEV) {
        xxx_reset_bus(softc);
    } else {
        xxx_abort_ccb(hcb->ccb, CAM_CMD_TIMEOUT);
    }
}
```

When we abort a request all the other disconnected requests to the same target/LUN get aborted too. So there appears a question, should we return them with status CAM_REQ_ABORTED or CAM_CMD_TIMEOUT? The current drivers use CAM_CMD_TIMEOUT. This seems logical because if one request got timed out then probably something really bad is happening to the device, so if they would not be disturbed they would time out by themselves.

Chapter 13. USB Devices

Written by Nick Hibma.
Modifications for Handbook made by Murray Stokely.

13.1. Introduction

The Universal Serial Bus (USB) is a new way of attaching devices to personal computers. The bus architecture features two-way communication and has been developed as a response to devices becoming smarter and requiring more interaction with the host. USB support is included in all current PC chipsets and is therefore available in all recently built PCs. Apple's introduction of the USB-only iMac has been a major incentive for hardware manufacturers to produce USB versions of their devices. The future PC specifications specify that all legacy connectors on PCs should be replaced by one or more USB connectors, providing generic plug and play capabilities. Support for USB hardware was available at a very early stage in NetBSD and was developed by Lennart Augustsson for the NetBSD project. The code has been ported to FreeBSD and we are currently maintaining a shared code base. For the implementation of the USB subsystem a number of features of USB are important.

Lennart Augustsson has done most of the implementation of the USB support for the NetBSD project. Many thanks for this incredible amount of work. Many thanks also to Ardy and Dirk for their comments and proofreading of this paper.

- Devices connect to ports on the computer directly or on devices called hubs, forming a treelike device structure.

- The devices can be connected and disconnected at run time.

- Devices can suspend themselves and trigger resumes of the host system

- As the devices can be powered from the bus, the host software has to keep track of power budgets for each hub.

- Different quality of service requirements by the different device types together with the maximum of 126 devices that can be connected to the same bus, require proper scheduling of transfers on the shared bus to take full advantage of the 12Mbps bandwidth available. (over 400Mbps with USB 2.0)

- Devices are intelligent and contain easily accessible information about themselves

The development of drivers for the USB subsystem and devices connected to it is supported by the specifications that have been developed and will be developed. These specifications are publicly available from the USB home pages. Apple has been very strong in pushing for standards based drivers, by making drivers for the generic classes available in their operating system MacOS and discouraging the use of separate drivers for each new device. This chapter tries to collate essential information for a basic understanding of the USB 2.0 implementation stack in FreeBSD/NetBSD. It is recommended however to read it together with the relevant 2.0 specifications and other developer resources:

- USB 2.0 Specification (http://www.usb.org/developers/docs/usb20_docs/)

- Universal Host Controller Interface (UHCI) Specification (ftp://ftp.netbsd.org/pub/NetBSD/misc/blymn/uhci11d.pdf)

- Open Host Controller Interface (OHCI) Specification(ftp://ftp.compaq.com/pub/supportinformation/papers/hcir1_0a.pdf)

- Developer section of USB home page (http://www.usb.org/developers/)

13.1.1. Structure of the USB Stack

The USB support in FreeBSD can be split into three layers. The lowest layer contains the host controller driver, providing a generic interface to the hardware and its scheduling facilities. It supports initialisation of the hardware, scheduling of transfers and handling of completed and/or failed transfers. Each host controller driver implements a virtual hub providing hardware independent access to the registers controlling the root ports on the back of the machine.

The middle layer handles the device connection and disconnection, basic initialisation of the device, driver selection, the communication channels (pipes) and does resource management. This services layer also controls the default pipes and the device requests transferred over them.

The top layer contains the individual drivers supporting specific (classes of) devices. These drivers implement the protocol that is used over the pipes other than the default pipe. They also implement additional functionality to make the device available to other parts of the kernel or userland. They use the USB driver interface (USBDI) exposed by the services layer.

13.2. Host Controllers

The host controller (HC) controls the transmission of packets on the bus. Frames of 1 millisecond are used. At the start of each frame the host controller generates a Start of Frame (SOF) packet.

The SOF packet is used to synchronise to the start of the frame and to keep track of the frame number. Within each frame packets are transferred, either from host to device (out) or from device to host (in). Transfers are always initiated by the host (polled transfers). Therefore there can only be one host per USB bus. Each transfer of a packet has a status stage in which the recipient of the data can return either ACK (acknowledge reception), NAK (retry), STALL (error condition) or nothing (garbled data stage, device not available or disconnected). Section 8.5 of the USB 2.0 Specification explains the details of packets in more detail. Four different types of transfers can occur on a USB bus: control, bulk, interrupt and isochronous. The types of transfers and their characteristics are described below.

Large transfers between the device on the USB bus and the device driver are split up into multiple packets by the host controller or the HC driver.

Device requests (control transfers) to the default endpoints are special. They consist of two or three phases: SETUP, DATA (optional) and STATUS. The set-up packet is sent to the device. If there is a data phase, the direction of the data packet(s) is given in the set-up packet. The direction in the status phase is the opposite of the direction during the data phase, or IN if there was no data phase. The host controller hardware also provides registers with the current status of the root ports and the changes that have occurred since the last reset of the status change register. Access to these registers is provided through a virtualised hub as suggested in the USB specification. The virtual hub must comply with the hub device class given in chapter 11 of that specification. It must provide a default pipe through which device requests can be sent to it. It returns the standard andhub class specific set of descriptors. It should also provide an interrupt pipe that reports changes happening at its ports. There are currently two specifications for host controllers available: Universal Host Controller Interface (UHCI) from Intel and Open Host Controller Interface (OHCI) from Compaq, Microsoft, and National Semiconductor. The UHCI specification has been designed to reduce hardware complexity by requiring the host controller driver to supply a complete schedule of the transfers for each frame. OHCI type controllers are much more independent by providing a more abstract interface doing a lot of work themselves.

13.2.1. UHCI

The UHCI host controller maintains a framelist with 1024 pointers to per frame data structures. It understands two different data types: transfer descriptors (TD) and queue heads (QH). Each TD represents a packet to be communicated to or from a device endpoint. QHs are a means to groupTDs (and QHs) together.

Each transfer consists of one or more packets. The UHCI driver splits large transfers into multiple packets. For every transfer, apart from isochronous transfers, a QH is allocated. For every type of transfer these QHs are collected at a QH for that type. Isochronous transfers have to be executed first because of the fixed latency requirement and are directly referred to by the pointer in the framelist. The last isochronous TD refers to the QH for interrupt transfers for that frame. All QHs for interrupt transfers point at the QH for control transfers, which in turn points at the QH for bulk transfers. The following diagram gives a graphical overview of this:

This results in the following schedule being run in each frame. After fetching the pointer for the current frame from the framelist the controller first executes the TDs for all the isochronous packets in that frame. The last of these TDs refers to the QH for the interrupt transfers for thatframe. The host controller will then descend from that QH to the QHs for the individual interrupt transfers. After finishing that queue, the QH for the interrupt transfers will refer the controller to the QH for all control transfers. It will execute all the subqueues scheduled there, followed by all the transfers queued at the bulk QH. To facilitate the handling of finished or failed transfers different types of interrupts are generated by the hardware at the end of each frame. In the last TD for a transfer the Interrupt-On Completion bit is set by the HC driver to flag an interrupt when the transfer has completed. An error interrupt is flagged if a TD reaches its maximum error count. If the short packet detect bit is set in a TD and less than the set packet length is transferred this interrupt is flagged to notify the controller driver of the completed transfer. It is the host controller driver's task to find out which transfer has completed or produced an error. When called the interrupt service routine will locate all the finished transfers and call their callbacks.

Refer to the UHCI Specification for a more elaborate description.

13.2.2. OHCI

Programming an OHCI host controller is much simpler. The controller assumes that a set of endpoints is available, and is aware of scheduling priorities and the ordering of the types of transfers in a frame. The main data structure used by the host controller is the endpoint descriptor (ED) to which a queue of transfer descriptors (TDs) is attached. The ED contains the maximum packet size allowed for an endpoint and the controller hardware does the splitting into packets. The pointers to the data buffers are updated after each transfer and when the start and end pointer are equal, the TD is retired to the done-queue. The four types of endpoints (interrupt, isochronous, control, and bulk) have their own queues. Control and bulk endpoints are queued each at their own queue. Interrupt EDs are queued in a tree, with the level in the tree defining the frequency at which they run.

The schedule being run by the host controller in each frame looks as follows. The controller will first run the non-periodic control and bulk queues, up to a time limit set by the HC driver. Then the interrupt transfers for that frame number are run, by using the lower five bits of the frame number as an index into level 0 of the tree of interrupts EDs. At the end of this tree the isochronous EDs are connected and these are traversed subsequently. The isochronous TDs contain the frame number of the first frame the transfer should be run in. After all the periodic transfers have been run, the control and bulk queues are traversed again. Periodically the interrupt service routine is called to process the done queue and call the callbacks for each transfer and reschedule interrupt and isochronous endpoints.

See the UHCI Specification for a more elaborate description. The middle layer provides access to the device in a controlled way and maintains resources in use by the different drivers and the services layer. The layer takes care of the following aspects:

- The device configuration information

- The pipes to communicate with a device

- Probing and attaching and detaching form a device.

13.3. USB Device Information

13.3.1. Device Configuration Information

Each device provides different levels of configuration information. Each device has one or more configurations, of which one is selected during probe/attach. A configuration provides power and bandwidth requirements. Within each configuration there can be multiple interfaces. A device interface is a collection of endpoints. For example USB speakers can have an interface for the audio data (Audio Class) and an interface for the knobs, dials and buttons (HID Class). All interfaces in a configuration are active at the same time and can be attached to by different drivers. Each interface can have alternates, providing different quality of service parameters. In for example cameras this is used to provide different frame sizes and numbers of frames per second.

Within each interface, 0 or more endpoints can be specified. Endpoints are the unidirectional access points for communicating with a device. They provide buffers to temporarily store incoming or outgoing data from the device. Each endpoint has a unique address within a configuration, the endpoint's number plus its direction. The default endpoint, endpoint 0, is not part of any interface and available in all configurations. It is managed by the services layer and not directly available to device drivers.

This hierarchical configuration information is described in the device by a standard set of descriptors (see section 9.6 of the USB specification). They can be requested through the Get Descriptor Request. The services layer caches these descriptors to avoid unnecessary transfers on the USB bus. Access to the descriptors is provided through function calls.

- Device descriptors: General information about the device, like Vendor, Product and Revision Id, supported device class, subclass and protocol if applicable, maximum packet size for the default endpoint, etc.

- Configuration descriptors: The number of interfaces in this configuration, suspend and resume functionality supported and power requirements.

- Interface descriptors: interface class, subclass and protocol if applicable, number of alternate settings for the interface and the number of endpoints.

- Endpoint descriptors: Endpoint address, direction and type, maximum packet size supported and polling frequency if type is interrupt endpoint. There is no descriptor for the default endpoint (endpoint 0) and it is never counted in an interface descriptor.

- String descriptors: In the other descriptors string indices are supplied for some fields.These can be used to retrieve descriptive strings, possibly in multiple languages.

Class specifications can add their own descriptor types that are available through the GetDescriptor Request.

Pipes Communication to end points on a device flows through so-called pipes. Drivers submit transfers to endpoints to a pipe and provide a callback to be called on completion or failure of the transfer (asynchronous transfers) or wait for completion (synchronous transfer). Transfers to an endpoint are serialised in the pipe. A transfer can either complete, fail or time-out (if a time-out has been set). There are two types of time-outs for transfers. Time-outs can happen due to time-out on the USBbus (milliseconds). These time-outs are seen as failures and can be due to disconnection of the device. A second form of time-out is implemented in software and is triggered when a transfer does not complete within a specified amount of time (seconds). These are caused by a device acknowledging negatively (NAK) the transferred packets. The cause for this is the device not being ready to receive data, buffer under- or overrun or protocol errors.

If a transfer over a pipe is larger than the maximum packet size specified in the associated endpoint descriptor, the host controller (OHCI) or the HC driver (UHCI) will split the transfer into packets of maximum packet size, with the last packet possibly smaller than the maximum packet size.

Sometimes it is not a problem for a device to return less data than requested. For example abulk-in-transfer to a modem might request 200 bytes of data, but the modem has only 5 bytes available at that time. The driver can set the short packet (SPD) flag. It allows the host controller to accept a packet even if the amount of data transferred is less than requested. This flag is only valid for in-transfers, as the amount of data to be sent to a device is always known beforehand. If an unrecoverable error occurs in a device during a transfer the pipe is stalled. Before any more data is accepted or sent the driver needs to resolve the cause of the stall and clear the endpoint stall condition through send the clear endpoint halt device request over the default pipe. The default endpoint should never stall.

There are four different types of endpoints and corresponding pipes: - Control pipe / default pipe: There is one control pipe per device, connected to the default endpoint (endpoint 0). The pipe carries the device requests and associated data. The difference between transfers over the default pipe and other pipes is that the protocol for the transfers is described in the USB specification. These requests are used to reset and configure the device. A basic set of commands that must be supported by each device is provided in chapter 9 of the USB specification. The commands supported on this pipe can be extended by a device class specification to support additional functionality.

- Bulk pipe: This is the USB equivalent to a raw transmission medium.

- Interrupt pipe: The host sends a request for data to the device and if the device has nothing to send, it will NAK the data packet. Interrupt transfers are scheduled at a frequency specified when creating the pipe.

- Isochronous pipe: These pipes are intended for isochronous data, for example video or audio streams, with fixed latency, but no guaranteed delivery. Some support for pipes of this type is available in the current implementation. Packets in control, bulk and interrupt transfers are retried if an error occurs during transmission or the device acknowledges the packet negatively (NAK) due to for example lack of buffer space to store the incoming data. Isochronous packets are however not retried in case of failed delivery or NAK of a packet as this might violate the timing constraints.

The availability of the necessary bandwidth is calculated during the creation of the pipe. Transfers are scheduled within frames of 1 millisecond. The bandwidth allocation within a frame is prescribed by the USB specification, section 5.6 [2]. Isochronous and interrupt transfers are allowed to consume up to 90% of the bandwidth within a frame. Packets for control and bulk transfers are scheduled after all isochronous and interrupt packets and will consume all the remaining bandwidth.

More information on scheduling of transfers and bandwidth reclamation can be found in chapter 5 of the USB specification, section 1.3 of the UHCI specification, and section 3.4.2 of the OHCI specification.

13.4. Device Probe and Attach

After the notification by the hub that a new device has been connected, the service layer switches on the port, providing the device with 100 mA of current. At this point the device is in its default state and listening to device address 0. The services layer will proceed to retrieve the various descriptors through the default pipe. After that it will send a Set Address request to move the device away from the default device address (address 0). Multiple device drivers might be able to support the device. For example a modem driver might be able to support an ISDN TA through the AT compatibility interface. A driver for that specific model of the ISDN adapter might however be able to provide much better support for this device. To support this flexibility, the probes return priorities indicating their level of support. Support for a specific revision of a product ranks the highest and the generic driver the lowest priority. It might also be that multiple drivers could attach to one device if there are multiple interfaces within one configuration. Each driver only needs to support a subset of the interfaces.

The probing for a driver for a newly attached device checks first for device specific drivers. If not found, the probe code iterates over all supported configurations until a driver attaches in a configuration. To support devices with multiple drivers on different interfaces, the probe iterates over all interfaces in a configuration that have not yet been claimed by a driver. Configurations that exceed the power budget for the hub are ignored. During attach the driver should initialise the device to its proper state, but not reset it, as this will make the device disconnect itself from the bus and restart the probing process for it. To avoid consuming unnecessary bandwidth should not claim the interrupt pipe at attach time, but should postpone allocating the pipe until the file is opened and the data is actually used. When the file is closed the pipe should be closed again, even though the device might still be attached.

13.4.1. Device Disconnect and Detach

A device driver should expect to receive errors during any transaction with the device. The design of USB supports and encourages the disconnection of devices at any point in time. Drivers should make sure that they do the right thing when the device disappears.

Furthermore a device that has been disconnected and reconnected will not be reattached at the same device instance. This might change in the future when more devices support serial numbers (see the device descriptor) or other means of defining an identity for a device have been developed.

The disconnection of a device is signaled by a hub in the interrupt packet delivered to the hub driver. The status change information indicates which port has seen a connection change. The device detach method for all device drivers for the device connected on that port are called and the structures cleaned up. If the port status indicates that in the mean time a device has been connected to that port, the procedure for probing and attaching the device will be started. A device reset will produce a disconnect-connect sequence on the hub and will be handled as described above.

13.5. USB Drivers Protocol Information

The protocol used over pipes other than the default pipe is undefined by the USB specification. Information on this can be found from various sources. The most accurate source is the developer's section on the USB home pages. From these pages, a growing number of deviceclass specifications are available. These specifications specify what a compliant device should look like from a driver perspective, basic functionality it needs to provide and the protocol that is to be used over the communication channels. The USB specification includes the description of the Hub Class. A class specification for Human Interface Devices (HID) has been created to cater for keyboards, tablets, bar-code readers, buttons, knobs, switches, etc. A third example is the class specification for mass storage devices. For a full list of device classes see the developers section on the USB home pages.

For many devices the protocol information has not yet been published however. Information on the protocol being used might be available from the company making the device. Some companies will require you to sign a Non - Disclosure Agreement (NDA) before giving you the specifications. This in most cases precludes making the driver open source.

Another good source of information is the Linux driver sources, as a number of companies have started to provide drivers for Linux for their devices. It is always a good idea to contact the authors of those drivers for their source of information.

Example: Human Interface Devices The specification for the Human Interface Devices like keyboards, mice, tablets, buttons, dials,etc. is referred to in other device class specifications and is used in many devices.

For example audio speakers provide endpoints to the digital to analogue converters and possibly an extra pipe for a microphone. They also provide a HID endpoint in a separate interface for the buttons and dials on the front of the device. The same is true for the monitor control class. It is straightforward to build support for these interfaces through the available kernel and userland libraries together with the HID class driver or the generic driver. Another device that serves as an example for interfaces within one configuration driven by different device drivers is a cheap keyboard with built-in legacy mouse port. To avoid having the cost of including the hardware for a USB hub in the device, manufacturers combined the mouse data received from the PS/2 port on the back of the keyboard and the key presses from the keyboard into two separate interfaces in the same configuration. The mouse and keyboard drivers each attach to the appropriate interface and allocate the pipes to the two independent endpoints.

Example: Firmware download Many devices that have been developed are based on a general purpose processor with an additional USB core added to it. Because the development of drivers and firmware for USB devices is still very new, many devices require the downloading of the firmware after they have been connected.

The procedure followed is straightforward. The device identifies itself through a vendor and product Id. The first driver probes and attaches to it and downloads the firmware into it. After that the device soft resets itself and the driver is detached. After a short pause the device announces its presence on the bus. The device will have changed its vendor/product/revision Id to reflect the fact that it has been supplied with firmware and as a consequence a second driver will probe it and attach to it.

An example of these types of devices is the ActiveWire I/O board, based on the EZ-USB chip. For this chip a generic firmware downloader is available. The firmware downloaded into the ActiveWire board changes the revision Id. It will then perform a soft reset of the USB part of the EZ-USB chip to disconnect from the USB bus and again reconnect.

Example: Mass Storage Devices Support for mass storage devices is mainly built around existing protocols. The Iomega USB Zipdrive is based on the SCSI version of their drive. The SCSI commands and status messages are wrapped in blocks and transferred over the bulk pipes to and from the device, emulating a SCSI controller over the USB wire. ATAPI and UFI commands are supported in a similar fashion.

The Mass Storage Specification supports 2 different types of wrapping of the command block.The initial attempt was based on sending the command and status through the default pipe and using bulk transfers for the data to be moved between the host and the device. Based on experience a second approach was designed that was based on wrapping the command and status blocks and sending them over the bulk out and in endpoint. The specification specifies exactly what has to happen when and what has to be done in case an error condition is encountered. The biggest challenge when writing drivers for these devices is to fit USB based protocol into the existing support for mass storage devices. CAM provides hooks to do this in a fairly straight forward way. ATAPI is less simple as historically the IDE interface has never had many different appearances.

The support for the USB floppy from Y-E Data is again less straightforward as a new command set has been designed.

Chapter 14. Newbus

Written by Jeroen Ruigrok van der Werven (asmodai) and Hiten Pandya.

Special thanks to Matthew N. Dodd, Warner Losh, Bill Paul, Doug Rabson, Mike Smith, Peter Wemm and Scott Long.

This chapter explains the Newbus device framework in detail.

14.1. Device Drivers

14.1.1. Purpose of a Device Driver

A device driver is a software component which provides the interface between the kernel's generic view of a peripheral (e.g., disk, network adapter) and the actual implementation of the peripheral. The *device driver interface (DDI)* is the defined interface between the kernel and the device driver component.

14.1.2. Types of Device Drivers

There used to be days in UNIX®, and thus FreeBSD, in which there were four types of devices defined:

- block device drivers

- character device drivers

- network device drivers

- pseudo-device drivers

Block devices performed in a way that used fixed size blocks [of data]. This type of driver depended on the so-called *buffer cache*, which had cached accessed blocks of data in a dedicated part of memory. Often this buffer cache was based on write-behind, which meant that when data was modified in memory it got synced to disk whenever the system did its periodical disk flushing, thus optimizing writes.

14.1.3. Character Devices

However, in the versions of FreeBSD 4.0 and onward the distinction between block and character devices became non-existent.

14.2. Overview of Newbus

Newbus is the implementation of a new bus architecture based on abstraction layers which saw its introduction in FreeBSD 3.0 when the Alpha port was imported into the source tree. It was not until 4.0 before it became the default system to use for device drivers. Its goals are to provide a more object-oriented means of interconnecting the various busses and devices which a host system provides to the *Operating System*.

Its main features include amongst others:

- dynamic attaching

- easy modularization of drivers

- pseudo-busses

One of the most prominent changes is the migration from the flat and ad-hoc system to a device tree layout.

At the top level resides the *"root"* device which is the parent to hang all other devices on. For each architecture, there is typically a single child of "root" which has such things as *host-to-PCI bridges*, etc. attached to it. For x86, this "root" device is the *"nexus"* device. For Alpha, various different models of Alpha have different top-level devices corresponding to the different hardware chipsets, including *lca, apecs, cia* and *tsunami*.

A device in the Newbus context represents a single hardware entity in the system. For instance each PCI device is represented by a Newbus device. Any device in the system can have children; a device which has children is often called a *"bus"*. Examples of common busses in the system are ISA and PCI, which manage lists of devices attached to ISA and PCI busses respectively.

Often, a connection between different kinds of bus is represented by a *"bridge"* device, which normally has one child for the attached bus. An example of this is a *PCI-to-PCI bridge* which is represented by a device *pcibN* on the parent PCI bus and has a child *pciN* for the attached bus. This layout simplifies the implementation of the PCI bus tree, allowing common code to be used for both top-level and bridged busses.

Each device in the Newbus architecture asks its parent to map its resources. The parent then asks its own parent until the nexus is reached. So, basically the nexus is the only part of the Newbus system which knows about all resources.

Tip

An ISA device might want to map its IO port at `0x230`, so it asks its parent, in this case the ISA bus. The ISA bus hands it over to the PCI-to-ISA bridge which in its turn asks the PCI bus, which reaches the host-to-PCI bridge and finally the nexus. The beauty of this transition upwards is that there is room to translate the requests. For example, the `0x230` IO port request might become memory-mapped at `0xb0000230` on a MIPS box by the PCI bridge.

Resource allocation can be controlled at any place in the device tree. For instance on many Alpha platforms, ISA interrupts are managed separately from PCI interrupts and resource allocations for ISA interrupts are managed by the Alpha's ISA bus device. On IA-32, ISA and PCI interrupts are both managed by the top-level nexus device. For both ports, memory and port address space is managed by a single entity - nexus for IA-32 and the relevant chipset driver on Alpha (e.g., CIA or tsunami).

In order to normalize access to memory and port mapped resources, Newbus integrates the **bus_space** APIs from NetBSD. These provide a single API to replace inb/outb and direct memory reads/writes. The advantage of this is that a single driver can easily use either memory-mapped registers or port-mapped registers (some hardware supports both).

This support is integrated into the resource allocation mechanism. When a resource is allocated, a driver can retrieve the associated **bus_space_tag_t** and **bus_space_handle_t** from the resource.

Newbus also allows for definitions of interface methods in files dedicated to this purpose. These are the `.m` files that are found under the `src/sys` hierarchy.

The core of the Newbus system is an extensible "object-based programming" model. Each device in the system has a table of methods which it supports. The system and other devices uses those methods to control the device and request services. The different methods supported by a device are defined by a number of "interfaces". An "interface" is simply a group of related methods which can be implemented by a device.

In the Newbus system, the methods for a device are provided by the various device drivers in the system. When a device is attached to a driver during *auto-configuration*, it uses the method table declared by the driver. A device can later *detach* from its driver and *re-attach* to a new driver with a new method table. This allows dynamic replacement of drivers which can be useful for driver development.

The interfaces are described by an interface definition language similar to the language used to define vnode operations for file systems. The interface would be stored in a methods file (which would normally be named foo_if.m).

Example 14.1. Newbus Methods

```
    # Foo subsystem/driver (a comment...)

  INTERFACE foo

METHOD int doit {
  device_t dev;
};

# DEFAULT is the method that will be used, if a method was not
# provided via: DEVMETHOD()

METHOD void doit_to_child {
  device_t dev;
  driver_t child;
} DEFAULT doit_generic_to_child;
```

When this interface is compiled, it generates a header file "foo_if.h" which contains function declarations:

```
    int FOO_DOIT(device_t dev);
    int FOO_DOIT_TO_CHILD(device_t dev, device_t child);
```

A source file, "foo_if.c" is also created to accompany the automatically generated header file; it contains implementations of those functions which look up the location of the relevant functions in the object's method table and call that function.

The system defines two main interfaces. The first fundamental interface is called *"device"* and includes methods which are relevant to all devices. Methods in the *"device"* interface include *"probe"*, *"attach"* and *"detach"* to control detection of hardware and *"shutdown"*, *"suspend"* and *"resume"* for critical event notification.

The second, more complex interface is *"bus"*. This interface contains methods suitable for devices which have children, including methods to access bus specific per-device information [1], event notification (*child_detached*, *driver_added*) and resource management (*alloc_resource*, *activate_resource*, *deactivate_resource*, *release_resource*).

Many methods in the "bus" interface are performing services for some child of the bus device. These methods would normally use the first two arguments to specify the bus providing the service and the child device which is requesting the service. To simplify driver code, many of these methods have accessor functions which lookup the parent and call a method on the parent. For instance the method BUS_TEARDOWN_INTR(device_t dev, device_t child, ...) can be called using the function bus_teardown_intr(device_t child, ...).

Some bus types in the system define additional interfaces to provide access to bus-specific functionality. For instance, the PCI bus driver defines the "pci" interface which has two methods *read_config* and *write_config* for accessing the configuration registers of a PCI device.

14.3. Newbus API

As the Newbus API is huge, this section makes some effort at documenting it. More information to come in the next revision of this document.

---

[1]bus_generic_read_ivar(9) and bus_generic_write_ivar(9)

14.3.1. Important Locations in the Source Hierarchy

src/sys/[arch]/[arch] - Kernel code for a specific machine architecture resides in this directory. For example, the i386 architecture, or the SPARC64 architecture.

src/sys/dev/[bus] - device support for a specific [bus] resides in this directory.

src/sys/dev/pci - PCI bus support code resides in this directory.

src/sys/[isa|pci] - PCI/ISA device drivers reside in this directory. The PCI/ISA bus support code used to exist in this directory in FreeBSD version 4.0.

14.3.2. Important Structures and Type Definitions

devclass_t - This is a type definition of a pointer to a struct devclass.

device_method_t - This is the same as kobj_method_t (see src/sys/kobj.h).

device_t - This is a type definition of a pointer to a struct device. device_t represents a device in the system. It is a kernel object. See src/sys/sys/bus_private.h for implementation details.

driver_t - This is a type definition which references struct driver. The driver struct is a class of the device kernel object; it also holds data private to the driver.

```
struct driver {
KOBJ_CLASS_FIELDS;
void *priv;   /* driver private data */
};
```

Figure 14.1. *driver_t* Implementation

A device_state_t type, which is an enumeration, device_state. It contains the possible states of a Newbus device before and after the autoconfiguration process.

```
/*
 * src/sys/sys/bus.h
 */
 typedef enum device_state {
DS_NOTPRESENT, /* not probed or probe failed */
DS_ALIVE,  /* probe succeeded */
DS_ATTACHED, /* attach method called */
DS_BUSY   /* device is open */
 } device_state_t;
```

Figure 14.2. Device States *device_state_t*

Chapter 15. Sound Subsystem

Contributed by Jean-Francois Dockes.

15.1. Introduction

The FreeBSD sound subsystem cleanly separates generic sound handling issues from device-specific ones. This makes it easier to add support for new hardware.

The pcm(4) framework is the central piece of the sound subsystem. It mainly implements the following elements:

- A system call interface (read, write, ioctls) to digitized sound and mixer functions. The ioctl command set is compatible with the legacy *OSS* or *Voxware* interface, allowing common multimedia applications to be ported without modification.

- Common code for processing sound data (format conversions, virtual channels).

- A uniform software interface to hardware-specific audio interface modules.

- Additional support for some common hardware interfaces (ac97), or shared hardware-specific code (ex: ISA DMA routines).

The support for specific sound cards is implemented by hardware-specific drivers, which provide channel and mixer interfaces to plug into the generic pcm code.

In this chapter, the term pcm will refer to the central, common part of the sound driver, as opposed to the hardware-specific modules.

The prospective driver writer will of course want to start from an existing module and use the code as the ultimate reference. But, while the sound code is nice and clean, it is also mostly devoid of comments. This document tries to give an overview of the framework interface and answer some questions that may arise while adapting the existing code.

As an alternative, or in addition to starting from a working example, you can find a commented driver template at http://people.FreeBSD.org/~cg/template.c

15.2. Files

All the relevant code lives in /usr/src/sys/dev/sound/ , except for the public ioctl interface definitions, found in /usr/src/sys/sys/soundcard.h

Under /usr/src/sys/dev/sound/ , the pcm/ directory holds the central code, while the pci/, isa/ and usb/ directories have the drivers for PCI and ISA boards, and for USB audio devices.

15.3. Probing, Attaching, etc.

Sound drivers probe and attach in almost the same way as any hardware driver module. You might want to look at the ISA or PCI specific sections of the handbook for more information.

However, sound drivers differ in some ways:

- They declare themselves as pcm class devices, with a struct snddev_info device private structure:

```
static driver_t xxx_driver = {
    "pcm",
```

```
        xxx_methods,
        sizeof(struct snddev_info)
};

    DRIVER_MODULE(snd_xxxpci, pci, xxx_driver, pcm_devclass, 0, 0);
    MODULE_DEPEND(snd_xxxpci, snd_pcm, PCM_MINVER, PCM_PREFVER,PCM_MAXVER);
```

Most sound drivers need to store additional private information about their device. A private data structure is usually allocated in the attach routine. Its address is passed to pcm by the calls to pcm_register() and mixer_init(). pcm later passes back this address as a parameter in calls to the sound driver interfaces.

- The sound driver attach routine should declare its MIXER or AC97 interface to pcm by calling mixer_init(). For a MIXER interface, this causes in turn a call to xxxmixer_init().

- The sound driver attach routine declares its general CHANNEL configuration to pcm by calling pcm_register(dev, sc, nplay, nrec), where sc is the address for the device data structure, used in further calls from pcm, and nplay and nrec are the number of play and record channels.

- The sound driver attach routine declares each of its channel objects by calls to pcm_addchan(). This sets up the channel glue in pcm and causes in turn a call to xxxchannel_init().

- The sound driver detach routine should call pcm_unregister() before releasing its resources.

There are two possible methods to handle non-PnP devices:

- Use a device_identify() method (example: sound/isa/es1888.c). The device_identify() method probes for the hardware at known addresses and, if it finds a supported device, creates a new pcm device which is then passed to probe/attach.

- Use a custom kernel configuration with appropriate hints for pcm devices (example: sound/isa/mss.c).

pcm drivers should implement device_suspend, device_resume and device_shutdown routines, so that power management and module unloading function correctly.

15.4. Interfaces

The interface between the pcm core and the sound drivers is defined in terms of kernel objects.

There are two main interfaces that a sound driver will usually provide: *CHANNEL* and either *MIXER* or *AC97*.

The *AC97* interface is a very small hardware access (register read/write) interface, implemented by drivers for hardware with an AC97 codec. In this case, the actual MIXER interface is provided by the shared AC97 code in pcm.

15.4.1. The CHANNEL Interface

15.4.1.1. Common Notes for Function Parameters

Sound drivers usually have a private data structure to describe their device, and one structure for each play and record data channel that it supports.

For all CHANNEL interface functions, the first parameter is an opaque pointer.

The second parameter is a pointer to the private channel data structure, except for channel_init() which has a pointer to the private device structure (and returns the channel pointer for further use by pcm).

15.4.1.2. Overview of Data Transfer Operations

For sound data transfers, the pcm core and the sound drivers communicate through a shared memory area, described by a struct snd_dbuf .

struct snd_dbuf is private to pcm, and sound drivers obtain values of interest by calls to accessor functions (sndbuf_getxxx()).

The shared memory area has a size of sndbuf_getsize() and is divided into fixed size blocks of sndbuf_getblksz() bytes.

When playing, the general transfer mechanism is as follows (reverse the idea for recording):

- pcm initially fills up the buffer, then calls the sound driver's xxxchannel_trigger() function with a parameter of PCMTRIG_START.

- The sound driver then arranges to repeatedly transfer the whole memory area (sndbuf_getbuf(), sndbuf_getsize()) to the device, in blocks of sndbuf_getblksz() bytes. It calls back the chn_intr() pcm function for each transferred block (this will typically happen at interrupt time).

- chn_intr() arranges to copy new data to the area that was transferred to the device (now free), and make appropriate updates to the snd_dbuf structure.

15.4.1.3. channel_init

xxxchannel_init() is called to initialize each of the play or record channels. The calls are initiated from the sound driver attach routine. (See the probe and attach section).

```
static void *
xxxchannel_init(kobj_t obj, void *data,
    struct snd_dbuf *b, struct pcm_channel *c, int dir)❶
{
    struct xxx_info *sc = data;
    struct xxx_chinfo *ch;
    ...
    return ch;❷
}
```

❶ b is the address for the channel struct snd_dbuf. It should be initialized in the function by calling sndbuf_alloc(). The buffer size to use is normally a small multiple of the 'typical' unit transfer size for your device.

c is the pcm channel control structure pointer. This is an opaque object. The function should store it in the local channel structure, to be used in later calls to pcm (ie: chn_intr(c)).

dir indicates the channel direction (PCMDIR_PLAY or PCMDIR_REC).

❷ The function should return a pointer to the private area used to control this channel. This will be passed as a parameter to other channel interface calls.

15.4.1.4. channel_setformat

xxxchannel_setformat() should set up the hardware for the specified channel for the specified sound format.

```
static int
xxxchannel_setformat(kobj_t obj, void *data, u_int32_t format)❶
{
    struct xxx_chinfo *ch = data;
    ...
    return 0;
}
```

❶ format is specified as an AFMT_XXX value (soundcard.h).

15.4.1.5. channel_setspeed

xxxchannel_setspeed() sets up the channel hardware for the specified sampling speed, and returns the possibly adjusted speed.

```
    static int
    xxxchannel_setspeed(kobj_t obj, void *data, u_int32_t speed)
    {
        struct xxx_chinfo *ch = data;
        ...
        return speed;
    }
```

15.4.1.6. channel_setblocksize

xxxchannel_setblocksize() sets the block size, which is the size of unit transactions between pcm and the sound driver, and between the sound driver and the device. Typically, this would be the number of bytes transferred before an interrupt occurs. During a transfer, the sound driver should call pcm's chn_intr() every time this size has been transferred.

Most sound drivers only take note of the block size here, to be used when an actual transfer will be started.

```
    static int
    xxxchannel_setblocksize(kobj_t obj, void *data, u_int32_t blocksize)
    {
        struct xxx_chinfo *ch = data;
        ...
        return blocksize;❶
    }
```

❶   The function returns the possibly adjusted block size. In case the block size is indeed changed, sndbuf_resize() should be called to adjust the buffer.

15.4.1.7. channel_trigger

xxxchannel_trigger() is called by pcm to control data transfer operations in the driver.

```
    static int
    xxxchannel_trigger(kobj_t obj, void *data, int go)❶
    {
        struct xxx_chinfo *ch = data;
        ...
        return 0;
    }
```

❶   go defines the action for the current call. The possible values are:

- PCMTRIG_START: the driver should start a data transfer from or to the channel buffer. If needed, the buffer base and size can be retrieved through sndbuf_getbuf() and sndbuf_getsize().

- PCMTRIG_EMLDMAWR / PCMTRIG_EMLDMARD: this tells the driver that the input or output buffer may have been updated. Most drivers just ignore these calls.

- PCMTRIG_STOP / PCMTRIG_ABORT : the driver should stop the current transfer.

Note

If the driver uses ISA DMA, sndbuf_isadma() should be called before performing actions on the device, and will take care of the DMA chip side of things.

15.4.1.8. channel_getptr

xxxchannel_getptr() returns the current offset in the transfer buffer. This will typically be called by chn_intr(), and this is how pcm knows where it can transfer new data.

15.4.1.9. channel_free

xxxchannel_free() is called to free up channel resources, for example when the driver is unloaded, and should be implemented if the channel data structures are dynamically allocated or if sndbuf_alloc() was not used for buffer allocation.

15.4.1.10. channel_getcaps

```
struct pcmchan_caps *
xxxchannel_getcaps(kobj_t obj, void *data)
{
    return &xxx_caps;❶
}
```

❶   The routine returns a pointer to a (usually statically-defined) pcmchan_caps structure (defined in sound/pcm/channel.h. The structure holds the minimum and maximum sampling frequencies, and the accepted sound formats. Look at any sound driver for an example.

15.4.1.11. More Functions

channel_reset(), channel_resetdone(), and channel_notify() are for special purposes and should not be implemented in a driver without discussing it on the FreeBSD multimedia mailing list.

channel_setdir() is deprecated.

15.4.2. The MIXER Interface

15.4.2.1. mixer_init

xxxmixer_init() initializes the hardware and tells pcm what mixer devices are available for playing and recording

```
static int
xxxmixer_init(struct snd_mixer *m)
{
    struct xxx_info    *sc = mix_getdevinfo(m);
    u_int32_t v;

    [Initialize hardware]

    [Set appropriate bits in v for play mixers]❶
    mix_setdevs(m, v);
    [Set appropriate bits in v for record mixers]
    mix_setrecdevs(m, v)

    return 0;
}
```

❶   Set bits in an integer value and call mix_setdevs() and mix_setrecdevs() to tell pcm what devices exist.

Mixer bits definitions can be found in soundcard.h (SOUND_MASK_XXX values and SOUND_MIXER_XXX bit shifts).

15.4.2.2. mixer_set

xxxmixer_set() sets the volume level for one mixer device.

```
static int
xxxmixer_set(struct snd_mixer *m, unsigned dev,
                unsigned left, unsigned right)❶
{
    struct sc_info *sc = mix_getdevinfo(m);
    [set volume level]
    return left | (right << 8);❷
}
```

❶   The device is specified as a SOUND_MIXER_XXX value

The volume values are specified in range [0-100]. A value of zero should mute the device.

❷   As the hardware levels probably will not match the input scale, and some rounding will occur, the routine returns the actual level values (in range 0-100) as shown.

15.4.2.3. mixer_setrecsrc

xxxmixer_setrecsrc() sets the recording source device.

```
static int
xxxmixer_setrecsrc(struct snd_mixer *m, u_int32_t src)❶
{
    struct xxx_info *sc = mix_getdevinfo(m);

    [look for non zero bit(s) in src, set up hardware]

    [update src to reflect actual action]
    return src;❷
}
```

❶   The desired recording devices are specified as a bit field
❷   The actual devices set for recording are returned. Some drivers can only set one device for recording. The function should return -1 if an error occurs.

15.4.2.4. mixer_uninit, mixer_reinit

xxxmixer_uninit() should ensure that all sound is muted and if possible mixer hardware should be powered down

xxxmixer_reinit() should ensure that the mixer hardware is powered up and any settings not controlled by mixer_set() or mixer_setrecsrc() are restored.

15.4.3. The AC97 Interface

The *AC97* interface is implemented by drivers with an AC97 codec. It only has three methods:

- xxxac97_init() returns the number of ac97 codecs found.

- ac97_read() and ac97_write() read or write a specified register.

The *AC97* interface is used by the AC97 code in pcm to perform higher level operations. Look at sound/pci/maestro3.c or many others under sound/pci/ for an example.

Chapter 16. PC Card

This chapter will talk about the FreeBSD mechanisms for writing a device driver for a PC Card or CardBus device. However, at present it just documents how to add a new device to an existing pccard driver.

16.1. Adding a Device

Device drivers know what devices they support. There is a table of supported devices in the kernel that drivers use to attach to a device.

16.1.1. Overview

PC Cards are identified in one of two ways, both based on the *Card Information Structure* (CIS) stored on the card. The first method is to use numeric manufacturer and product numbers. The second method is to use the human readable strings that are also contained in the CIS. The PC Card bus uses a centralized database and some macros to facilitate a design pattern to help the driver writer match devices to his driver.

Original equipment manufacturers (OEMs) often develop a reference design for a PC Card product, then sell this design to other companies to market. Those companies refine the design, market the product to their target audience or geographic area, and put their own name plate onto the card. The refinements to the physical card are typically very minor, if any changes are made at all. To strengthen their brand, these vendors place their company name in the human readable strings in the CIS space, but leave the manufacturer and product IDs unchanged.

Because of this practice, FreeBSD drivers usually rely on numeric IDs for device identification. Using numeric IDs and a centralized database complicates adding IDs and support for cards to the system. One must carefully check to see who really made the card, especially when it appears that the vendor who made the card might already have a different manufacturer ID listed in the central database. Linksys, D-Link, and NetGear are a number of US manufacturers of LAN hardware that often sell the same design. These same designs can be sold in Japan under names such as Buffalo and Corega. Often, these devices will all have the same manufacturer and product IDs.

The PC Card bus code keeps a central database of card information, but not which driver is associated with them, in **/sys/dev/pccard/pccarddevs** . It also provides a set of macros that allow one to easily construct simple entries in the table the driver uses to claim devices.

Finally, some really low end devices do not contain manufacturer identification at all. These devices must be detected by matching the human readable CIS strings. While it would be nice if we did not need this method as a fallback, it is necessary for some very low end CD-ROM players and Ethernet cards. This method should generally be avoided, but a number of devices are listed in this section because they were added prior to the recognition of the OEM nature of the PC Card business. When adding new devices, prefer using the numeric method.

16.1.2. Format of `pccarddevs`

There are four sections in the `pccarddevs` files. The first section lists the manufacturer numbers for vendors that use them. This section is sorted in numerical order. The next section has all of the products that are used by these vendors, along with their product ID numbers and a description string. The description string typically is not used (instead we set the device's description based on the human readable CIS, even if we match on the numeric version). These two sections are then repeated for devices that use the string matching method. Finally, C-style comments enclosed in /* and */ characters are allowed anywhere in the file.

The first section of the file contains the vendor IDs. Please keep this list sorted in numeric order. Also, please coordinate changes to this file because we share it with NetBSD to help facilitate a common clearing house for this information. For example, here are the first few vendor IDs:

```
vendor FUJITSU    0x0004  Fujitsu Corporation
vendor NETGEAR_2  0x000b  Netgear
```

```
vendor PANASONIC  0x0032 Matsushita Electric Industrial Co.
vendor SANDISK    0x0045 Sandisk Corporation
```

Chances are very good that the NETGEAR_2 entry is really an OEM that NETGEAR purchased cards from and the author of support for those cards was unaware at the time that Netgear was using someone else's ID. These entries are fairly straightforward. The vendor keyword denotes the kind of line that this is, followed by the name of the vendor. This name will be repeated later in pccarddevs, as well as used in the driver's match tables, so keep it short and a valid C identifier. A numeric ID in hex identifies the manufacturer. Do not add IDs of the form 0xffffffff or 0xffff because these are reserved IDs (the former is "no ID set" while the latter is sometimes seen in extremely poor quality cards to try to indicate "none"). Finally there is a string description of the company that makes the card. This string is not used in FreeBSD for anything but commentary purposes.

The second section of the file contains the products. As shown in this example, the format is similar to the vendor lines:

```
/* Allied Telesis K.K. */
product ALLIEDTELESIS LA_PCM 0x0002 Allied Telesis LA-PCM

/* Archos */
product ARCHOS ARC_ATAPI 0x0043 MiniCD
```

The product keyword is followed by the vendor name, repeated from above. This is followed by the product name, which is used by the driver and should be a valid C identifier, but may also start with a number. As with the vendors, the hex product ID for this card follows the same convention for 0xffffffff and 0xffff. Finally, there is a string description of the device itself. This string typically is not used in FreeBSD, since FreeBSD's pccard bus driver will construct a string from the human readable CIS entries, but it can be used in the rare cases where this is somehow insufficient. The products are in alphabetical order by manufacturer, then numerical order by product ID. They have a C comment before each manufacturer's entries and there is a blank line between entries.

The third section is like the previous vendor section, but with all of the manufacturer numeric IDs set to -1, meaning "match anything found" in the FreeBSD pccard bus code. Since these are C identifiers, their names must be unique. Otherwise the format is identical to the first section of the file.

The final section contains the entries for those cards that must be identified by string entries. This section's format is a little different from the generic section:

```
product ADDTRON AWP100  { "Addtron", "AWP-100&spWireless&spPCMCIA", "Version&sp01.02", ↵
NULL }
product ALLIEDTELESIS WR211PCM { "Allied&spTelesis&spK.K.", "WR211PCM", NULL, NULL } ↵
Allied Telesis WR211PCM
```

The familiar product keyword is followed by the vendor name and the card name, just as in the second section of the file. Here the format deviates from that used earlier. There is a {} grouping, followed by a number of strings. These strings correspond to the vendor, product, and extra information that is defined in a CIS_INFO tuple. These strings are filtered by the program that generates pccarddevs.h to replace &sp with a real space. NULL strings mean that the corresponding part of the entry should be ignored. The example shown here contains a bad entry. It should not contain the version number unless that is critical for the operation of the card. Sometimes vendors will have many different versions of the card in the field that all work, in which case that information only makes it harder for someone with a similar card to use it with FreeBSD. Sometimes it is necessary when a vendor wishes to sell many different parts under the same brand due to market considerations (availability, price, and so forth). Then it can be critical to disambiguating the card in those rare cases where the vendor kept the same manufacturer/product pair. Regular expression matching is not available at this time.

16.1.3. Sample Probe Routine

To understand how to add a device to the list of supported devices, one must understand the probe and/or match routines that many drivers have. It is complicated a little in FreeBSD 5.x because there is a compatibility layer for OLDCARD present as well. Since only the window-dressing is different, an idealized version will be presented here.

```
static const struct pccard_product wi_pccard_products[] = {
  PCMCIA_CARD(3COM, 3CRWE737A, 0),
  PCMCIA_CARD(BUFFALO, WLI_PCM_S11, 0),
  PCMCIA_CARD(BUFFALO, WLI_CF_S11G, 0),
  PCMCIA_CARD(TDK, LAK_CD011WL, 0),
  { NULL }
};

static int
wi_pccard_probe(dev)
  device_t dev;
{
  const struct pccard_product *pp;

  if ((pp = pccard_product_lookup(dev, wi_pccard_products,
      sizeof(wi_pccard_products[0]), NULL)) != NULL) {
    if (pp->pp_name != NULL)
      device_set_desc(dev, pp->pp_name);
    return (0);
  }
  return (ENXIO);
}
```

Here we have a simple pccard probe routine that matches a few devices. As stated above, the name may vary (if it is not `foo_pccard_probe()` it will be `foo_pccard_match()`). The function `pccard_product_lookup()` is a generalized function that walks the table and returns a pointer to the first entry that it matches. Some drivers may use this mechanism to convey additional information about some cards to the rest of the driver, so there may be some variance in the table. The only requirement is that each row of the table must have a `struct pccard_product` as the first element.

Looking at the table `wi_pccard_products`, one notices that all the entries are of the form `PCMCIA_CARD(foo, bar, baz)`. The `foo` part is the manufacturer ID from `pccarddevs`. The `bar` part is the product ID. `baz` is the expected function number for this card. Many pccards can have multiple functions, and some way to disambiguate function 1 from function 0 is needed. You may see `PCMCIA_CARD_D`, which includes the device description from `pccarddevs`. You may also see `PCMCIA_CARD2` and `PCMCIA_CARD2_D` which are used when you need to match both CIS strings and manufacturer numbers, in the "use the default description" and "take the description from pccarddevs" flavors.

16.1.4. Putting it All Together

To add a new device, one must first obtain the identification information from the device. The easiest way to do this is to insert the device into a PC Card or CF slot and issue `devinfo -v`. Sample output:

```
        cbb1 pnpinfo vendor=0x104c device=0xac51 subvendor=0x1265 subdevice=0x0300 ↵
class=0x060700 at slot=10 function=1
        cardbus1
        pccard1
          unknown pnpinfo manufacturer=0x026f product=0x030c cisvendor="BUFFALO" ↵
cisproduct="WLI2-CF-S11" function_type=6 at function=0
```

`manufacturer` and `product` are the numeric IDs for this product, while `cisvendor` and `cisproduct` are the product description strings from the CIS.

Since we first want to prefer the numeric option, first try to construct an entry based on that. The above card has been slightly fictionalized for the purpose of this example. The vendor is BUFFALO, which we see already has an entry:

```
vendor BUFFALO    0x026f BUFFALO (Melco Corporation)
```

But there is no entry for this particular card. Instead we find:

```
/* BUFFALO */
product BUFFALO WLI_PCM_S11 0x0305 BUFFALO AirStation 11Mbps WLAN
product BUFFALO LPC_CF_CLT 0x0307 BUFFALO LPC-CF-CLT
```

```
product BUFFALO LPC3_CLT 0x030a BUFFALO LPC3-CLT Ethernet Adapter
product BUFFALO WLI_CF_S11G 0x030b BUFFALO AirStation 11Mbps CF WLAN
```

To add the device, we can just add this entry to `pccarddevs`:

```
product BUFFALO WLI2_CF_S11G 0x030c BUFFALO AirStation ultra 802.11b CF
```

Once these steps are complete, the card can be added to the driver. That is a simple operation of adding one line:

```
static const struct pccard_product wi_pccard_products[] = {
 PCMCIA_CARD(3COM, 3CRWE737A, 0),
 PCMCIA_CARD(BUFFALO, WLI_PCM_S11, 0),
 PCMCIA_CARD(BUFFALO, WLI_CF_S11G, 0),
+ PCMCIA_CARD(BUFFALO, WLI_CF2_S11G, 0),
 PCMCIA_CARD(TDK, LAK_CD011WL, 0),
 { NULL }
};
```

Note that I have included a '+' in the line before the line that I added, but that is simply to highlight the line. Do not add it to the actual driver. Once you have added the line, you can recompile your kernel or module and test it. If the device is recognized and works, please submit a patch. If it does not work, please figure out what is needed to make it work and submit a patch. If the device is not recognized at all, you have done something wrong and should recheck each step.

If you are a FreeBSD src committer, and everything appears to be working, then you can commit the changes to the tree. However, there are some minor tricky things to be considered. `pccarddevs` must be committed to the tree first. Then `pccarddevs.h` must be regenerated and committed as a second step, ensuring that the right $FreeBSD$ tag is in the latter file. Finally, commit the additions to the driver.

16.1.5. Submitting a New Device

Please do not send entries for new devices to the author directly. Instead, submit them as a PR and send the author the PR number for his records. This ensures that entries are not lost. When submitting a PR, it is unnecessary to include the `pccardevs.h` diffs in the patch, since those will be regenerated. It is necessary to include a description of the device, as well as the patches to the client driver. If you do not know the name, use OEM99 as the name, and the author will adjust OEM99 accordingly after investigation. Committers should not commit OEM99, but instead find the highest OEM entry and commit one more than that.

Part III. Appendices

Table of Contents

Bibliography

[1] Marshall Kirk McKusick, Keith Bostic, Michael J Karels, and John S Quarterman. Copyright © 1996 Addison-Wesley Publishing Company, Inc.. 0-201-54979-4. Addison-Wesley Publishing Company, Inc.. *The Design and Implementation of the 4.4 BSD Operating System.* 1-2.

Index